APPLIED MACHINE LEARNING

A CASE-BASED APPROACH

APPLIED MACHINE LEARNING

A CASE-BASED APPROACH

Prof. Santosh Purushottam Tamboli
Prof. (Dr.) Umakant Dinkar Butkar
Dr. Kalyanapu Srinivas
Prof. Rohit S.Barve

NAMYA PRESS.com

Published by

Namya Press

India: 213, Vardan House, 7/28 Ansari Road Darya Ganj - Delhi India 110002
USA: 10685-B Hazelhurst Dr. # 31013 Houston, Texas USA - 77043
Email: namyapress@gmail.com
Website: https://namyapress.com

Edition	:	First Published in 2023 (Namya Press)
Title	:	Applied Machine Learning: A Case-Based Approach
Authors	:	Prof. Santosh Purushottam Tamboli Prof. (Dr.) Umakant Dinkar Butkar, Dr. Kalyanapu Srinivas Prof. Rohit S.Barve
ISBN	:	978-93-5545-218-4

Dedicated to

Our Family

&

Our Current Working

Organization

Preface

This book provides an introduction to Machine Learning and its related concepts and techniques. It has been written with an emphasis on practical applications and the methods used to solve real-world problems. It is a case-based approach and begins with an introduction to the field of Machine Learning, followed by descriptions of various related concepts and algorithms. After that, it thoroughly works through worked examples on how they can be applied. This book is designed to offer an appropriate level of technical detail for practitioners as well as academics, and assumes no prior knowledge or experience with Machine Learning. The goal is to teach readers the concepts of Machine Learning in a practical way.

Contents

1

Introduction of Machine Learning

1.1. UNDERSTANDING MACHINE LEARNING'S FUNDAMENTALS

Machine learning (ML) is a subfield of artificial intelligence (AI) that focuses on the development of algorithms and techniques that enable computers to learn from data and make predictions or decisions without special programming. In other words, ML algorithms learn patterns and relationships from examples or past experiences and use that knowledge to make informed predictions or decisions based on new, unseen data. The basic principle of machine learning is that computers can learn from data and improve their performance over time by recognizing patterns and making predictions or decisions based on those patterns. ML algorithms are designed to automatically learn and adapt to data without being individually programmed for each specific task. This makes ML particularly useful in complex and data-rich domains where traditional rule-based programming methods may be difficult or impractical to apply. To better understand machine learning, let's delve into its basic components, types, and learning. Parts of Machine Learning:

- **Data:** Data is the foundation of machine learning. It consists of examples or cases that the ML algorithm uses to learn patterns and make predictions or decisions. Data can take different forms, such as structured data (e.g. databases, spreadsheets) or unstructured data (e.g. text documents, images, videos).
- **Features:** Features are individual measurable properties or characteristics of the data that the ML algorithm uses to make predictions or decisions. Features are selected or extracted from the raw data and serve as inputs to the ML model. Feature

quality and relevance play a crucial role in the performance of an ML algorithm.

- **ML Model:** An ML model is a mathematical or computer representation of the relationships and patterns learned from data. A model captures a description between input properties and output predictions or decisions. It is a core component of an ML system and is responsible for making predictions or decisions based on new, unseen information.
- **Training:** Training feeds the ML model with labelled data to learn patterns and relationships. Tagged data consists of input properties and their corresponding actual output values or target identifiers. During training, the ML algorithm adj u sts the internal parameters of the model to minimize the difference between the predicted outputs and the actual outputs.
- **Evaluation:** Evaluation evaluates the performance of the trained ML model with new, unseen data. Model predictions or decisions are compared with actual values or records in the assessment data. Evaluation metrics such as precision, accuracy, recall, or root mean square error are used to measure the performance of an ML model.

Types of Machine Learning

Machine learning can be divided into three main types based on the learning process and the availability of labelled data:

- **Supervised learning:** Supervised learning algorithms learn from labelled data, where each instance of the training data has a corresponding target entity or result value. The goal is to learn how to map input functions to output identifiers so that you can make predictions or make decisions based on new, unseen data. Common supervised learning tasks include classification and regression.
- **Unsupervised learning:** Unsupervised learning algorithms learn from unlabelled data where only input features are provided without target labels or output values. The goal of unsupervised learning is to find inherent patterns, structures, or relationships in data. Clustering and dimensionality reduction are typical tasks in unsupervised learning.
- **Reinforcement learning:** Reinforcement learning means that the agent learns to interact with the environment and make decisions to maximize the cumulative reward. The agent learns through trial and error and receives feedback on its actions

in the form of rewards or punishments. The goal is to learn the optimal policy or strategy to achieve long-term benefits. Reinforcement learning is often applied to sequential decision tasks.

Machine Learning Process

The machine learning process consists of several interrelated steps that turn data into a trained ML model capable of making predictions or decisions. Typical steps in the ML process are:

- **Data preprocessing:** In this step, the raw data is prepared and converted into a suitable format for the ML algorithm. This includes tasks such as cleaning data by handling missing values, handling outliers, and normalizing or scaling data to ensure consistency.
- **Feature Selection/Extraction:** Feature selection or extraction is the process of identifying the most important and informative features from the data. Its purpose is to reduce the dimensionality of the data and remove pale or unnecessary features that can hinder learning. Feature extraction techniques such as principal component analysis (PCA) or word embedding can be used to transform the data into a lower dimensional representation.
- **Model selection:** Model selection involves the appropriate ML algorithm or model that best fits the given problem. The choice of model depends on the type of task (classification, regression, clustering, etc.), the nature of the data and the available resources.
- **Training:** In the training phase, the selected ML model is trained using labelled data. A model is presented with its input properties and their corresponding target identifiers or output values. The model iteratively adjusts its internal parameters using optimization algorithms to minimize the difference between predicted outputs and actual outputs.
- **Evaluation:** After training, the performance of the ML model is evaluated using evaluation data that the model did not see during training. Evaluation metrics are used to measure model accuracy, precision, recall, or other performance metrics. This step helps assess the generalizability of the model and its ability to make accurate predictions or decisions based on new, unseen data.
- **Model optimization and hyperparameter tuning:** Model optimization involves fine-tuning the ML algorithm to improve

its performance. The hyperparameters that determine the behaviour and complexity of the ML model are tuned for optimal performance. Techniques such as grid search, random search or Bayesian optimization can be used to explore different combinations of hyperparameters and find the best settings for the model.

- **Prediction/Decision Making:** Once an ML model is trained and optimized, it can be used to make predictions or decisions based on new, unseen data. The model takes inputs as input and produces corresponding predictions or decisions as output. Predictions or decisions can be further analysed or used to take appropriate actions in real applications.

Challenges and Future Directions in Machine Learning

Although machine learning has made significant progress, researchers and practitioners are actively considering a number of challenges and future trends.

1. **Data quality and quantity:** Availability of high-quality, labelled data is critical to training accurate ML models. Collecting, cleaning, and labelling large data sets can be time-consuming and expensive. Techniques for handling limited labelled data, knowledge augmentation and generative models are being developed to address this challenge.
2. **Interpretability and explain ability:** As ML models become more complex, interpreting and explaining their decisions or predictions becomes difficult. The goal of interpretive ML research is to develop techniques that provide transparency and explanations for ML algorithms so that users understand and trust model outputs.
3. **Ethical and justice considerations:** ML algorithms can inadvertently reinforce biases and discriminate against certain groups if not carefully developed and used. Ensuring fairness, accountability and transparency in ML algorithms is an ongoing challenge. Methods to identify and mitigate bias, as well as guidelines and regulations, are being developed to address the ethical implications.
4. **Deep Learning and Beyond:** Deep Learning, a subfield of ML based on neural networks, has shown significant success in several areas. Future directions include addressing challenges in training deep learning models for limited labelled data, reducing computational requirements and improving interpretability. Alternative learning paradigms such as reinforcement learning

and unsupervised learning are also being explored for more efficient and effective learning algorithms.

Machine learning is a powerful approach to data analysis and decision making that allows computers to learn from data and make predictions or decisions without special programming. It includes a variety of algorithms, techniques and processes that make it possible to extract valuable insights from data. By understanding the components of ML, the different types of learning and the ML process, we can understand the basics of this exciting field.

Machine learning continues to advance rapidly, and ongoing research focuses on challenges related to data quality, interpretability, fairness, and ethical considerations. The exciting development of deep learning and alternative learning paradigms is shaping the future of machine learning, making it a dynamic and promising field for innovation and applications in various fields.

DIFFERENT MACHINE LEARNING TECHNIQUES

Machine learning (ML) can be classified into three main types based on the learning process and the availability of labelled data supervised learning, unsupervised learning, and reinforcement learning. Each type has its own characteristics, algorithms and applications. Let's examine these types in more detail:

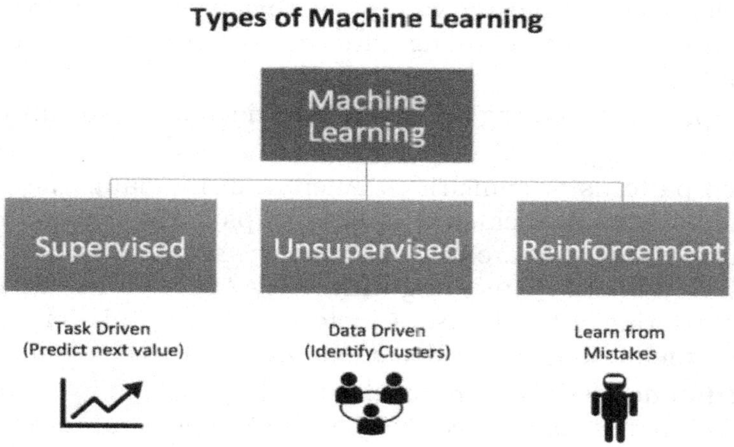

1. Supervised learning: Supervised learning is the most common and widely used type of machine learning. In supervised learning, the ML algorithm learns from labelled data, where each instance of the training dataset has a corresponding target label or output value. The goal is to learn the mapping between input features and output titles, allowing the algorithm to make predictions or make decisions based on new, unseen information.

Supervised learning tasks can be divided into two subtypes:

- **Classification:** In classification tasks, the ML algorithm learns to classify input data into predefined classes or classes. For example, based on features representing email attributes, a classification algorithm can be trained to predict whether we have spam or not. Common classification algorithms include logistic regression, support vector machines (SVM), decision trees, and random forests.
- **Regression:** In regression tasks, the ML algorithm learns to predict continuous numerical values or quantities. Regression is used when the output variable is a continuous value, such as predicting housing prices based on characteristics such as floor space, number of rooms, etc. Linear r e gression, polynomial regression, and neural networks are commonly used algorithms for regression tasks.

Supervised learning requires labelled data for training, and the quality and quantity of labelled data greatly affect the performance of the ML model. The trained model can then generalize the learned patterns and make predictions based on new, unseen data.

2. Unsupervised learning: Unsupervised learning refers to learning from unlabelled data where only input features are provided without target identifiers or output values. In this type of learning, the ML algorithm examines underlying patterns, structures, or relationships in the data.

Unsupervised learning tasks can be divided into two subtypes:

- **Clustering:** Clustering algorithms group similar cases based on patterns or similarities inherent in the data. The goal is to identify natural clusters or subgroups in the dataset. K-means clustering, hierarchical clustering, and DBSCAN (Density-Based Spatial Clustering with Noisy Applications) are common clustering algorithms. Clustering is useful for customer segmentation, outlier detection, and pattern recognition.
- **Dimensionality reduction:** Dimensionality reduction techniques aim to reduce the number of input features while preserving important information. It helps visualize high-dimensional data and extract the most important features. Principal component analysis (PCA) and t-SNE (t-Distributed Stochastic Neighbour Embedding) are popular dimensionality reduction algorithms.

Unsupervised learning is valuable when there is no identified data or when the goal is to find unknown patterns or insights in the data.

3. Reinforcement learning: Reinforcement learning (RL) is a subfield of machine learning that focuses on training agents to make sequential decisions in an environment to maximize cumulative reward. It is inspired by how humans and animals learn through trial and error while interacting with the world. RL algorithms allow an agent to learn optimal strategies through exploration and exploitation without explicit inspection or labeled datasets.

Main Parts of Reinforcement Learning

- **Agent:** Learner or decision maker who interacts with the environment. It monitors the current situation, takes action and receives feedback in the form of rewards.
- **Environment:** The external system with which the agent interacts. It gives the agent states, accepts actions, and provides rewards or punishments based on the actions of the agent.
- **State:** Representation of the environment at a given moment. It collects important information that the agent needs to make decisions.
- **Action:** The options available to the agent in each mode. An agent chooses actions based on its policy, which maps states to actions. 5. Reward: a feedback signal indicating the desirability of an agent's action. The agent's goal is to maximize cumulative benefits over time.
- **Practice:** Strategy or behavior of an agent that maps states into actions. It guides the agent's decision-making process.
- **Value function:** the value of a state or state-action pair that represents the expected cumulative reward that an agent can obtain from that state or state-action pair. It directs the agent to evaluate the desirability of various actions or states.

Algorithms of Amplification

- **Q-Learning:** Q-Learning is a model-free RL algorithm that learns an action value function (Q-function). It iteratively updates Q values based on observed benefits and estimated future benefits. The agent uses the Q values to determine the best course of action in a given state.
- **Practicing gradient methods:** These algorithms optimize practice by directly estimating gradients using a sample. They learn by repeatedly adjusting practice to increase the

likelihood that performing actions will lead to higher rewards. Practical gradient methods include REINFORCE, Proximal Policy Optimization (PPO), and Trust Region Policy Optimization (TRPO).

- **Deep Q-Network (DQN):** DQN combines Q-learning with deep neural networks to deal with high-dimensional spatial spaces. It uses a deep neural network known as a Q network to approximate the Q values. DQN introduces repetition of experiences and target networks to stabilize and improve the learning.
- **Actor-critical methods:** Actor-critical algorithms maintain both a policy (actor) and a value function (critic). The actor proposes policy-based actions, the critic evaluates the action using a value function. That approach allows the agent to learn from both political effectiveness and the evaluations of critics.

Applications of Reinforcement Learning

Reinforcement learning has found applications in several areas, including:

- **Gaming:** RL algorithms have achieved significant success in playing games such as chess, Go and video games, surpassing human performance.
- **Robotics:** RL is used to train robots to perform complex tasks such as grasping objects, navigating dynamic environments or mastering locomotive skills.
- **Autonomous vehicles:** RL trains self-driving cars to make decisions based on the environment and traffic conditions.
- **Recommender systems:** RL algorithms can be used to adapt recommendations to users by learning their preferences and optimizing long-term rewards.
- **Healthcare:** RL is used to optimize treatment strategies, drug dosing and resource allocation in healthcare settings. Reinforcement learning provides agents with an efficient framework for making optimal decisions in sequential decision problems. This allows for independent learning, adaptability, and the ability to handle complex tasks without direct supervision.

Hybrid Methods and Other Variations

In addition to the three main types mentioned above, there are hybrid approaches and varieties of machine learning that combine different types of elements:

- **Semi-supervised learning:** Semi-supervised learning combines labelled and unlabelled information for training. It uses both a small amount of labelled data and a larger amount of unlabelled data to improve learning. Semi-supervised learning is useful when labelling large datasets is expensive or time-consuming.
- **Transfer learning:** Transfer learning uses knowledge learned in one task or domain to improve learning in another related task or domain. The pretrained knowledge of the source task is transferred and refined by the limited labelled information of the target task. Transfer learning reduces the need for extensive training for the target task and enables faster learning.
- **Online Learning:** Also known as incremental learning or lifelong learning, online learning involves learning from a continuous stream of incoming data. The ML model is constantly updated as new information emerges, allowing the model to adapt and learn in real time. Online learning is useful when the distribution of information changes over time or when new cases need to be handled incrementally.
- **Deep Learning:** Deep learning is a subfield of ML that focuses on using multilayer neural networks to learn hierarchical representations of data. Deep learning has made significant progress in various fields such as image recognition, natural language processing, and speech synthesis. Deep learning models such as Convolutional Neural Networks (CNNs) and Recurrent Neural Networks (RNNs) learn complex patterns and relationships in data, enabling powerful predictions and decisions.

Machine learning includes different types, each with its own characteristics, algorithms and applications. Supervised learning, unsupervised learning and reinforcement learning are the main types of ML. Supervised learning learns from labelled data to make predictions or make decisions, while unsupervised learning examines patterns in unlabelled data. Reinforcement learning focuses on learning by interacting with the environment to maximize rewards. Hybrid methods and variants such as semi-supervised learning, transfer learning, online learning and deep learning expand the capabilities and applications of machine learning. With this kind of understanding, researchers and practitioners can choose the most appropriate approach to solve specific problems and unlock the potential of machine learning in various fields.

1.3. REINFORCEMENT, SUPERVISED, AND UNSUPERVISED LEARNING

Reinforcement learning (RL) is a type of machine learning in which an agent learns how to interact with the environment to maximize cumulative reward. An agent works in an environment and based on received feedback or reward, it learns to act optimally to achieve long-term goals. The learning process of reinforcement learning can be visualized using the following diagram:

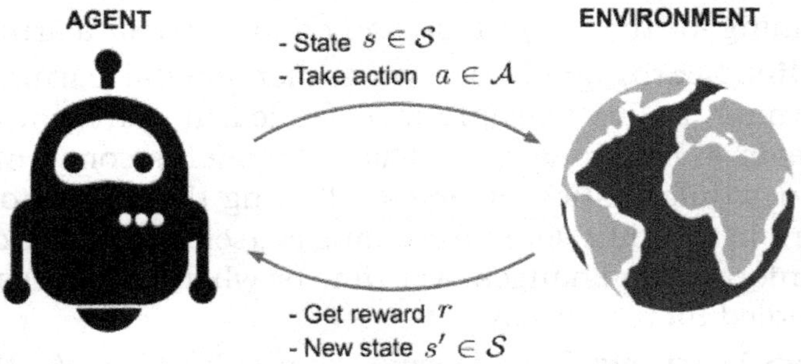

Reinforcement learning

In RL, an agent interacts with the environment by monitoring its current state, choosing an action to perform, and receiving feedback in the form of rewards or punishments. The goal of the agent is to learn a policy that represents a mapping of states and actions that maximize the cumulative reward over time. Politics can be deterministic or stochastic depending on whether it chooses actions deterministically or probabilistically. Reinforcement learning is typically used for sequential decision-making tasks where an agent must learn how to behave in an environment to achieve a certain goal. Examples include training an autonomous vehicle to navigate traffic, teaching a robot to perform complex tasks, or developing strategies to play games such as chess or go.

Supervised Learning

Supervised learning refers to a guided approach where learners receive structured guidance and support throughout the learning process. This involves providing learners with precise instructions, scaffolding and feedback so that they can effectively acquire new knowledge and skills. This approach is often used in educational settings, training programs, and online courses to improve learning outcomes.

In Supervised learning, the teacher or tutor takes an active role in guiding students through the material. They provide clear instructions, break complex concepts into smaller, more manageable chunks, and provide support when students encounter difficulties. The goal is to gradually transfer responsibility from the teacher to the student, encouraging independent learning over time.

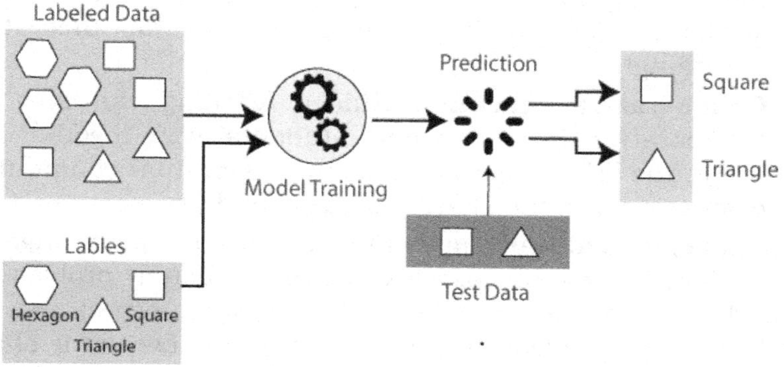

Supervised Learning

Supervised learning can take different forms depending on the context and learning objectives. Here are some of the more common strategies and techniques used in supervised learning:

- **Direct instruction:** The teacher presents information or clearly demonstrates his skills and gives step-by-step instructions and examples. Learners observe and imitate the actions of the teacher and gradually develop their understanding and competence.
- **Scaffolding:** The teacher provides temporary support to help students bridge the gap between current knowledge and desired learning outcomes. This support may include prompts, suggestions, models, graphic organizers, or partial solutions that gradually disappear as students acquire skills.
- **Modelling:** The teacher models the desired behaviour or thought process and shows the students how to approach the task or problem. Learners observe the activity and then try to imitate or reproduce it.
- **Think aloud:** The teacher talks about his thought process when solving a problem or completing a task. This technique helps learners understand cognitive stages and promotes metacognitive skills.

- **Guided Exercise:** Students participate in structured exercises under the guidance and supervision of a teacher. The teacher gives feedback, corrects misunderstandings and gives suggestions for improvement.
- **Formative assessment:** The instructor assesses students' progress during the learning process and provides feedback on their strengths and areas of development. This feedback helps students identify their learning gaps and adjust their strategies accordingly.
- **Collaborative Learning:** Guided learning can also include collaborative activities where students work together in pairs or groups. This approach encourages mutual communication, discussion and the sharing of ideas and perspectives.

Benefits of guided learning include increased student engagement, better understanding of complex concepts, better problem-solving skills and improved self-confidence. By providing structured support and guidance, guided learning can help learners overcome challenges and achieve deeper learning outcomes. It is worth noting that guided learning is not intended to replace other teaching methods such as inquiry-based learning or independent study. Instead, it can be used in conjunction with these approaches to create a balanced and effective learning experience that meets the needs of diverse learners.

Unsupervised Learning

Unsupervised learning is a type of machine learning where a model learns patterns and structures in data without special supervision or labelled examples. Unlike supervised learning, which relies on labelled data to make predictions or classifications, unsupervised learning algorithms operate on unlabelled data and attempt to find patterns, relationships, and structures inherent in the dataset.

The goal of unsupervised learning is to explore and extract valuable insights, uncover hidden patterns, and better understand the underlying structure of data. It is often used for tasks such as clustering, dimensionality reduction, and outlier detection.

Here are some of the more common techniques used in unsupervised learning:

- **Clustering:** Clustering algorithms group similar data points based on their characteristics. The goal is to identify clusters or groups of data points that are similar to each other and different from data points in other clusters. K-means, hierarchical clustering, and DBSCAN are popular clustering algorithms.

- **Dimensionality reduction:** Dimensionality reduction techniques aim to reduce the number of features or variables in a dataset while preserving important information. This helps visualize high-dimensional data and remove noise or irrelevant features. Principal component analysis (PCA) and t-SNE (t-Distributed Stochastic Neighbor Embedding) are commonly used dimensionality reduction techniques.
- **Anomaly detection:** Anomaly detection identifies rare or unusual data points or patterns that do not conform to the standard. This technique is useful for detecting fraudulent activities, identifying anomalies in data sets or diagnosing system failures. One-class SVM, Isolated Forest, and Autoencoders are popular methods for outlier detection.

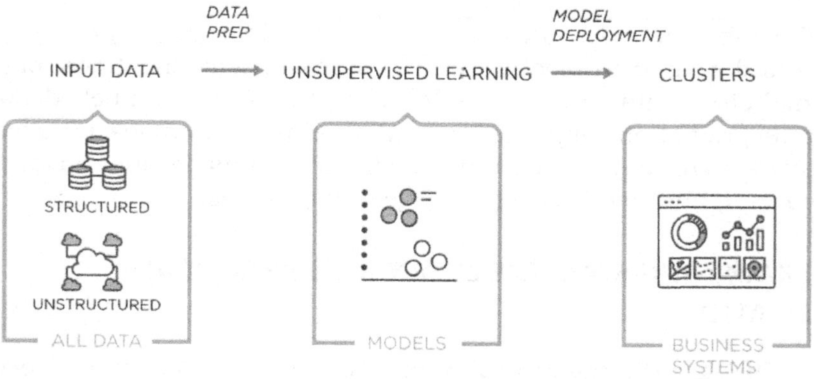

Unsupervised Learning

- **Learning Association Rules:** Learning association rules identifies interesting relationships or patterns between variables in large data sets. It is often used in market basket analysis, where the goal is to find relationships or dependencies between products that are often purchased together. Apriori and FP growth algorithms are widely used to learn association rules. Unsupervised learning has a wide range of applications in various fields, including data mining, image and text analysis, recommendation systems, and natural language processing. It enables the exploration and discovery of patterns in unstructured or unlabeled data, providing valuable insights and enabling better decisions.

Table 1: Comparison of Reinforcement Learning, Supervised Learning, and Unsupervised Learning

Type	Learning Approach	Labelled Data Required?	Main Tasks
Reinforcement Learning	Learn through interaction with an environment to maximize rewards	No	Sequential decision-making, game playing, robotics
Supervised Learning	Learn from labelled data to make predictions or decisions	Yes	Classification, regression
Unsupervised Learning	Learn from unlabelled data to discover patterns or relationships	No	Clustering, dimensionality reduction

The table provides an overview of each learning style's essential traits and primary objectives. Unsupervised learning finds patterns in unlabelled data, supervised learning learns from labelled data to generate predictions or judgements, and reinforcement learning focuses on learning through interaction. Each variety has distinct advantages, drawbacks, and uses across a range of industries.

1.4. EXAMINING MACHINE LEARNING'S PRACTICAL APPLICATIONS

- **Disease diagnosis and prognosis:** Machine learning algorithms can analyze patient data, including medical histories, symptoms and test results, to help accurately diagnose diseases. These algorithms can also predict the probability of disease occurrence based on risk factors and patient profiles.
- **Personalized medicine and treatment optimization:** Machine learning models can analyze genetic and clinical data to determine the most effective treatments for specific patients. By considering factors such as genetic markers, medical history and demographic information, individualized treatment plans can be developed.
- **Analysis and interpretation of medical images:** Machine learning techniques such as deep learning have shown significant success in analyzing medical images, including X-rays, MRIs and CT scans. These models can help radiologists identify abnormalities, segment organs, and provide quantitative assessments.

- **Drug discovery and development:** Machine learning is used in drug development to analyze large data sets, including molecular structures and biological interactions. These algorithms help identify potential drug candidates, predict their efficacy, and optimize molecular structures.

Financial Services

Financial services refer to the range of economic activities and products that financial institutions or intermediaries make available to individuals, businesses and governments. These services cover various aspects of money management, investments and financial transactions. They play a key role in promoting economic growth, supporting businesses and managing the financial well-being of individuals.

Here are some of the main areas of financial services:

- **Banking:** Banks are central to the financial system and offer services such as savings and checking accounts, loans, mortgages, credit cards and investment products. They provide a safe place to store money, facilitate transactions and provide financial advice.
- **Insurance:** Insurance companies provide coverage and protection against a variety of risks, including life insurance, health insurance, property insurance, auto insurance, and liability insurance. They pool the risks of policyholders and provide financial compensation for covered events.
- **Investment management:** Investment firms and investment managers help individuals and institutions invest their money in various financial instruments such as stocks, bonds, mutual funds, exchange-traded funds (ETFs) and alternative investments. Their goal is to generate income while covering risks according to the clients' goals.
- **Financial Planning:** Financial planners or advisors help individuals and businesses create comprehensive financial plans to achieve their financial goals. He analyzes financial situations, guides budgeting, tax planning, retirement planning, estate planning and investment strategies.
- **Exchange and Trading:** Exchanges facilitate buying and selling of shares of listed companies. Brokerage firms provide platforms for individuals to trade stocks, bonds, options, commodities and other securities. In addition, institutional investors use algorithmic trading, high-frequency trading and other advanced trading strategies.

- **Corporate finance:** Corporate finance includes activities related to financing and managing the capital structure of companies. This includes raising money by issuing shares or bonds, mergers and acquisitions, financial risk management and strategic financial planning.
- **Payment systems:** Financial services include a variety of payment methods, including traditional payment methods such as cash, checks and wire transfers, as well as electronic payment systems such as credit cards, debit cards, mobile wallets and digital currencies such as Bitcoin.
- **Retirement Planning:** Financial institutions offer retirement plans such as mutual funds, 401(k) plans, Individual Retirement Accounts (IRAs) and annuities. These plans help people save and invest money to secure their financial future after retirement.
- **Currency and currency exchange services:** Companies and individuals engaged in international business need currency exchange services. Banks and specialized currency service providers offer currency conversion, hedging and other currency-related services. 10. Risk management. Financial services also include risk management activities such as underwriting, actuarial services, hedging strategies and derivatives trading. They help individuals and organizations reduce financial risks associated with uncertain events.

It is important to note that financial services are regulated by government agencies and must comply with applicable laws and regulations to ensure consumer protection, financial stability and fair market practices. Some offers and policies may vary by country and region.

Production

- **Predictive maintenance and asset management:** Machine learning models can analyze sensor data, maintenance logs and historical failures to predict equipment failures and plan maintenance proactively. This approach minimizes downtime, reduces maintenance costs and extends asset life.
- **Quality control and defect detection:** Machine learning algorithms can analyze sensor data, images or audio signals to detect defects or deviations in manufacturing processes. By identifying problems early, manufacturers can maintain product quality and reduce waste.
- **Supply chain optimization and demand planning:** Machine learning techniques are used to optimize supply chain

operations, including inventory, demand forecasting and logistics planning. These models help minimize costs, improve efficiency and increase customer satisfaction.

- **Detection of anomalies in Manufacturing Processes:** Machine learning algorithms can identify unusual patterns or anomalies in manufacturing data, indicating potential quality problems or process anomalies. Early detection of deviations enables timely corrective actions that improve product quality and process efficiency.

Transportation

Transport refers to the movement of people, goods and services from one place to another. It plays a key role in connecting individuals, communities and economies by facilitating trade, enabling travel and tourism and supporting various industries.

Transport Methods

- **Road Transport:** This includes vehicles such as cars, buses, trucks and motorcycles that travel on roads and highways. Road transport is the most common way to transport short distances and goods in cities and regions. 2. Rail transport: Rail systems use trains and rails to transport passengers and goods. Trains can carry large quantities of goods over long distances and are known for their efficiency and cost effectiveness. Rail transport is generally used for freight and public transport.
- **Air Transport:** Air travel involves the use of airplanes, helicopters and other aircraft to transport people and goods. It is the fastest mode of transport for long distances and is crucial for international travel and time-sensitive cargo.
- **Water transport:** waterways such as rivers, canals, lakes and oceans are used for transport. Ships, boats and ferries transport goods and passengers across waterways. Water transport is essential for international trade, bulk transport and cruise tourism.
- **Pipeline Transportation:** Pipelines are used to transport liquids and gases such as oil, natural gas and water. This form of transport is efficient for long-distance transport and is often used in the energy industry.

Importance of Transport

- **Economic Development:** Efficient transportation systems are essential for economic growth. They facilitate the movement of goods, allowing companies to obtain raw materials, enter markets and deliver products to customers. Transport also enables industries such as manufacturing, agriculture and retail to operate.

- **Accessibility and Mobility:** Transport provides people with access to education, healthcare, employment opportunities and various services. It increases mobility and enables travel for work, leisure and social interaction. Public transport systems play a key role in ensuring accessibility for all.
- **Trade and Globalization:** International transportation networks connect countries and enable global trade. Ships, aircraft and logistics systems facilitate the cross-border movement of goods and support international trade and economic integration. 4. Social bonds: Transport helps create and strengthen social bonds, connecting individuals, families and communities. It allows people to visit friends and relatives, participate in cultural events and discover new places.

Traffic Problems

- **Traffic Congestion:** Growing population and urbanization have increased traffic congestion in many cities, causing delays, increased fuel consumption and environmental pollution. Solving traffic congestion requires infrastructure improvements, effective traffic management and alternative traffic solutions.
- **Environmental effects:** Traffic is a major factor in greenhouse gas emissions, air pollution and noise pollution. Encouraging the use of sustainable transport options such as electric vehicles, public transport and cycling is crucial to mitigating environmental impacts.
- **Maintenance and expansion of infrastructure:** Aging infrastructure and the need for expansion present challenges to many transportation systems. Sufficient funding and planning are essential to maintain existing infrastructure and develop new transport networks to meet growing needs.
- **Safety:** Ensuring the safety of transport systems is a constant challenge. Measures such as strict regulations, advanced vehicle safety features and advanced security protocols are required to protect passengers and goods. 5. Access and Equity: Access to transportation services may be limited in certain areas, especially in rural and poor communities. Ensuring fair transport links is essential to closing social and economic inequalities.

The transportation industry is constantly evolving with technology and innovation. Concepts such as autonomous vehicles, high-speed rail and hyperloop systems could revolutionize transportation in the future, offering greater efficiency, sustainability and convenience.

Marketing

Marketing is a broad term that includes various strategies and techniques used to promote products, services or ideas to a target audience. This includes understanding customer needs, creating value and effectively communicating the benefits of a product or service.

In today's highly competitive business environment, effective marketing is essential for businesses to reach their target markets, increase brand awareness and increase sales. Here are some key aspects of marketing:

- **Market research:** before starting a marketing campaign, it is important to conduct market research to understand your target audience, their preferences and buying behavior. It helps to develop effective marketing strategies and identify opportunities in the market.
- **Segmentation and targeting:** Not all customers are the same. Market segmentation means dividing a larger market into smaller, more manageable segments based on similar characteristics or needs. Once segments are identified, companies can target specific segments with tailored marketing messages and strategies.
- **Branding:** A strong brand is a powerful asset for any business. It represents the company's identity and differentiates it from its competitors. Branding involves creating a unique brand image, logo, tagline and consistent communication across various marketing channels.
- **Product positioning:** Positioning involves creating a clear perception of the product or service in the target audience. It focuses on highlighting the unique selling propositions and benefits that differentiate the product from the competition.
- **Marketing Channels:** Marketing is carried out through various channels such as traditional advertising (TV, radio, print), digital marketing (websites, social media, email marketing), content marketing, influencer marketing and more. The choice of channels depends on the target group and marketing objectives.
- **Marketing Mix:** Marketing mix refers to the combination of product, price, place (distribution) and promotions. These

elements work together to create a comprehensive marketing strategy that addresses product features, pricing strategies, distribution channels, and promotional activities.

- **Marketing Communication:** Effective communication is crucial in marketing. It involves creating persuasive messages and using persuasive techniques to engage the target audience. This can be done through advertising, public relations, sales promotion, direct marketing and other means of communication.
- **Market analysis:** With the development of technology, marketing analytics has become important in measuring and optimizing marketing activities. This includes collecting and analyzing data to gain insight into consumer behavior, campaign effectiveness, return on investment (ROI) and informed decision making. Overall, marketing is a dynamic and ever-evolving field that requires creativity, strategic thinking and a deep understanding of customer behavior. It plays an important role for businesses in connecting with their target audience, generating leads and promoting business growth.

1.5. MACHINE LEARNING ETHICAL CONSIDERATIONS

Fairness and Impartiality

Fairness in machine learning refers to the absence of discrimination or bias in the models' predictions or decisions. However, machine learning algorithms can inadvertently maintain biases in the training data, leading to discriminatory results. Bias can be caused by a number of factors, such as unbalanced data representation, historical bias, or distorted records. For example, if a loan approval model is trained on historical data that shows biases against certain demographic groups, the model may unfairly reject loan applications from those groups. Addressing fairness and bias in machine learning involves several approaches. Algorithmic fairness techniques aim to mitigate biases by adjusting the learning process or decision boundaries of the models. These methods include pre-processing methods to reduce bias in the training data, modifying loss functions to add fairness constraints, or using post-processing methods to adjust model predictions. Fairness metrics such as differential effect analysis or smoothed coefficients can be used to analyze and monitor the fairness of machine learning algorithms.

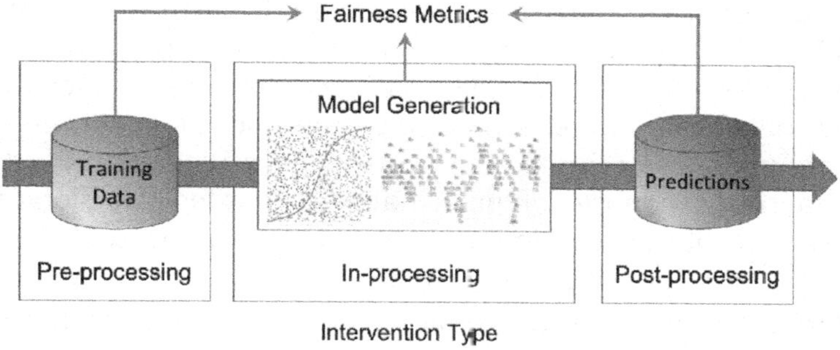

Fairness in ML

- **Privacy:** Privacy is a critical ethical consideration when handling sensitive or personal data in machine learning. Machine learning often requires processing large amounts of data, including personally identifiable information (PII) or other sensitive data. Protecting privacy and ensuring data security are paramount to maintaining trust and meeting legal requirements.

  To protect privacy, organizations must implement privacy-preserving technologies. Data anonymization techniques, such as k-anonymity or differential privacy, can be used to protect individual identities while preserving the usefulness of the data. Encryption methods, such as homomorphic encryption or secure multiparty computation, allow encrypted data to be computed without revealing the raw data. In addition, organizations must obtain informed consent from data, clearly state the purpose and use of the data, and implement secure data handling practices to prevent unauthorized access or misuse.

- **Transparency:** Transparency refers to the ability to understand and explain how machine learning models predict or make decisions. As machine learning algorithms, such as deep neural networks, become more complex, their decision-making processes can be difficult to interpret. Lack of transparency can hinder trust and accountability, especially in critical areas such as health care, finance or criminal justice.

  Translation techniques can be used to increase transparency. Interpretable machine learning methods, such as decision trees, rule-based models or linear models, provide human-understandable explanations for their predictions. Model-agnostic interpretation techniques such as LIME (Local Interpretable Model-agnostic Explanations) or SHAP (SHapley-additive Explanations) can provide post-hoc explanations for some black-box models. These methods help stakeholders understand and evaluate the rationale behind the predictions, identify potential biases, and detect errors or unwanted behaviors in the models. 4. Accountability: Accountability is necessary to ensure that the use of machine learning technology is responsible and meets ethical standards. When machine learning systems make automated decisions that can have a significant impact on individuals or society, creating accountability becomes critical.

Organizations should implement mechanisms to monitor and evaluate the performance of machine learning models. Regular audits and evaluations help identify potential mistakes, misunderstandings or unintended consequences. Feedback loops should be in place so that continuous improvements and improvements can be made. Transparent management frameworks that define roles, responsibilities and procedures for handling errors or solving problems ensure that appropriate action can be taken in the event of errors or adverse effects. In addition, organizations must actively involve relevant stakeholders and domain experts in decision-making processes to ensure the responsible adoption of machine learning models.

- **Data management:** Data governance refers to the overall management and control of data throughout its lifecycle, including collection, storage, use and sharing. Responsible data management practices are necessary to ensure the ethical use of machine learning technology.

  Organizations must establish clear guidelines and standards for data collection to ensure that data collection is based on appropriate consent and in compliance with relevant data protection regulations. Data quality control mechanisms should be in place to ensure data accuracy and reliability. Deploying strong data access controls and security measures protect against unauthorized access and misuse of data. Regular data checks and corrections help identify and correct potential risks or weaknesses. Adherence to data governance principles promotes transparency, security and responsible data handling throughout the machine learning lifecycle.

  It is important to note that the ethical aspects of machine learning are an ongoing work of research and development. As the field evolves, practitioners and researchers continue to explore new techniques, frameworks, and best practices to address ethical issues and promote the responsible and reliable use of machine learning systems. Collaboration between data scientists, policy makers, domain experts, ethicists and other stakeholders is essential to develop guidelines, standards and regulatory frameworks that promote the responsible and ethical use of machine learning technologies.

Ethical Considerations

Ethical aspects of machine learning refer to the responsible and fair use of machine learning algorithms and systems. As artificial intelligence (AI) and machine learning technologies advance, they offer both enormous potential and significant ethical challenges. Here are some important points to consider:

- **Bias and Fairness:** Machine learning algorithms can inadvertently maintain biases present in the data they are trained on. This can lead to discriminatory outcomes or reinforce existing social prejudices. It is important to carefully analyze training data, identify biases and take steps to mitigate them to ensure fairness and equal treatment for all individuals.
- **Transparency and explainability:** Machine learning models often act like black boxes, making it difficult to understand how they make their decisions. Lack of transparency can lead to mistrust and concern about accountability. The effort is to develop explainable artificial intelligence methods that can provide insight into the decision-making process of these models.
- **Privacy and data protection:** Machine learning algorithms require large amounts of data to train effectively. Ensuring the privacy and security of personal data is crucial. Organizations must adhere to legal and ethical standards when collecting, storing and using information, including obtaining informed consent and implementing robust security measures.
- **Algorithmic accountability:** When machine learning models are deployed in critical areas such as healthcare or criminal justice, accountability frameworks must be established. This includes monitoring and auditing algorithms to identify and correct potential biases, errors or unintended consequences.
- **Impact on employment:** Automation of machine learning can eliminate certain jobs, leading to social and economic consequences. It is important to address these issues by investing in retraining and education programs and exploring how AI can create new job opportunities.
- **Social impacts and inequality:** Machine learning technologies can exacerbate existing social inequalities, such as biased

recruitment practices or access to essential services. Evaluating broader social impacts and actively working to reduce inequality are critical ethical considerations.

- **Dual Use Dilemma:** Machine learning algorithms can be used for both beneficial and harmful purposes. Ethical considerations include promoting the responsible use of AI and preventing its misuse, for example in surveillance or autonomous weapon systems.
- **Cooperation and management:** Collaboration between researchers, policy makers, industry professionals and the public is essential to effectively address ethical challenges. Establishing government frameworks, standards and regulations can help ensure the responsible development and deployment of machine learning technologies.

These are just some of the main ethical considerations in machine learning. As AI technology advances, it is important to continue to discuss, evaluate, and refine ethical principles to guide the development and use of these powerful tools in ways that are consistent with social values and promote the common good.

1.6. MACHINE LEARNING FRAMEWORKS AND TOOLS

Tools an d frameworks for machine learning are essential for creating, refining, and deploying machine learning models. They offer the tools, frameworks, and infrastructure required to simplify machine learning workflow and speed up model creation. Let's examine some well-liked machine learning frameworks and tools:

Frameworks

In the field of machine learning, frameworks are software tools or librarie s that provide predefined functions, algorithms, and utilities to simplify the development and implementation of machine learning models. T his framework provides an advanced user interface for building, training and evaluating models, as well as handling data pre- and post-processing operations.

Here are some popular machine learning frameworks.

- **TensorFlow:** Developed by Google, TensorFlow is one of the most widely used machine learning frameworks. It provides a complete ecosystem for building and deploying machine learning models. TensorFlow supports both deep learning and traditional machine learning approaches, and provides advanced APIs such as Keras to facilitate model development.

- **PyTorch:** Developed by Facebook's AI research lab, PyTorch is another popular deep learning framework. It features dynamic calculation graphics, making it easy to define and edit models on the fly. PyTorch is known for its flexibility and is often preferred by researchers and practitioners in the deep learning community.
- **scikit-learn:** scikit-learn is a widely used machine learning library in Python. It provides a wealth of algorithms and tools for various tasks, including classification, regression, clustering, dimensionality reduction, and more. scikit-learn is known for its ease of use and well-documented API.
- **Keras:** While Keras is often used as a high-level API in TensorFlow, it can also function as a standalone deep learning framework. Keras focuses on simplicity and ease of use, while providing powerful capabilities for building deep learning models. It provides a user-friendly interface for designing and training neural networks.
- **MXNet:** MXNet is a flexible and powerful deep learning framework that supports both imperative and symbolic programming. It offers dynamic computer graphics that enable efficient memory usage and dynamic network architectures. MXNet is known for its scalability and is often used for large-scale distributed training.
- **Caffe:** Caffe is a deep learning framework developed by Berkeley AI Research (BAIR). It excels in speed and efficiency, especially in convolutional neural networks (CNN) used in computer vision tasks. Caffe is a simple and expressive architecture definition language that makes it easy to define network structures.
- **Theano:** Theano is a Python library that enables efficient mathematical computation using multidimensional arrays. It is often used as a backend for a deep learning framework like Keras. Theano provides a low-level interface for building and optimizing mathematical expressions, useful for researchers and developers who need precise control of their models. These are just a few examples of the many machine learning frameworks available. Each framework has its own strengths and focuses on different aspects of machine learning. The choice of framework depends on factors such as the task at hand, level of expertise, community support and specific project requirements.

Table 2: Popular Machine Learning Frameworks and Tools

Framework/Tool	Description
TensorFlow	TensorFlow is an open-source machine learning framework developed by Google. It provides a comprehensive ecosystem for building and deploying machine learning models.
PyTorch	PyTorch is an open-source machine learning library developed by Facebook's AI Research Lab. It is widely used for developing dynamic neural networks and supports efficient model training and deployment.
Scikit-learn	Scikit-learn is a popular machine learning library in Python that provides a wide range of algorithms and tools for machine learning tasks such as classification, regression, clustering, and dimensionality reduction.
Keras	Keras is a high-level deep learning library that runs on top of TensorFlow or Theano. It offers a user-friendly interface for building and training neural networks.
Microsoft Azure	Microsoft Azure is a cloud-based platform that provides various machine learning services, including automated machine learning, model deployment, and scalable infrastructure for machine learning projects.
IBM Watson	IBM Watson is a comprehensive AI platform that offers a range of services, including machine learning, natural language processing, computer vision, and data analytics.

TensorFlow

TensorFlow is an open-source library widely used for machine learning and deep learning. Developed by the Google Brain team, TensorFlow provides a flexible and comprehensive ecosystem for building and deploying various machine learning models.

Basically, TensorFlow is based on the concept of computer graph. A computer graph is a directed graph where nodes represent mathematical operations and edges represent the flow of data between those operations. In TensorFlow, the nodes of a graph are called "ops" and the edges are called "tensors", which are multi-dimensional arrays. Here are some key features and components of TensorFlow:

- **Flexible Architecture:** TensorFlow provides a flexible architecture that allows users to define and customize their own models. It supports both high-level APIs like Keras, as well as low-level APIs that provide more control over model design.
- **Automatic differentiation:** TensorFlow can automatically calculate gradients to optimize model parameters using techniques such as back propagation. This makes training complex neural networks easier.

- **Extensive Model Collection:** TensorFlow provides a lot of ready-made models and layers through its advanced APIs. These models can be used for various tasks such as image classification, object recognition, natural language processing and more.
- **Distributed Computing:** TensorFlow supports distributed computing across multiple devices, machines and GPUs. This allows you to efficiently scale your models and training processes, making it suitable for large machine learning tasks.
- **Tensor Board:** TensorFlow includes Tensor Board, a web-based tool for visualizing and analyzing computer graphics, training progress, and model performance. This helps in tracking and debugging models.
- **Deployment Options:** TensorFlow provides several options for model deployment, including serving models on cloud platforms, mobile devices, browsers, and embedded systems. TensorFlow Lite is a lightweight version of TensorFlow designed for mobile and edge devices.
- **Community and Ecosystem:** TensorFlow has a large and active community that contributes to the development of new features, models and tools. It also integrates with popular libraries such as NumPy, scikit-learn and OpenCV, making TensorFlow easy to integrate into existing workflows.

PyTorch

PyTorch is a popular open-source machine learning framework widely used to develop and train deep learning models. Developed by Facebook's AI research lab, it provides a dynamic computer graphics approach that enables flexible and efficient model development.

Here are some key aspects and features of PyTorch for machine learning:

- **Dynamic computer graph:** PyTorch uses dynamic computer graph, which means that the graph is generated and evaluated continuously at runtime. This dynamic nature provides flexibility in building complex models with different architectures and input sizes. It also allows for easier debugging and makes it easier to use Python's standard debugging tools.
- **Computing tensors:** PyTorch represents data using multidimensional arrays called tensors. PyTorch tensors are similar to NumPy arrays, but with additional features and optimizations for GPU acceleration. Tensors in PyTorch can be easily manipulated and manipulated using various

mathematical operations, making them powerful for numerical computations related to machine learning.

- **Automatic differentiation:** PyTorch includes a technique called automatic differentiation that allows you to efficiently compute gradients. Gradients are crucial for training deep learning models using techniques such as back propagation. PyTorch's automatic differentiation engine, called Autograd, tracks tensor functions and automatically calculates gradients, making it easy to implement and train complex models.
- **Neural Network Modules:** PyTorch provides a rich set of ready-made modules and functions for building neural networks. These modules contain different layers, activation functions, loss functions and optimization algorithms. PyTorch's modular structure makes it easy to create and customize neural network architectures using these modules.
- **GPU acceleration:** PyTorch integrates seamlessly with graphics processing units (GPUs) to accelerate calculations. It provides CUDA support that allows GPUs to perform operations efficiently. Using GPUs can significantly speed up the training and inference processes, especially for large deep learning models that involve heavy matrix operations.
- **Easy debugging and prototyping:** PyTorch's no-nonsense programming style enables intuitive model development, debugging and prototyping. Developers can seamlessly use Python's native control flow expressions, debugging tools, and libraries in their PyTorch code. This flexibility makes it easy to experiment with different model architectures, loss functions, and optimization techniques.
- **Vast Ecosystem:** PyTorch has a thriving community and a rich ecosystem of libraries and tools built around it. Many popular deep learning libraries, such as TorchVision for computer vision tasks and TorchText for natural language processing, are built on top of PyTorch. In addition, PyTorch integrates seamlessly with other machine learning libraries and frameworks, allowing users to tap into a wide variety of resources.

Overall, PyTorch's dynamic computational graphics, tensor computing capabilities, automatic differentiation, modular design, GPU acceleration, and ease of use make it a powerful framework for developing and training machine learning models. Its popularity among researchers and practitioners continues to grow due to its flexibility, simplicity and strong community support.

- **Scikit-learn:** Scikit-learn is a powerful machine learning library in Python. It provides a wide range of algorithms and tools for tasks such as classification, regression, clustering and dimensionality reduction. Scikit-learn is known for its user-friendly API, robust documentation, and powerful implementations of machine learning algorithms. It is commonly used for exploratory data analysis, model evaluation, and building machine learning pipelines.
- **Keras:** Keras is an advanced deep learning library that runs on TensorFlow or Theano. It provides a user-friendly and intuitive interface for building and training neural networks. Keras strips away the low-level details and provides a simplified API for rapid prototyping of deep learning models. Its ease of use and flexibility have made it a popular choice among beginners and seasoned professionals alike.
- **Microsoft Azure:** Microsoft Azure is a cloud-based platform that offers a wide range of machine learning services. It provides tools and infrastructure for large-scale development, training and deployment of machine learning models. Azure Machine Learning enables data scientists to create and manage machine learning workflows, providing capabilities such as automated machine learning and model deployment in production environments.
- **IBM Watson:** IBM Watson is a comprehensive artificial intelligence platform that provides various services for machine learning, natural language processing, computer vision and data analytics. It provides a set of tools and APIs to develop intelligent applications and gain insights from data. IBM Watson services are designed to facilitate the development of AI-based solutions across industries and sectors. Among other things, these frameworks and tools allow data scientists and developers to harness the power of machine learning and create advanced models for a wide range of applications. They provide the building blocks, libraries, and infrastructure needed to accelerate the development process and deploy sustainable machine learning solutions.

2

Regression Analysis: A Comprehensive Guide to Statistical Modeling

Regression analysis is a statistical modeling technique widely used in machine learning and data analysis to understand the relationship between a dependent variable and one or more independent variables. This is especially useful for making predictions based on input variables or estimating numerical values.

In regression analysis, the dependent variable is often called the target variable or the response variable, while the independent variables are called the predictor variables or characteristics. The goal is to develop a mathematical model that can accurately predict the target variable based on predetermined predictors.

The basic idea of regression analysis is to fit the regression model to the available data by minimizing the difference between the predicted values of the target variable and the actual values. This process is usually done by estimating the parameters of a regression equation using various statistical techniques, such as ordinary least squares (OLS), gradient descent, or maximum likelihood estimation.

There are different regression analysis techniques, each suitable for different scenarios:

- **Simple Linear Regression:** This technique is used when there is a linear relationship between the target variable and one of the predictor variables. The model assumes a linear relationship between the variables, which allows to estimate the slope and intercept of the line.
- **Multiple linear regression:** Multiple linear regression extends simple linear regression by considering multiple predictor variables. This assumes a linear relationship between the

target variable and all predictors, allowing us to estimate the coefficients for each predictor.

- **Polynomial regression:** Polynomial regression is an extension of linear regression where the relationship between the target variable and the predictors is modelled as an nth degree polynomial equation. It can capture non-linear relationships between variables by adding higher terms.
- **Ridge regression and lasso regression:** These methods are used to deal with multicollinearity (correlation) of predictor variables. Ridge regression adds a penalty to the least-squares method to reduce coefficient estimates, while Lasso regression performs variable selection by setting some coefficients to zero.
- **Logistic regression:** Although logistic regression is called regression, it is mainly used for binary classification problems. It models the relationship between the target variable and the predictors using a logistic function that maps the inputs with a probability value between 0 and 1.
- **Time-series regression:** Time-series regression is used in processing time-dependent data, when the target variable is influenced by its past values and other time-related factors. Methods such as autoregressive i ntegrated moving average (ARIMA) or seasonal time series decomposition (STL) can be used.

2.1. UNDERSTANDING REGRESSION ANALYSIS

Regression analysis can be broadly divided into two main types: simple linear regression and multiple linear regression.

1. Simple linear regression:

Simple linear regression involves examining the relationship between a single independent variable (X) and a dependent variable (Y). The relationship is assumed to be linear, meaning that a straight line can adequately represent the data.

A simple linear regression equation is usually expressed as:

$Y = \beta_0 \beta_1 X \varepsilon$

Where:

- Y is the dependent variable
- X is the independent variable
- β_0 is the y-intercept (value of Y when X is zero)
- β_1 is the slope (change in Y with unit change in X)
- ε is the error term (difference between predicted and actual value of Y)

The purpose of simple linear regression is to estimate the values of β_0 and β_1 that best fit the data, minimizing the sum of squared errors. So we can make predictions for Y based on given X values.

In the example mentioned earlier, the simple linear regression equation was:

Exam points = 55 5 * Lessons

Here, the y-intercept (β_0) is 55, indicating that if the student did not study at all (Lessons = 0), the estimated exam score is 55. The slope (β_1) is 5, which means that for each additional lesson, the exam score is expected to increase by 5 per point.

2. Multiple linear regression:

Multiple linear regression involves examining the relationship between a dependent variable (Y) and two or more independent variables (X1, X2, ..., Xn). It extends the concept of simple linear regression to include multiple predictors.

The multiple linear regression equation is given as:

$Y = \beta_0\ \beta_1 X_1\ \beta_2 X_2\ ...\ \beta_n X_n\ \varepsilon$

Where:

- Y is the dependent variable
- X_1, X2, ..., X_n are independent variables
- β_0 is the y-intercept
- β_1, β_2, ..., β_n are the slopes corresponding to each independent variable
- ε is the error term

The purpose of linear multiple regression is to estimate the values of β_0, β_1, β_2, ..., β_n that best fit the data by minimizing the sum of the squared errors. This allows predictions to be made for Y based on given values X1, X2, ..., Xn.

Linear r egression can often be used to analyze more complex relationships between variables. This allows us to examine how different independent variables affect the variation in the dependent variable.

Both simple linear regression and multiple linear regression use statisti c al measures to assess the quality and significance of the regression model. Here are some key steps.

R-Square (Coefficient of Determination): R-squared, also known as coeffi cient of determination, is a statistical quantity commonly used in m achine learning and regression analysis to evaluate the performance of a predictive model. It shows how well the model fits the observed data.

The R-square value varies between 0 and 1 and represents the proportion of variance in the dependent variable that can be explained by the independent variables in the model. In other words, it measures the percentage of variation in the response variable captured by the model.

The following steps are usually taken to calculate the R-squared:

- **Model fitting:** Use a regression algorithm to fit a model to the training data, using the independent variables to predict the dependent variable.
- **Calculate the total sum of squares (SST):** Calculate the total change in the dependent variable by summing the differences between each true value and the mean of the dependent variable.
- **Calculate the residual sum of squares (SSE):** Calculate the sum of the squared differences between each predicted value and the corresponding true value.
- **Calculate R-Square:** Subtract SSE from SST and divide the result by SST. The formula is:

  R-squared = 1 - (SSE / SST)

  R-squared = 1 - (SSE / SST)

  The resulting value ranges from 0 to 1. A value of 0 indicates that the model explains none of the variation in the dependent variable, while a value of 1 indicates that the model explains all of the variation.

  The interpretation of R-squared can be subjective and has some limitations. Here are some points to consider.

- **Higher is better:** A higher R-squared value usually means a better fit. But "fit" can vary depending on the problem domain and the nature of the data.
- **Superfitting:** R-squared increases as more independent variables are included in the model, even if they have no significant relationship with the dependent variable. This can lead to overfitting, where the model performs well on the training data but poorly on the unseen data.
- **Context matters:** R-squared should always be interpreted in the context of a specific problem and research area. Some fields may have more variable data, making it more difficult to achieve a high R-squared value.
- **Comparisons:** R-squared is useful for comparing different models. If two models have similar R-squared values, this indicates that they explain the same amount of variation in the

dependent variable. However, R-squared alone should not be the sole basis for model selection.

In summary, R-squared measures how well a regression model fits the observed data. Although this is a useful metric, it should be interpreted with caution and in conjunction with other evaluation metrics and domain knowledge to evaluate the overall performance of a machine learning model.

p-values: In machine learning, the concept of p-values is not used as often as in traditional statistical hypothesis testing. Machine learning models focus on predictive accuracy and generalization rather than hypothesis testing. However, P-values are still important in some areas of machine learning research and practice, especially when it comes to interpretability or model comparison.

Here is a brief description of p-values and what they mean in machine learning:

- **What is a p-value?:** The p-value is a statistical measure that helps evaluate the strength of the evidence against the null hypothesis. It quantifies the probability of obtaining the observed data or more extreme data, assuming that the null hypothesis is true.
- **Traditional hypothesis testing:** In traditional statistics, p-values are usually used to determine whether there is enough evidence to reject the null hypothesis in favor of an alternative hypothesis. This requires specifying a level of significance (often indicated as alpha, e.g. 0.05) and if the calculated p-value is less than alpha, the null hypothesis is rejected.
- **Machine learning and p-values:** In machine learning, p-values are not typically used to test hypotheses in the same way as in traditional statistics. This is because machine learning models are often complex and contain many variables and interactions. Instead, the focus is on model performance, such as accuracy, precision, recall, or other metrics.
- **Interpretability and feature selection:** In some cases, p-values can be useful for interpreting machine learning models or selecting relevant features. For example, in linear regression, p-values can help identify which features are statistically significant in predicting the target variable. Care should be taken, however, as p-values may not provide the full picture, especially in high-dimensional settings.
- **Multiple hypothesis testing:** Machine learning often involves testing multiple hypotheses simultaneously, such as comparing

the performance of multiple models or selecting features. In these cases, traditional p-values may not be appropriate because they do not take into account the problem of multiple comparisons. Methods such as Bonferroni correction or false discovery rate (FDR) control can be used to solve this problem.

- **Model comparison and evaluation:** When comparing different models or algorithms, p-values are not necessarily directly applicable. Instead, practitioners typically use resampling techniques (such as cross-validation or bootstrapping) or statistical tests designed specifically to compare models, such as the t-test or ANOVA. It is important to note that the field of machine learning has evolved to emphasize other evaluation and validation techniques such as cross-validation, A/B testing, or out-of-sample performance. These methods focus on evaluating model performance with unseen data, rather than relying solely on p-values for hypothesis testing.

Standard Errors

In machine learning, standard errors are statistical measures that provide an estimate of the uncertainty or variability associated with model parameters or predictions. They are commonly used to assess the reliability of a machine learning model and to make inferences about the population from which the training data was sampled.

Here are a few key points to elaborate on the topic of standard errors in machine learning:

1. **Model Parameters:** In many machine learning algorithms, the goal is to estimate a set of parameters that define the model. For example, in linear regression, the model parameters are the regression coefficients. Standard errors can be calculated for these parameters to determine how much they are likely to vary if the model is fit on different subsets of the training data. The standard errors provide a measure of uncertainty around the estimated parameter values.
2. **Model Evaluation:** Standard errors can also be used to evaluate the performance of a machine learning model. When assessing the predictive performance of a model, standard errors can be calculated for various evaluation metrics such as accuracy, precision, recall, or F1 score. These standard errors help quantify the uncertainty in the model's performance and can be used to compare different models or variations of the same model.
3. **Confidence Intervals:** Standard errors are often used to construct confidence intervals, which provide a range of

plausible values for an unknown population parameter. Confidence intervals indicate the level of confidence (e.g., 95% confidence) that the true parameter value falls within the specified range. By calculating the standard error and using appropriate statistical distributions (e.g., t-distribution or normal distribution), confidence intervals can be derived for model parameters or predictions.

4. **Resampling Methods:** One common approach to estimating standard errors in machine learning is through resampling methods such as bootstrapping or cross-validation. Bootstrapping involves drawing random samples with replacement from the original training data to create multiple bootstrap samples. The model is then fitted on each bootstrap sample, and the standard deviation of the parameter estimates across the bootstrap samples provides an estimate of the standard error. Cross-validation involves partitioning the data into multiple subsets (e.g., k-fold cross-validation) and iteratively fitting the model on different combinations of training and validation sets. The variability in model performance across these iterations can be used to estimate standard errors.
5. **Interpretation and Inference:** Standard errors play a crucial role in statistical inference. They help determine the significance of model parameters or features by calculating test statistics such as t-values or z-scores. These test statistics are computed by dividing the estimated parameter value by its standard error. If the test statistic exceeds a certain threshold (e.g., based on a significance level), it suggests that the parameter is statistically significant and likely to have a meaningful effect.

Overall, standard errors in machine learning provide valuable insights into the uncertainty associated with model parameters and predictions. They help assess model reliability, make comparisons between models, construct confidence intervals, and facilitate statistical inference. Understanding and appropriately accounting for standard errors are essential for sound model interpretation and decision-making.

Confidence Intervals

Confidence intervals provide a range of values within which the true value of the coefficient is likely to fall at a given confidence level. These statistical measures help interpret the results of the regression analysis and give an idea of the strength and significance of the relationships between the variables. In addition, regression analysis can be extended to include other variables such as polynomial regression (for non-linear relationships) and logistic regression (for binary outcomes). Remember that regression analysis is a powerful tool, but it depends on certain assumptions such as linearity, independence of errors, homoscedasticity, and the absence of multicollinearity. It is important to check these assumptions and consider the limitations of the analysis.

2.2. LINEAR REGRESSION

The relationship between a dependent variable and one or more independent variablescan be modelled statistically using linear regression. The dependent variable can be written as a linear combination of the independent variables because it is assumed that there is a linear relationship between them.

In the example we discussed earlier, the goal was to explore the relationship between the number of hours studied and exam scores. To perform linear regression, we use the data table provided:

Hours Studied (X)	Exam Scores (Y)
2	60
4	70
6	75
8	80
10	90

We now proceed to fit the linear regression model to the data. The model equation is obtained as follows:

$Y = \beta_0 \; \beta_1 X \; \varepsilon$

Here is the breakdown of the terms in the equation:

- Y is the dependent variable (test results)
- X is the independent variable (hours studied)
- β_0 is the y-intercept (value of Y when X is zero)
- β_1 is the slope (change in Y with unit change in X)
- ε is the error term (difference between predicted and actual value of Y)

The goal is to estimate the values of β_0 and β_1 that best fit the data, minimizing the difference between the predicted and actual test result values. In our sample data, a linear regression model might yield the following equation:

Exam points = 55 5 * Lessons

This equation means that the y-intercept (β_0) is 55, which indicates that if the student did not study at all (lessons = 0), the estimated exam score is 55. The slope (β_1) is 5, which means that for each lesson an increase in exam results by 5 points is expected. To visualize the linear regression line with scatter, we add a line representing the model equation.

The line represents the best-fit data point. This describes the general trend that as the number of lessons increases, so do exam scores. In addition to the fitted line, linear regression provides statistical measures to assess model quality and significance. Let's briefly discuss these measures.

1. Coefficient of Determination (R-squared)

The coefficient of determination, often called R-squared or R^2, is a statistical quantity used to evaluate the goodness of fit of a regression model. It quantifies the proportion of variance in the dependent variable that can be explained by the independent variables in the model. In the context of machine learning, R-squared is often used as an evaluation metric to determine how well a model fits the observed data.

To understand R-squared, let's look at a simple linear regression model where we have a dependent variable (Y) and an independent variable (X). The goal of the model is to find the best linear relationship between X and Y. R-squared measures the portion of the total variation in Y that can be explained by a linear relationship with X.

The R-squared value varies between 0 and 1. This means:

R-squared = 0: The model explains nothing about the variation in the dependent variable. It doesn't fit the data at all. - R-squared = 1: the model perfectly explains the observed variation in the dependent variable. It fits the data perfectly.

However, it is important to note that a high R-squared value does not necessarily mean a good model. R-squared only shows how well the model fits the data used to build it. It does not guarantee the predictive accuracy of the model for unseen data or the absence of other problems such as overfitting.

R-square can be interpreted as the proportion of variance in the dependent variable that can be predicted by the independent variables. Mathematically, this is calculated as:

R-squared = 1 - (SSR/SST)

where SSR is the sum of squared residuals (the difference between the predicted and actual values of the dependent variable) and SST is the sum of squares (the sum of the squared differences between the actual values of the dependent variable and the mean of the dependent variable).

A higher R-squared value indicates that the model explains more of the variance in the dependent variable. However, if the model becomes too complex and overfits the data, the R-squared can become artificially inflated, giving a misleading impression of the model's performance. Therefore, it is important to look at R-squared along with other evaluation measures and assess the generalizability of the model.

2. P-values

P-values are statistical measures commonly used in hypothesis testing to assess the strength of evidence against the null hypothesis. Although p-values are widely used in traditional statistical analysis, their interpretation and role in machine learning is slightly different.

In traditional statistical hypothesis testing, the p-value represents the probability that the test statistic is as extreme as the calculated one, assuming that the null hypothesis is true. Typically, if the p-value is below a predetermined significance level (eg, 0.05), the null hypothesis is rejected in favor of the alternative hypothesis.

In the context of machine learning, p-values are less often used directly because machine learning algorithms focus on predictive accuracy rather than hypothesis testing. However, they can be useful in some cases:

- **Feature Selection:** In some machine learning algorithms, feature selection methods may use statistical tests such as chi-square test or t-test to evaluate the importance of each feature. In these cases, p-values help determine which functions to include in the model based on their statistical significance.
- **Interpretability:** In some machine learning models, especially linear models such as linear regression or logistic regression, p-values can provide information about the significance of individual predictors. A low p-value for a predictor indicates a strong association with the target variable.
- **Model evaluation:** In cases where a machine learning model is compared to a baseline model or an alternative model, statistical tests can be used to determine if there is a significant difference in performance. P values can help assess the statistical significance of observed differences.

It is important to note that although p-values can be informative in these cases, they should not be the only criteria for making machine learning decisions. Other factors should also be considered, such as effect size, practical relevance, and familiarity with the field.

Additionally, it is worth mentioning that some machine learning methods, such as deep learning, are less dependent on statistical tests and p-values. These models tend to focus more on learning complex patterns directly from the data, rather than relying on explicit hypothesis testing.

3. Standard Errors

In machine learning, standard errors are statistical measures used to quantify the uncertainty or variability associated with a model's estimates or predictions. They provide valuable information about the reliability and precision of the model's results. While standard errors are commonly used in statistical inference, their interpretation and application in machine learning may differ slightly due to the nature of the field.

Here are a few key points to elaborate on standard errors in machine learning:

- **Model Coefficients:** In linear models, such as linear regression, the standard errors are often used to assess the uncertainty associated with the estimated coefficients. The standard error of a coefficient measures the average distance between the estimated coefficient and the true population value it represents. A smaller standard error indicates greater precision and confidence in the estimated coefficient.
- **Model Evaluation:** Standard errors can also be used in model evaluation to estimate the uncertainty around the performance metrics, such as accuracy, precision, recall, or F1 score. For example, when evaluating a classification model, you can calculate the standard error of the accuracy to understand how much the estimated accuracy may vary if the model were trained on different datasets.
- **Cross-Validation:** Cross-validation is a commonly used technique for model evaluation and selection. When performing cross-validation, multiple training and testing sets are created from the available data. The standard errors of the performance metrics computed across these different folds can give an indication of the variability in the model's performance.
- **Bootstrapping:** Bootstrapping is a resampling technique used to estimate the sampling distribution of a statistic. It involves generating multiple bootstrap samples by randomly sampling with replacement from the original dataset. By calculating the standard deviation of the estimates obtained from these

bootstrap samples, one can estimate the standard error of the statistic.

- **Confidence Intervals:** Standard errors are often used to construct confidence intervals, which provide a range of plausible values for an unknown parameter. Confidence intervals give an indication of the precision of the estimated parameter. The width of the interval is determined by the standard error: a smaller standard error results in a narrower confidence interval.
- **Generalization and Prediction:** In machine learning, the goal is often to build models that generalize well to unseen data. Standard errors can provide insights into how well the model might generalize. For instance, if the standard error of the model's performance on a validation set is high, it suggests that the model's predictions might be more uncertain or variable when applied to new, unseen data.

It's important to note that standard errors are not the only measure of uncertainty in machine learning. Other techniques, such as Bayesian inference or ensemble methods, can also provide valuable insights into uncertainty estimation. Nonetheless, standard errors remain a useful tool for understanding the variability and reliability of machine learning models and their predictions.

Confidence Intervals

Confidence intervals provide a range of values within which the true value of the coefficient is likely to fall at a given confidence level. They help estimate the uncertainty of the estimated coefficients. These statistical measures help interpret the results of linear regression, assess the significance of the relationship between variables and understand the quality of the model. Linear regression is widely used in various fields, including economics, finance, social sciences, and engineering. It provides insight into the effect of the independent variables on the dependent variable and allows predictions to be made based on the observed data. However, it is important to note that linear regression requires certain assumptions such as linearity, independence of errors, homoscedasticity (constant variance), and absence of multicollinearity. Violations of these assumptions may require alternative regression techniques or transformations to capture more complex relationships

2.3. POLYNOMIAL REGRESSION

A development of linear regression that can also account for non-linear relationships between variables is polynomial regression.

It entails adding polynomial terms (exponents) of the independent variable(s) to the regression equation in order to fit a polynomial function to the data.

We intended to investigate the connection between years of work experience and an employee's wage in the prior scenario. Our data table for polynomial regression looked like this:

Table 1

Years of Experience (X)	Salary (Y)
1	30,000
3	40,000
5	50,000
7	60,000
9	70,000

To fit the polynomial regression model, we included the polynomial terms of the independent variable in the regression equation. We used a quadratic (quadratic) polynomial regression equation of the form:

$Y = \beta_0\ \beta_1 X\ \beta_2 X^2\ \varepsilon$

Here is the breakdown of the terms in the equation:

- Y is the dependent variable (salary)
- X is the independent variable (years of experience)
- β_0 is the y-intercept (value of Y when X is zero)
- β_1 is the coefficient of the first order term (linear coefficient)
- β_2 is the coefficient of the second term (quadratic factor)
- ε is the error term (difference between predicted and actual value of Y)

The goal is to estimate the values of β_0, β_1, and β_2 that best fit the data, minimizing the difference between predicted and actual wage values. For our sample data, the polynomial regression model produced the following equation:

Salary = 20,000 5,000 * work experience 2,000 * years of experience^2 this equation means that the y-intercept (β_0) is 20,000, indicating that the estimated salary for a worker with zero years of experience is 20,000. The linear coefficient (β_1) is 5,000, which means that for each additional year of work, the salary increases by 5,000. The squared coefficient (β_2) is 2000, indicating that the relationship between work experience and earnings is non-linear and that the rate of wage increase can change with increasing experience.

The curve represents the best-fit data points and represents the non-linear relationship between years of experience and salary. In addition to the fitted curve, polynomial regression provides statistical measures to assess model quality and significance. These measurements are similar to linear regression measurements, including coefficient of determination (R-squared), p-values, standard errors, and confidence intervals. Polynomial regression is useful when the relationship between variables is non-linear and allows more flexibility in modelling complex patterns in the data. It can capture curves, turns and turning points that linear regression cannot.

However, it is important to note that polynomial regression has its limitations. Using higher-order polynomials can lead to overfitting, where the model fits the training data too closely but performs poorly on new, unseen data. It is very important to strike a balance between the complexity of the polynomial equation and the risk of overfitting.

2.4. SUPPORT VECTOR REGRESSION

A supervised learning algorithm called Support Vector Regression (SVR) is utilised for regression analysis. It is a version of the classification-focused Support Vector Machines (SVM) technique. By identifying a regression function that best approximates the data while maximising the margin between the data points and the regression function, SVR extends SVM to tackle regression difficulties.

Let's go back to the earlier example of property pricing based on house size to better grasp SVR.

Consider the following dataset:

Table 2

House Size (X)	Price (Y)
1000	250
1500	400
2000	450
2500	500
3000	550

First, we plot the data points on a scatterplot, with house size on the x-axis and price on the y-axis:

The goal of SVR is to find a regression function that fits the data but allows for tolerance around the function. This margin is the area within which errors or deviations from the regression line are allowed. The goal is to maximize this margin while keeping errors within a specified tolerance.

SVR accomplishes this by identifying a subset of data points, called support vectors, that are closest to the margin. These support vectors play a crucial role in defining the regression function. In SVR, data points are mapped to a higher-dimensional feature space using a kernel function. This transformation allows SVR to capture non-linear relationships between variables.

Some common kernel functions used in SVR are linear, polynomial, Gaussian radial basis function (RBF), and sigmoid. The choice of kernel function depends on the data set and the desired complexity of the regression function. Different kernels have different properties and store different types of associations. Once the support vectors and regression function are defined, SVR can be used to predict new, unseen data points. The regression function represents the line or curve of best fit that approximates the data, maximizing the margin. To illustrate this, we can plot the regression function derived from SVR applied to the house price data.

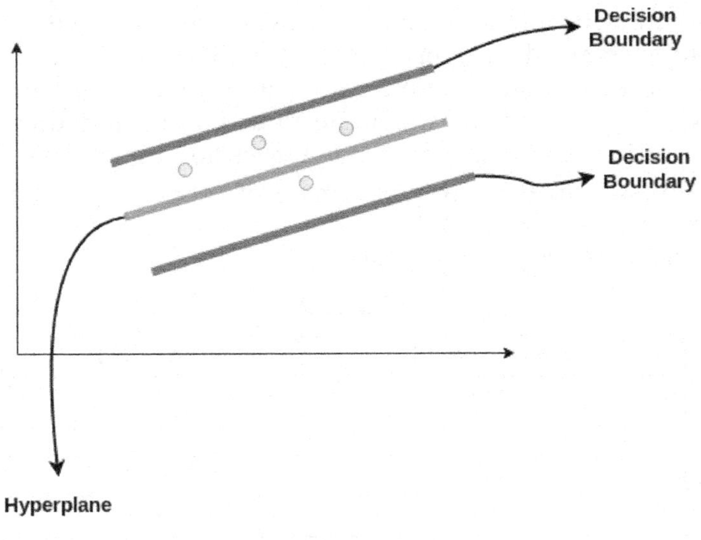

Support Vector Regression

The red line represents the regression function determined by SVR. The shaded area around the line represents the tolerance limit. Data points within this range are considered marginal, while data points outside the range are considered errors. SVR provides additional parameters to adjust margin width and error tolerance, allowing fine-tuning of the model performance. It is important to note that SVR, like all machine learning algorithms, has assumptions and limitations. SVR assumes that data points are independent and identically distributed and may be sensitive to outliers. Care must be taken to properly preprocess the data and select appropriate kernel functions. In general, SVR is a powerful algorithm for regression tasks, especially in situations where there are nonlinear relationships between variables. It is widely used in various fields such as finance, economics and engineering. I hope this review provides a comprehensive overview of SVR and its application to regression problems.

2.5. DECISION TREE REGRESSION

Decision Tree Regression is a machine learning approach that simulates associations between features and the target variable in regression tasks using a decision tree structure. It divides the feature space into segments and gives each segment a prediction value.

Let's go back to the ice cream sales depending on temperature example to demonstrate the procedure:

Table 2

Temperature (X)	Ice Cream Sales (Y)
25	200
28	250
32	320
35	400
30	280

To build a decision tree regression model, the algorithm goes through the following steps.

- **Selecting the best partition:** In machine learning, selecting the best partition refers to dividing the dataset into training and testing subsets to evaluate the performance of the machine learning model. This is an important step in model development because it helps assess how well the model generalizes to unseen data.
- **The most common way to split a data set is a "train-test split", where the data set is split into two parts:** a training set and a test (or validation) set. The training set is used to train the model, while the test set is used to evaluate its performance. Here are some key considerations for choosing the best distribution for machine learning.
- **Size of data:** The size of data plays an important role in determining the distribution ratio. If the dataset is large, a smaller portion (eg 70:30) can be reserved for testing. However,

if the data set is limited, it is recommended to reserve a larger portion (eg 80:20 or 90:10) for testing to obtain more reliable estimates of performance.

- **Data distribution:** It is important to ensure that the data reflects the real scenarios that the model will encounter. If the dataset has class imbalance problems, where certain classes are underrepresented, it is important to use methods such as stratified sampling to ensure that the distribution preserves the distribution of classes in both the training and test set.
- **Randomness:** The distribution should be random to avoid bias in the selection of samples. Random selection ensures that data from both the training and testing sets are representative of the entire data set and reduces the risk of overfitting the data to certain models.
- **Temporal considerations:** If the data set has a temporal component, such as time series data, it is important to consider the temporal order when splitting. Typically, the training set should contain data from earlier periods and the test set should contain data from later periods to assess the model's ability to make accurate predictions in the future.
- **Cross-validation:** In addition to distribution train tests, cross-validation can be used to obtain more reliable performance estimates. Cross-validation involves dividing the data set into several subsets (skills), training a model with a combination of these skills, and evaluating its performance with the rest of the skills. This process is repeated several times and the performance results are averaged to obtain a more reliable estimate of the model's performance.
- **Domain knowledge:** Prior knowledge of the problem domain and data set can help in choosing the appropriate section. Understanding the characteristics of the data and potential challenges can help guide decisions such as distribution ratio, handling missing data or dealing with outliers. It is important to note that model performance on the test set should not be used to measure the generalization of the final model. To obtain a more reliable estimate of model performance, after model development and parameter tuning, it is critical to analyze the model with completely unseen data (e.g., a hold data set or real-world data). In summary, choosing the best distribution in machine learning requires consideration of factors such as dataset size, data distribution, randomness, time considerations, and the use of

techniques such as cross-validation. This requires a balance between efficiently training the model and fairly evaluating its performance with unseen data.

- **Tree building:** Machine learning tree building refers to the process of building decision trees, which are widely used models for classification and regression tasks. Decision trees are predictive models that learn a series of hierarchical decisions or rules from training data to make predictions or decisions about new, unseen data points.

Creating a decision tree involves two main steps: tree induction and tree pruning.

- **Wood induction:** The process starts with the root node, which represents the entire training data set. - At each internal node, a decision rule or test condition is applied to split the data based on certain attribute values. - The goal is to create distributions that maximize the homogeneity or purity of the data in each resulting subset. Common metrics for measuring purity are the Gini Addendum and Data Validation. - The separation process continues recursively until certain stopping criteria are met, such as maximum depth, minimum number of samples per page or a significant improvement in purity.
- **Tree pruning:** Once the original tree is built, it can be too complex and prone to overfitting, meaning it performs well on training data but generalizes poorly to new data. - Pruning is a technique used to reduce the complexity of a tree and improve its generalizability. - One method of pruning is post-pruning, where the tree is grown to its maximum size and then nodes or branches are removed based on their estimated effect on the tree's performance in the validation set. - Another approach is pre-cutting, where tree construction is stopped early due to certain conditions, such as impurity reduction or accuracy below a threshold. There are different algorithms for building trees, such as ID3, C4.5, CART (Classification and Regression Trees) and Random Forests. Each algorithm has its own specific details, but they all follow the general framework of tree induction and pruning. Decision trees have several advantages, including interpretability, as the resulting tree structure can be easily visualized and understood. They can handle both numerical and categorical properties and can capture complex non-linear relationships.

However, decision trees are prone to exaggeration, especially when they grow very deep, and may not always be the most accurate models compared to more advanced techniques such as ensemble methods or deep learning models. In general, tree building in machine learning is the basic process of creating decision trees that can effectively model and make predictions from a given data set.

- **Determination of predictive values:** Predictive values are important metrics used in machine learning to evaluate the performance and reliability of a predictive model. They give an idea of how well the model's predictions match the actual results. There are two types of forecasts: positive predictive value (PPV) and negative predictive value (NPV). The positive predictive value (PPV) measures the proportion of the positive predictions of the model that are true positive cases. It helps answer the question, "How likely is it that the forecast is correct?" A high PPV indicates that the positive predictions of the model are reliable and accurate. The negative predictive value (NPV) measures the proportion of negative predictions made by the model that are true negatives. It answers the question, "How likely is a negative forecast to be true?" A high NPV indicates that the negative predictions of the model are reliable and accurate. To determine these values, the performance of the prediction model is evaluated using a dataset labeled with known results. The dataset is usually divided into training and testing subsets. The model is trained on the training data and then used to make predictions on the test data. PPV and NPV can be calculated by comparing model predictions with actual results. PPV is calculated by dividing the number of true positive predictions by the total number of positive predictions made by the model. Mathematically, this can be expressed as:

  PPV = True Positives / (True Positives False Positives)

  Similarly, NPV is calculated by dividing the number of actual negative predictions by the total number of negative predictions made by the model:

  NPV = True Negatives / (True Negatives False Negatives)

  Both PPV and NPV provide valuable information about different aspects of a forecasting model's performance. While a high PPV indicates a model's ability to accurately identify positive cases, a high NPV reflects its ability to correctly exclude negative cases. These values help to assess the reliability and suitability of the model for specific applications. However, when interpreting and using these values, it is important to consider the specific context and requirements of the problem at hand, as they can be affected by factors such as class imbalance and the relative costs of false positives and false negatives.

- **Tree Pruning (Optional):** Pruning is the process of reducing the complexity of a decision tree by removing unnecessary branches that can cause overhang. Pruning techniques such as cost-intensive pruning or minimal impurity pruning aim to find an optimal log size that balances model complexity and predictive performance. The resulting decision tree can be visualized as a flowchart-like structure, where each internal node represents a feature-based decision and each leaf node represents a prediction value.

Here is an example of a decision tree regression model adapted to the data set of ice cream sales:

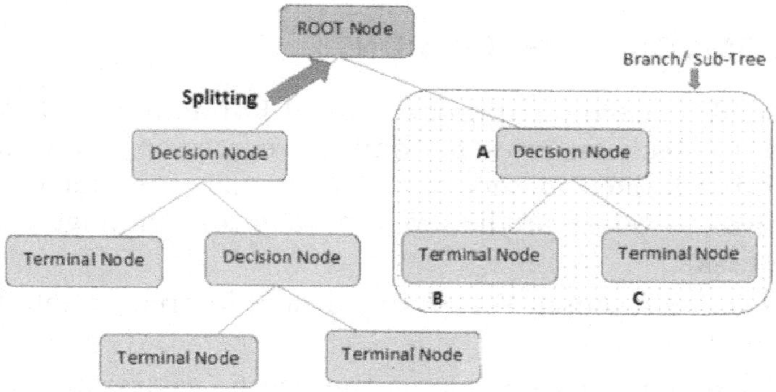

Decision Tree Regression

The decision tree starts with the root node, which represents the first distribution based on the temperature function. In this example, the tree divides the data into two segments: temperatures up to 27.5 degrees Celsius and temperatures above 27.5 degrees Celsius.

The process continues with subsequent splits until the stopping criteria are met. Each leaf node represents a segment of the feature space associated with a predictive value. In this example, the predicted values for the leaf nodes are 225, 300 and 360, which corresponds to the average ice cream sales for these segments.

One of the advantages of decision tree regression is its interpretability. With the help of the decision tree structure, we can understand the decision-making process and gain significant insights. Based on the decision tree, for example, it can be concluded that a temperature below 27.5 degrees Celsius will reduce sales of ice cream, while above 27.5

degrees will increase sales. However, decision tree regression also has some limitations. It tends to overfit the data, especially when the tree gets too deep or complex, and it picks up noise and specific patterns in the training data. Furthermore, decision trees generate piecewise constant predictions that lack unity of the predicted function.

Ensemble methods such as Random Forest and Gradient Boosting are often used to mitigate these limitations. These methods combine multiple decision trees to improve prediction accuracy and reduce overfitting. In summary, decision tree regression is an effective algorithm for regression tasks due to its interpretability and ability to capture non-linear relationships. Although it has certain limitations, there are techniques to overcome them and improve the performance of decision tree models. I hope this explanation provides a deeper understanding of regression decision tree and its application in regression analysis.

2.6. RANDOM FOREST REGRESSION

An ensemble learning approach called Random Forest Regression mixes various decision trees to conduct regression analysis. It is an effective and well-liked method that makes use of the idea of "wisdom of the crowd" to boost prediction accuracy and manage challenging regression tasks.

Let's examine Random Forest Regression in greater detail with the aid of an illustration.

Consider a dataset that relates the age (in years) and income (in thousands of dollars) of individuals:

Age (X)	Income (Y)
25	50
30	70
35	80
40	85
45	90
50	95

The algorithm follows the following steps to build a random forest regression model.

1. Random Sampling: Random sampling is a fundamental machine learning technique that plays an important role in a variety of tasks, including data processing, model training, and estimation. It involves selecting a subset of data points from a larger data set at random without any particular bias. This process helps mitigate potential biases in the data and ensures that the selected subset is representative of the entire population.

Data processing often uses random sampling to generate training and test data. By randomizing the data, we can ensure that both sets have similar sampling distributions, reducing the risk of overfitting and allowing the model to generalize well to unseen data. This method is particularly important when dealing with unbalanced data, where the number of occurrences in different classes is significantly unequal. Random sampling can help mitigate the problem of class imbalance by maintaining proportional representation of classes in selected subsets.

During model training, random sampling is often used in techniques such as stochastic gradient descent (SGD). SGD updates model parameters using a random set of mini-samples in each iteration, enabling efficient and scalable training for large datasets. Random sampling of a miniseries helps the model explore different parts of the data, allowing it to learn stronger and more generalizable representations. Random sampling also plays a role in estimation and model selection. When evaluating the performance of a machine learning model, it is important to avoid biased estimates. By randomly selecting subsets of the data to be estimated, we obtain more reliable estimates of model performance. In addition, methods such as k-fold cross-validation use random sampling to divide the data into multiple subsets or folds to ensure fair estimation by testing the model on different subsets of the data.

Overall, random sampling is a versatile machine learning technique that reduces bias, improves generalizability, and allows reliable estimation. Its application covers the different stages of machine learning, making it an indispensable tool for professionals in the field.

2. Create decision trees: Decision trees are a fundamental and widely used technique in machine learning. They are versatile models that can be applied to both classification and regression problems. The decision tree algorithm operates on smaller and more manageable regions of the partition function space based on input function values. These sections are represented as nodes in a tree structure, where each node represents a decision or condition of a function.

The process of building a decision tree involves recursively partitioning the data based on selected features with the goal of maximizing the benefit of the data or minimizing the impurities in each partition. Information gain measures the entropy or impurity reduction caused by a given cleavage. Different additive measures can be used, for example Gini additive or cross entropy.

A decision tree algorithm selects a function and a partition at each node that maximizes information gain. These partitioning divides the data into two or more subsets, each of which is then further partitioned recursively until a stopping criterion is met. The stopping criterion can be a maximum depth limit, a minimum number of samples required to split a node, or to reach a certain purity level in subsets. Once the decision tree is built, it can be used to predict new unseen data. Starting from the root node, the value of each property is compared with the distribution condition of the node and the corresponding branch is followed until a leaf node is reached. A leaf node represents a prediction or output for a given input.

Deciduous trees have several advantages that increase their popularity. They are easy to understand and interpret, as the resulting tree structure can be visualized and analysed. Decision trees can handle both categorical and numerical features and can capture complex relationships between input variables. In addition, decision trees can handle missing data and outliers without extensive pre-processing.

However, decision trees can suffer from overfitting, causing the model to become too complex and perform poorly with unseen information. Various techniques are used to mitigate this problem, such as tree trimming, hyperparameter fitting, or complex methods such as random forests or gradient boosting.

In conclusion, decision trees are effective machine learning models that provide a clear and interpretable framework for decision making. They are widely used due to their simplicity, handling different data types and capturing complex relationships. By understanding the principles and techniques behind decision trees, practitioners can effectively apply them to a variety of classification and regression problems.

3. Combining predictions: After all decision trees are created, predictions are made for new data points by combining predictions from individual trees. In regression problems, the average of the forecasts is usually calculated to obtain the final forecast. Here is an example of a random forest regression model fitted to the set and income data set:

The figure shows a simplified random forest with three decision trees. Each decision tree is built on a randomly selected subset of the training data, and the predictions from the individual trees are combined to obtain the final prediction.

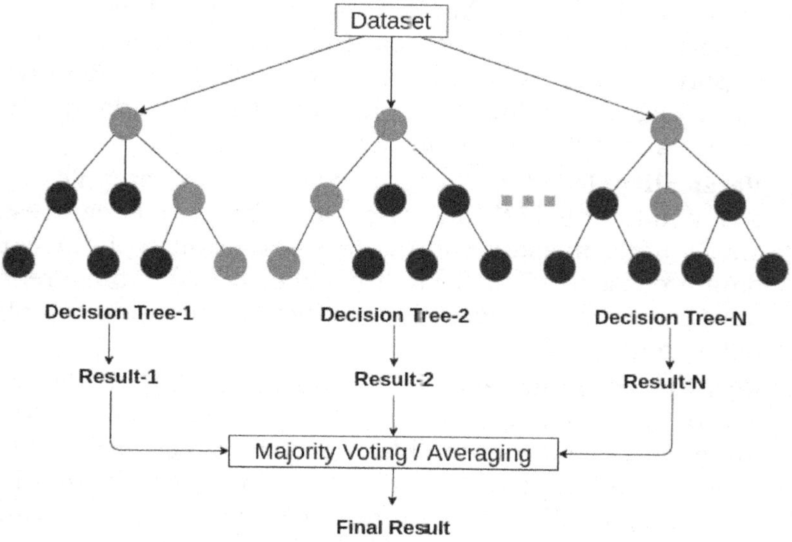

Random Forest Regression

Advantages of Random Forest Regression

1. **Better accuracy:** Random Forest Regression combines predictions from multiple decision trees to help improve overall prediction accuracy. Each decision tree learns different aspects of the data, and by combining their predictions, the model can make more reliable and accurate predictions. The general nature of the random forest reduces the effect of individual forest stands and provides a more reliable estimate of the target variable.
2. **Overfitting robustness:** Overfitting occurs when the model picks up noise or certain patterns in the training data, resulting in poor generalization to unseen data. Random forest regression reduces the risk of overfitting by introducing randomness into the model building process. Randomizing the data and selecting a subset of features in each distribution helps to correlate the trees and reduce the possibility of overfitting. As a result, Random Forest usually has better generalization ability than Single Decision Tree.
3. **Feature Importance:** Random Forest measures the feature importance, which shows which features have the greatest influence on the prediction. This information is obtained from the selection process for each tree. By analyzing the reduction in impurity or the increase in mean squared error at each

distribution point, Random Forest determines the relative importance of different features. This measure of feature importance can be useful for selecting features, identifying key variables, and gaining insight into the relationships between features and the target variable.

4. **Versatility:** Random Forest Regression is a versatile algorithm that can handle both numerical and categorical features. It can also handle missing values in the dataset without extensive data processing. This flexibility makes random forest regression suitable for many regression problems, including complex and heterogeneous datasets.
5. **Non-linear relationships:** Random forest regression can capture complex nonlinear relationships between traits and the target variable. An ensemble of decision trees allows the model to learn and approximate non-linear patterns in the data. By combining predictions from multiple trees, Random Forest can effectively model complex relationships that traditional linear regression models may not capture.
6. **Robustness to outliers:** Random Forest regression is relatively robust to outliers in the data. Because the model aggregates predictions from multiple trees, outliers have less impact on the final predictions compared to a single decision tree. The effect of ensemble averaging helps to minimize the influence of individual extreme data points, resulting in more reliable forecasts.
7. **Robustness to noise:** Random Forest regression is generally more robust to noisy data compared to other regression algorithms. Random steps introduced in model building, such as bootstrapping and feature subsets, help filter out noise and focus on underlying patterns in the data. With this robustness against noise, Random Forest is able to provide more stable and accurate predictions, even when there is noise in the data.

Overall, the advantages of Random Forest Regression make it a popular choice for regression tasks. It strikes a balance between accuracy, interpretability and robustness, making it suitable for many applications in various fields.

2.7. ASSESSING REGRESSION MODELS

1. Mean Square Error (MSE)

The mean squared error (MSE) is a commonly used evaluation metric in machine learning that quantifies the mean squared difference between the predicted values of a dataset and the true values. It is widely used to evaluate the performance of regression models that aim to predict continuous numerical values.

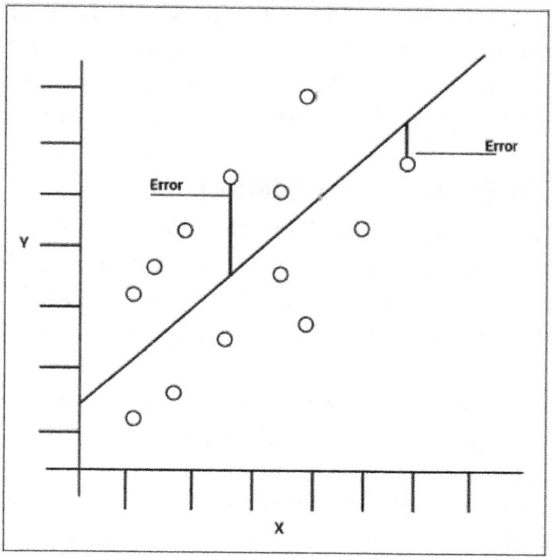

Mean Square Error

Calculation of MSE requires a data set with known actual values and corresponding predicted values generated by the regression model. For each data point, the squared difference between the actual value and the predicted value is calculated. These squared differences are then summed for all data points and divided by the total number of data points to obtain the mean squared difference. MSE measures the overall quality of the regression model's predictions. A lower MSE means that the model predictions are closer to the true values, which means better accuracy. On the other hand, a higher MSE indicates that the model predictions deviate more from the true values, indicating lower accuracy.

One advantage of using MSE is that it penalizes larger errors more due to the quadratic function. This means that outliers or significant deviations between predicted and actual values have a greater impact on MSE compared to other measures such as mean absolute error. As a result, MSE-optimized models tend to favour larger error reductions.

However, MSE has some limitations. Because it squares the errors, it amplifies the impact of outliers and gives them more weight in the evaluation process. Furthermore, the MSE value itself has no direct interpretation because it is in square units. Therefore, it is often used as a relative measure when comparing different models or evaluating model improvement after modifications. In summary, mean squared error is a widely used metric to evaluate regression models in machine learning. It determines the root mean square difference between the predicted and actual values, which helps in evaluating the accuracy and efficiency of the model. Although it has the advantage of penalizing larger errors, it should be used in conjunction with other evaluation metrics to provide a comprehensive understanding of model performance.

2. Root Mean Square Error (RMSE)

Root Mean Square Error (RMSE) is a widely used evaluation metric in machine learning that measures the average difference between predicted values and actual values. It is particularly common in regression tasks where the goal is to predict continuous numerical values.

To calculate RMSE, the differences between the predicted and actual values are squared, averaged, and then taken as the root mean square. This process ensures that negative and positive errors do not cancel each other out. RMSE represents the standard deviation of these errors and provides a single value that summarizes the performance of the model. RMSE is useful because it penalizes larger errors more severely than smaller errors due to the quadratic function. By taking the square root at the end, the RMSE returns the target variable to its original scale, which makes interpretation easier. The smaller the RMSE, the better the predictive ability of the model, because it indicates that the predictions are closer to the true values.

One of the advantages of RMSE is its ability to highlight outliers that have a significant effect on the total error. This feature makes it a solid metric in situations where it is important to consider the presence of extreme values. In addition, RMSE is a differentiable metric that is useful for optimization algorithms based on gradient-based techniques.

However, RMSE tends to emphasize larger errors, which can be problematic if some extreme values affect model performance. In such cases, alternative metrics such as mean absolute error (MAE) may be more appropriate. In addition, RMSE assumes a Gaussian distribution of errors, which may not be true in all scenarios.

3. Mean Absolute Error (MAE)

The mean absolute error (MAE) is a commonly used metric in machine learning to measure the accuracy of a regression model. It quantifies the average absolute difference between the predicted values of the target variable and the actual values. MAE provides a simple and intuitive measure of how well a model performs in terms of absolute errors.

MAE is calculated by calculating the absolute difference between each predicted value and the corresponding actual value. These differences are then averaged across all data points to produce a final MAE score. The MAE value represents the average size of the errors, regardless of their direction. It is expressed in the same units as the target variable, so it is easy to interpret and compare.

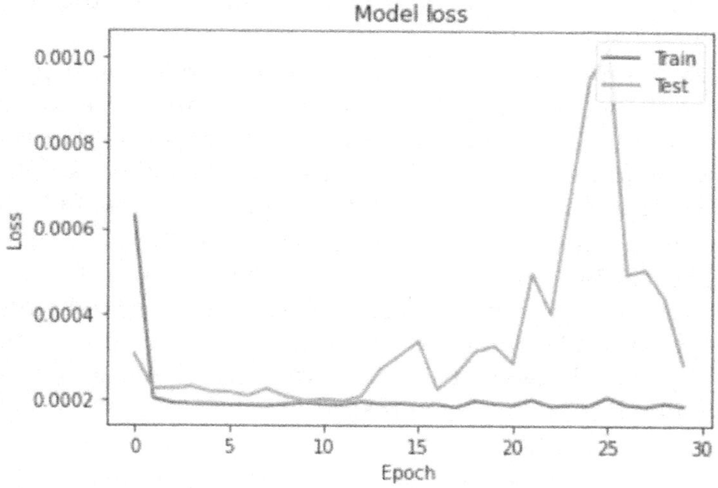

Mean Absolute Error

One of the advantages of MAE is its tolerance for deviations. Because the absolute difference is taken into account, extreme errors do not disproportionately affect the metric. This feature makes MAE particularly useful in scenarios where outliers can significantly affect performance evaluation. However, MAE has its limitations. It treats all errors equally regardless of their size. In situations where large errors are more critical than small errors, other metrics such as root mean square error (MSE) or root mean square error (RMSE) may be more relevant.

MAE is often used in model estimation, hyperparameter tuning, and model comparison. A lower MAE value indicates better accuracy, zero represents a perfect forecast. By comparing MAE scores between different models or different configurations of the same model, data scientists can make informed decisions about which approach produces the best results.

4. R-Square (R^2) Score

In machine learning, R-squared (R^2) is a statistical metric used to measure the goodness of fit of a regression model. It shows how well the model fits the observed data points. R-squared is a value between

0 and 1, where 1 represents a perfect fit and 0 means no relationship between the model and the data.

To understand R-squared, consider a regression model that predicts a target variable based on a set of input characteristics. The R-squared score determines the proportion of variance in the target variable explained by the model. In other words, it measures the percentage of the total variation in the data that is accounted for by the regression model.

A high R-squared score indicates that the model captures a large proportion of the variation in the target variable and suggests that the model predictions closely match the actual data points. On the other hand, a low R-squared score indicates that the model does not explain much of the variation in the data and may not be a good fit.

R-squared is calculated as the ratio of the explained sum of squares (ESS) to the total sum of squares (TSS). The ESS represents the sum of the mean squared differences between the predicted values and the target variable, while the TSS represents the sum of the mean squared differences between the actual values and the target variable. Mathematically, R-squared is expressed as:

R^2 = 1 - (ESS / TSS)

It is important to note that R-squared has its limitations. It does not provide information about the accuracy or reliability of individual predictions made by the model. A high R-squared score does not guarantee that the model always makes accurate predictions. In addition, R-squared tends to increase with the number of predictors in the model, even if they are not actually related to the target variable, which can lead to overfitting.

5. Modified R-Square

Adjusted R-squared, also known as adjusted R-squared, is a statistical measure commonly used in machine learning to evaluate the fit of a regression model. While the standard R-squared quantifies the proportion of variance in the dependent variable explained by the independent variables, the modified R-squared takes into account the number of predictors used in the model and adjusts the degrees of freedom.

Finding a balance between model complexity and overfitting is critical in machine learning. Standard R-squares tend to increase as more predictors are added, even if they are not truly informative. This can lead to overestimation of model performance and inclusion of irrelevant variables. Modified R-square solves this problem by penalizing the addition of unnecessary predictors.

The modified R-squared calculation includes the number of predictors and the sample size. As the number of predictors increases, the adjusted R-squared value adjusts downward to reflect the potential increase in model complexity. This adjustment is achieved by subtracting the penalty term from the standard R-squared. The penalty term is proportional to the number of predictors and the sample size, which provides a more accurate representation of the model's performance. Given the complexity of the model and the trade-off between the number of predictions and the sample size, the modified R-squared provides a more reliable measure of how well the model generalizes to unseen data. It helps evaluate and compare different models, allowing researchers and practitioners to choose the model that has the best balance between explanatory power and simplicity.

It is important to note that interpretation of the modified R-square must be done in conjunction with other assessment measures and domain information. Although a higher modified R-square indicates better model performance, it should be used in conjunction with other measures such as root mean square error, cross-validation, or data criteria to provide a comprehensive understanding of model accuracy and predictive ability.

- **Residual Analysis:** Residual analysis involves the study of residuals, which are the differences between predicted and actual values. Residual traces can be analyzed to analyze model assumptions and identify areas where the model may fail. Residual plots, such as scatter plots or histograms, can be used to check for residual patterns, non-linearity, heteroscedasticity or outliers. Deviations from random patterns or clear structures in residual plots indicate areas where the model can be improved.
- **Cross-validation:** Cross-validation is a technique used to evaluate the performance of a regression model on unseen data. This involves dividing the data set into several subsets, training a model on one subset, and evaluating it on the remaining subsets. Common cross-validation methods are k-fold cross-validation and holdout. Cross-validation provides a more reliable assessment of model performance and helps assess its generalizability.
- **Comparison with baseline models:** It is important to compare the performance of your regression model with baseline models or simple approaches. Basic models can be as simple as using the mean or median value of the target variable as predictors. Comparing the model's performance against these baselines helps to understand its performance and improve it compared to

simpler methods. Visualizations such as scatter plots, residual plots and distribution plots can complement evaluation metrics by providing a visual understanding of model performance and potential shortcomings.

Here's an example of a table summarizing the evaluation metrics for different regression models:

Model	MSE	RMSE	MAE
Model 1	10.12	3.18	2.51
Model 2	8.76	2.96	2.18
Model 3	7.52	2.74	2.04
Model	MSE	RMSE	MAE
Model 1	10.12	3.18	2.51

2.8. FEATURE SELECTION IN REGRESSION

1. Filtering methods

Filtering methods are based on evaluating the importance of features, independent of the regression model. These methods look at statistical measures such as correlation, mutual information or statistical tests to classify features. The following are some of the more commonly used filtering methods.

- **Correlation-based feature selection:** This method measures the linear relationship between each feature and the target variable. Features with high correlation values are considered more important. You can use techniques such as Pe a rson's correlation coefficient or Spearman's rank correlation coefficient.
- **Mutual information:** Mutual information measures the dependence between variables by evaluating how much information one variable contains about another. It considers both linear and non-linear relationships, so it is suitable for feature selection in regression.
- **Chi-square test:** This test is useful when the target variable is categorical. It assesses the independence of each trait and target variable by comparing observed frequencies with expected frequencies. Features with significant chi-square values are considered significant.

2. Envelopment methods

Envelopment methods estimate a subset of features by training and estimating a regression model using different combinations of features. These methods take into account the interaction between features and model performance. They involve an iterative process where features are added or removed based on a selected search algorithm and performance metrics. Some popular packaging methods include:

- **Forward Selection:** This method starts with an empty set of features and iteratively adds one feature at a time, choosing the one that improves the model the most.
- **Backward elimination:** This method starts with all features and removes the least important feature at each iteration based on model performance.
- **Recursive Feature Elimination (RFE):** RFE starts from all features and recursively eliminates the least important feature based on a selected metric until the desired number of features is reached. It typically uses cross-validation to assess the model's performance at each iteration.

3. Embedding methods

Embedding methods involve feature selection in the model creation process. These techniques select features by training the model, often adding a regularization term to the objective function. Some of the more common embedded methods include:

- **Lasso (minimum absolute shrinkage and selection operator):** Lasso regression adds an L1 penalty term to the objective function, which promotes sparsity of feature weights. This tends to reduce less significant features to zero, making feature selection efficient.
- **Ridge regression:** Ridge regression introduces an L2 penalty, which also favors small features, but does not lead to accurate feature selection. This can be useful if all functions are considered potentially important.
- **Elastic Network:** Elastic Network combines the L1 and L2 penalties of Lasso and Ridge regression. It balances between feature selection and decreasing coefficients, allowing groups of correlated features to be selected.

Here's a table illustrating the feature selection process using RFE:

Iteration	Selected Features	Model Performance (R-squared)	Iteration
1	Feature 1, 3, 6	0.65	1
2	Feature 1, 3, 4, 6, 9	0.78	2
3	Feature 1, 3, 4, 6, 7, 9	0.82	3
4	Feature 1, 2, 3, 4, 6, 7, 9	0.85	4
5	Feature 1, 2, 3, 4, 6, 7, 8, 9	0.86	5

Visualizations can also help to understand the selection of features. here are some samples:

Feature Importance Graph

In machine learning, feature importance refers to the process of determining the importance or contribution of each input feature in predicting the target variable. This is an important part of interpreting the model and understanding which features most affect the model's predictions. Feature importance helps select features, understand the underlying relationships in the data, and identify potential areas for improvement.

One common way to assess the importance of an item is to construct a feature importance graph or chart. This diagram illustrates the relative importance of different functions in a machine learning model. The specific technique used to calculate feature importance can vary depending on the algorithm used.

For example, in decision tree-based algorithms such as Random Forest or Gradient Boosting, the importance of a feature can be measured by analyzing how much the performance of the model degrades when a certain feature is removed. This performance degradation is often quantified using a metric such as Gini impurity, average reduced impurity, or average degraded accuracy. The greater the performance degradation, the more important the feature is considered to be.

Once the characteristic importance values are calculated, they can be plotted on a graph, usually in descending order of importance. This chart provides a visual representation of the relative importance of each feature. This allows analysts and data scientists to quickly identify the most effective features and gain insight into the data. Very important features may be considered key to model predictions, while minor features may have limited influence or be excluded without significant performance degradation.

Additionally, feature importance graphs can help in feature selection, especially in situations where the dataset contains many features. Analyzing the graph allows you to focus on the best features and possibly discard or reduce less important features, simplifying the model and reducing computational complexity. It is important to note that the meaning of the feature is highly dependent on the algorithm chosen and the specific data set being analyzed. Different algorithms can assign different importance scores to the same features, and the importance of features can change when different subsets of the data are used. Therefore, it is important to interpret the trait importance plot in the context of the specific model and dataset.

2. Recursive feature elimination plot: Recursive Feature Elimination (RFE) is a feature selection technique commonly used in machine learning to identify and remove unimportant or unnecessary features from a given dataset. It works by recursively removing features and building models on the remaining subset until an optimal feature is obtained.

The main goal of RFE is to improve model performance and interpretability by selecting the most informative features and discarding the least important. This method assigns an importance score to each feature based on how they affect the performance of the model. The procedure usually goes like this:

- **Feature Score:** RFE initially assigns an importance score to each feature in the dataset. It builds an initial model and ranks the features according to how they affect the performance of the model.
- **Feature removal:** RFE then removes the feature with the lowest importance score from the dataset. It reconstructs the model using the remaining functions.
- **Recursive iteration:** The previous feature classification and elimination steps are repeated recursively until a certain number of features remain or until predetermined performance criteria (e.g., threshold accuracy) are met.
- **Selection of optimal features:** After a recursive process, RFE provides a ranking of features based on their importance scores. The high-class features are considered the most informative and are selected as the optimal set to train the final model. RFE offers several advantages in machine learning. First, it can improve the generalizability of the model by reducing overfitting and capturing the most important information in the data. It also improves model interpretability by focusing on specific properties that have a significant impact on predictions. In addition, RFE can be used with different models or algorithms, allowing flexibility in the selection process.

A graphic called an "RFE chart" is often used to visualize RFE results. This chart shows the number of features on the x-axis and a performance metric (such as accuracy or area under the curve) on the y-axis. This shows how the performance of the model improves when features are gradually removed. The graph usually shows a downward trend, indicating that the performance of the model may decrease if fewer features are considered. However, there is often a tipping point where removing additional features results in minimal performance degradation. The figure helps determine the optimal number of features for the final model. In conclusion, recursive feature elimination is a useful technique for feature selection in machine learning. This helps to identify the most informative features, improve model performance and improve interpretability. The accompanying RFE table provides a visual representation of how the model's performance changes when features are removed, helping to select the optimal feature.

3

Classification Methods

3.1. INTRODUCTION TO CLASSIFICATION PROBLEMS

Classification is one of the main tasks of machine learning, which aims to categorize or name data into predetermined classes or classes based on their characteristics. It involves predicting the class or classes of a given input based on a training set of labeled examples. Classification problems can be found in various fields such as image recognition, text classification, fraud detection, medical diagnosis and others.

In this talk, we explore the concept of classification problems, the process involved, and some common algorithms used in classification tasks.

Table 1: Example Dataset for a Binary Classification Problem

Feature 1	Feature 2	Class
1.2	0.8	0
2.0	1.5	0
1.5	1.2	0
3.0	4.0	1
2.5	3.5	1
3.5	3.0	1

As an example dataset for a binary classification problem, let's look at Table 1. We have a class label that corresponds to each of the two features (Features 1 and 2). Using the feature values of new instances, one of the two classes (0 or 1) will be determined.

The steps we often take to tackle a classification problem are as follows:

1. Data Collection

Data collection is an important step in machine learning, which involves collecting and curating data for training and testing models. In this context, data refers to any structured or unstructured information, such as text, images, audio or numerical values, that are used to train an algorithm or make predictions. The quality and quantity of data collected greatly affects the effectiveness and accuracy of machine learning models.

During data collection, various methods are used to obtain the necessary information. This may include collecting information from websites, obtaining information from databases or using existing data sets. Depending on the specific problem and domain, data can be collected from different sources such as social media platforms, sensors, customer feedback or publicly available datasets.

It is important to ensure that the data collected is representative, diverse and unbiased to avoid introducing biased or biased patterns into machine learning models. An appropriate sample size must be selected and possible outliers or outliers that may affect the generalizability and effectiveness of the model must be considered.

Data collection also includes tagging and annotating data, especially in guided learning scenarios. This process requires human annotators to assign appropriate tags, categories, or labels to each data instance, which serve as the basis for training the models. The labeling process is critical because it directly affects the learnability and accurate predictions of the model.

In addition, ethical guidelines and data protection rules must be followed when collecting data. Organizations must ensure that data collection practices comply with legal requirements and maintain privacy and data protection to protect individuals' information.

2. Data Pre-processing

Data preprocessing is a key step in machine learning, where raw data is converted into a format suitable for analysis and model training. It is an integral part of the data pipeline as it helps improve data quality and reliability, which ultimately leads to better model performance.

The data processing process involves various techniques and tasks. One of the first steps is data cleaning, which involves dealing with missing values, outliers, and inconsistencies in the dataset. Missing values can be filled using methods such as imputation, where missing values are estimated from available data. Outliers, which are extreme values that differ significantly from the rest of the data, can be identified and removed or treated separately to prevent them from affecting model performa n ce. Data mismatches can be resolved by standardizing variables, correcting errors, or removing duplicate records.

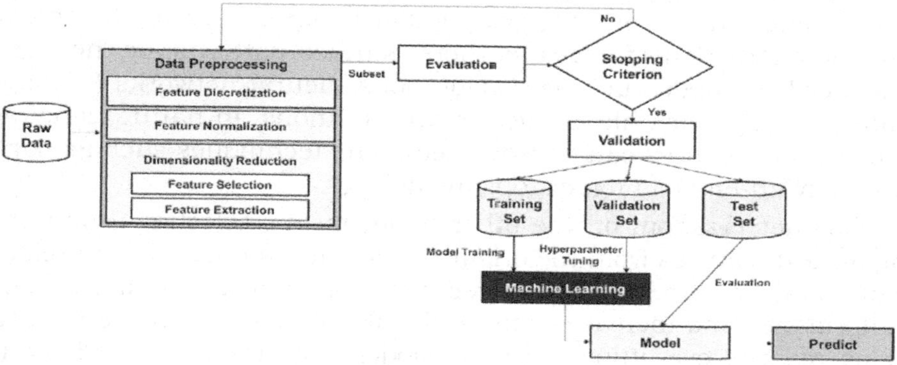

Data processing

Another important aspect of data processing is feature scaling or normalization. Since different features can have different scales and units, it is important to bring them to the same scale. This is usually achieved by techniques such as standardization (subtracting the mean and dividing by the standard deviation) or normalization (scaling the values to a certain range, often between 0 and 1). Normalization is particularly important for algorithms that are sensitive to the scale of the input features, such as distance-based algorithms.

Feature e ncoding is another preprocessing step that involves converti n g categorical variables into numerical representations that machine learning models can understand. This can be achieved using techniques such as one-time coding, where each category is converted to a binary vector, or tag coding, where each category is given a unique numerical identifier. The choice of coding technique depends on the nature of the data and the specific requirements of the model.

Feature Extraction/Selection

Feature extraction and feature selection are key steps in machine learning that involve the process of identifying and selecting relevant information from raw data to improve model performance.

Feature e xtraction is the process of transforming raw data into a more m a nageable and informative representation by extracting important features or characteristics. It aims to reduce data dimensions while pr e serving important information. This is particularly useful when dea l ing with high-dimensional data such as images or text, where the raw data may contain redundant or irrelevant information. By extracting significant features, the model can focus on the most characteristic aspects of the data, improving accuracy and efficiency. Depending on the type of data processed, there are several techniques for feature extraction. For example, popular image processing techniques are the extraction of edges, corners, surface patterns, or the use of advanced methods such as convolutional neural networks (CNNs) to automatically learn hierarchical representations. In natural language processing, features can be extracted using techniques such as bag of words, word-embedding, or topic modeling.

Characterization, on the other hand, means selecting a subset of significant features from the original function. Its purpose is to remove redundant or irrelevant features that can negatively affect model performance and increase computational complexity. Feature selection helps reduce overfitting, improve model interpretability, and reduce training.

There are different approaches to feature selection, including filter methods, wrapper methods, and nested methods. Filtering methods rely on statistical measurements or ranking criteria to evaluate the importance of features independently of the learning algorithm. Enveloping methods use a self-learning algorithm to evaluate subsets of features and select the best performer. Embedded methods involve feature selection as part of the learning process, where feature significance is determined during model training. The choice of feature extraction and selection techniques depends on the specific problem, the nature of the data, and the algorithms used. This requires a careful balance between preserving important information and reducing dimensions. Correct feature extraction and selection can significantly improve the performance, interpretability and effectiveness of machine learning models, leading to more accurate predictions and better insights into the data.

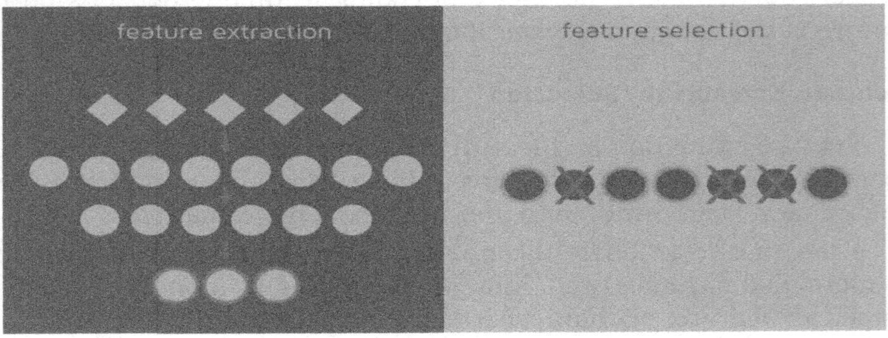

Feature Extraction/Selection

Model Selection

Model selection is a fundamental part of machine learning that involves choosing the most appropriate algorithm or model for a given task or problem. It is the process of evaluating and comparing different models to determine which one performs best in terms of accuracy, generalizability and robustness. The ultimate goal of model selection is to choose a model that can effectively capture the underlying patterns and relationships in the data while avoiding over- or under-fitting.

Model selection usually consists of several stages. First, a set of candidate models is identified based on a given problem, which may include different algorithms such as linear regression, decision trees, support vector machines or neural networks. These models differ in their assumptions, complexity, and predictive power.

The next step is to evaluate the performance of each model using appropriate evaluation measures. Commonly used metrics include precision, accuracy, recall, F1 score, and root mean square error. This evaluation is often done using techniques such as cross-validation, where the data is divided into multiple subsets for training and testing, ensuring that the performance of the model is evaluated at different data points.

Various model hyperparameters can also be tuned during the estimation process. Hyperparameters are configuration settings that are not learned from data but affect the behavior of the model. Examples of hyperparameters are learning rates, regularization parameters, and the number of hidden layers in a neural network. Hyperparameter tuning helps to find optimal settings for a particular model and improves its performance.

After evaluating and tuning the models, the final step is the best performing model based on the evaluation results. That choice can be subjective, taking into account factors such as interpretability, computer efficiency and domain-specific requirements. However, it is important to strike a balance between model complexity and generality to ensure that the chosen model performs well with unseen information.

Automated model selection techniques such as Bayesian optimization and genetic algorithms have gained popularity in recent years. These techniques automate the exploration of the hyperparameter search space, enabling more efficient and effective model selection.

Model Training

Model training is an important step in machine learning where a computer algorithm learns to make predictions or act on data. It involves the process of optimizing a mathematical model by adjusting its parameters to minimize errors or maximize the accuracy of its predictions. The purpose of model training is to enable the model to be generalized to very new, unprecedented data.

The first step in model training is to define the problem and the desired outcome. For this, it is necessary to choose an appropriate machine learning algorithm or model architecture that best suits the given task. There are different algorithms such as linear regression, decision trees, support vector machines and neural networks, each with their own strengths and weaknesses.

Once the algorithm or model architecture is chosen, the next step is to train the model using labeled data. Labeled data consists of input samples combined with their corresponding true initial or target values. During the training process, the model adjusts its internal parameters based on the provided data and iteratively refines its predictions or decision limits.

The training data is usually divided into two groups: the training set and the validation set. The training set is used to update model parameters, while the validation set is used to evaluate model performance and tune hyperparameters. Hyperparameters are settings that are not learned from the data but influence the training of the model, such as the learning rate, the strength of the regularity or the number of layers in the neural network.

The model training process includes an optimization algorithm that iteratively updates the model parameters based on the difference between its predictions and actual target values. This difference is quantified using a loss or cost function that measures the performance of the model. The optimization algorithm attempts to minimize this loss function by adjusting the parameters using techniques such as gradient descent or stochastic gradient descent. Training a model often requires multiple iterations or epochs where the entire training dataset is run through the model. At each time step, the model learns from the training data and adjusts its parameters to improve predictions. The number of epochs depends on the complexity of the problem, the amount of available data and the convergence of model performance.

After training is complete, the model is evaluated on a separate, unseen set of tests to evaluate its performance on new data. This evaluation helps determine how well the model has learned to generalize and predict data it has not encountered before. If the model performs well on the test set, it can be deployed and used to make predictions based on real, unseen data.

Model Evaluation

Model evaluation is an important part of machine learning that involves evaluating the effectiveness and efficiency of a trained model. It is very important to evaluate the performance of the model to determine its accuracy, reliability and generalizability before implementing it in real applications. The purpose of model evaluation is to understand how well the model has learned from the training data and how effectively it can make predictions or classifications based on new, unseen data.

One common method of model evaluation is the use of evaluation metrics. These metrics provide quantitative measures of model performance, allowing objective comparisons between different models or variants of the same model. Common evaluation metrics include precision, accuracy, recall, F1 score, and area under the curve (AUC) for classification tasks, while mean square error (MSE), root mean square error (RMSE), and mean absolute error (MAE) are often used for regression. tasks These metrics provide valuable information about various aspects of a model's performance, such as its ability to correctly classify cases or predict numerical values.

Cross-validation is another widely used model evaluation method. This involves dividing the available data into several subsets or folds and then iteratively training and evaluating the model on different combinations of these folds. Cross-validation helps assess the performance of the model on different subsets of the data and provides a more reliable assessment of its generalizability. In addition, model evaluation often involves visualization and analysis of model predictions and errors. This may include creating confusion matrices, ROC curves, or accuracy recovery curves that provide a deeper view of the model's performance at different classes or thresholds. By examining these visualizations, researchers and practitioners can identify potential biases, class imbalances, or areas where the model may have problems, allowing them to refine and improve the model accordingly.

Model evaluation is a continuous process, and reevaluation of the model is necessary when new information becomes available or the problem location changes. This allows the performance of the model to be continuously monitored and improved, ensuring its effectiveness and reliability over time. In summary, model evaluation is a crucial step in machine learning that evaluates the effectiveness, accuracy, and generalization of a trained model. This includes using assessment metrics, cross-validation techniques and visualizations to understand the model's strengths, weaknesses and areas for improvement. By conducting a thorough evaluation of the model, researchers and industry professionals can make informed decisions about the implementation of the model and use it reliably in real-world applications.

Model Deployment

Model deployment in machine learning refers to the process of making a trained machine learning model available for use in a production environment. It involves taking the model that has been developed, tested, and validated during the training phase and deploying it to a system or platform where it can receive input data, make predictions, and generate useful outputs.

The deployment of a machine learning model is a critical step in the overall machine learning workflow, as it bridges the gap between development and real-world application. During deployment, several considerations must be taken into account to ensure the model's reliability, scalability, and efficiency.

Firstly, the choice of deployment infrastructure is essential. It can range from traditional servers to cloud-based platforms, depending on factors such as computational requirements, scalability needs, and cost considerations. Cloud-based services like Amazon Web Services (AWS), Google Cloud Platform (GCP), and Microsoft Azure offer convenient options for deploying machine learning models.

Next, the model needs to be integrated into the deployment environment, which often involves writing code to expose the model as an application programming interface (API) or embedding it within an existing software system. The API allows other applications or services to send input data to the model for prediction and receive the model's output.

Security is a critical aspect of model deployment. Proper measures must be implemented to protect the model and its data from unauthorized access or malicious attacks. This includes ensuring secure communication channels, implementing user authentication and authorization mechanisms, and monitoring the system for potential security vulnerabilities.

Performance and scalability considerations are also vital during deployment. Models should be optimized for efficiency to handle real-time or near real-time predictions, especially in high-traffic scenarios. Techniques like model compression, quantization, and hardware acceleration can be applied to improve inference speed and reduce resource consumption.

Additionally, monitoring and maintenance of deployed models are crucial to ensure their continued effectiveness. Monitoring involves tracking model performance, detecting anomalies, and retraining or updating the model when necessary. It also involves versioning the deployed models to facilitate rollback or comparisons with new versions.

Finally, the deployment process should be automated and repeatable to ensure consistency and ease of updates. Techniques such as containerization, continuous integration and deployment (CI/CD) pipelines, and orchestration tools like Kubernetes can simplify the deployment and management of machine learning models.

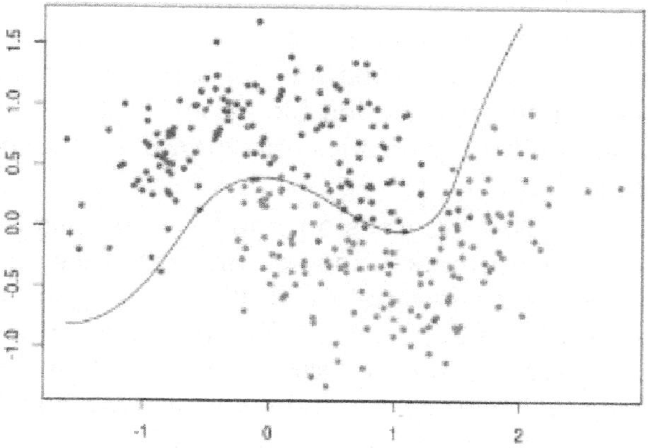

Decision Boundary of a Binary Classifier

In classification problems, models often create decision boundaries that separate different classes. Image 1 illustrates a decision boundary of a binary classifier. The blue points represent instances from class 0, while the red points represent instances from class 1. The decision boundary is the line that separates these two classes, allowing the model to make predictions based on the relative position of new data points to this boundary.

Classification problems play a crucial role in various real-world applications, enabling automated categorization and prediction. With the right data, preprocessing, feature engineering, and model selection, machine learning algorithms can effectively tackle classification tasks and provide valuable insights and predictions.

3.2 LOGISTIC REGRESSION

Logistic Regression Overview

Logistic regression is a popular and widely used classification algorithm in the field of machine learning. It is a statistical model used to predict binary or categorical outcomes based on a set of independent variables. The purpose of logistic regression is to find the relationship between input variables and the probability of a certain outcome.

In logistic regression, the dependent variable is binary, meaning that it can take one of two possible values, such as "yes" or "no", "0" or "1", or "true" or "false". Independent variables, also called traits, can be continuous or categorical. The logistic regression model assumes that the relationship between the independent variables and the logarithm of the result is linear. The logistic regression algorithm works by fitting a logistic function, also called a sigmoid function, to the training data. The sigmoid function maps any real-valued number to a value between 0 and 1 that represents the probability of a positive result. A logistic regression model calculates the log likelihood of an outcome using a linear combination of input variables and then uses a sigmoid function to obtain the likelihood.

To train the logistic regression model, the algorithm uses a technique called maximum likelihood estimation. Its goal is to find the coefficients of the linear combination that maximize the probability of observing the training data. These coefficients, also known as weights or parameters, determine the contribution of each input variable to the forecast. A logistic regression model can be trained using gradient descent optimization or other numerical methods.

Once a logistic regression model is trained, it can be used to predict new, previously unseen data. The model calculates the logarithmic coefficient using the learned weights and uses a sigmoid function to obtain the probability of a positive result. By choosing an appropriate threshold, the predicted probabilities can be converted into class identifiers. Logistic regression has several advantages in machine learning. It is relatively simple and interpretable compared to more complex algorithms, which makes the results easier to understand and explain. It can handle both continuous and categorical input variables and works well with large datasets. Logistic regression is also robust to data noise and outliers.

However, logistic regression has some limitations. This assumes a linear relationship between the input variables and the multiples of the logarithms, which may not be true in all cases. It can struggle with data sets that have complex relationships or interactions between variables. In addition, logistic regression is mostly designed for binary classification problems and may not be suitable for multiclass classification without modification.

In summary, logistic regression is an efficient and widely used algorithm for binary classification tasks in machine learning. It estimates the probability of a binary outcome based on a set of independent variables and uses a logistic function to map log odds to probabilities. Despite the assumptions and limitations, logistic regression remains a valuable tool in the machine learning toolbox.

Mathematical Formulation

Mathematical formulation plays a crucial role in machine learning because it provides a formal framework for posing and solving problems. Machine learning algorithms rely on mathematical concepts and techniques to process data, make predictions and learn from examples. At the heart of machine learning is formulating a problem such as an optimization or statistical inference task and then using mathematical models and algorithms to find an optimal solution.

One of the key aspects of the mathematical formulation of machine learning is data representation. Data are typically represented as matrices or vectors, where each entry corresponds to a function or attribute of a data event. By organizing data in this structured format, mathematical operations and transformations can be applied efficiently.

Another essential aspect of the mathematical formulation of machine learning is the definition of the objective or loss function. The objective function quantifies how well the model performs in a given task. It measures the difference between model predictions and actual values. The choice of objective function depends on the specific problem to be solved and can vary from simple error measures to more complex probability measures. In addition, mathematical design includes model design and optimization. Machine learning models are mathematical representations that capture relationships and patterns in data. They can range from simple linear models to complex deep neural networks. When designing a model, an appropriate mathematical structure is chosen and the parameters of the model are determined. Optimization techniques such as gradient descent are then used to find the parameter values that minimize the objective function. The mathematical formulation also includes regularization techniques that prevent overfitting and improve the generalization of machine learning models. Regularization adds additional terms to the objective function that penalize complex models or favor certain properties such as sparsity or smoothness. These regularization terms are formulated mathematically to balance the trade-off between model complexity and training data fit.

$$\log(odds) = \beta0 + \beta1*X1 + \beta2*X2 + ... + \beta n*Xn$$

where β0, β1, β2, ..., βn are the coefficients (weights) associated with the input features X1, X2, ..., Xn.

To convert the log-odds into a probability, we apply the logistic (sigmoid) function:

p(y=1|X) = 1 / (1 + exp(-log(odds)))

where p(y=1|X) is the probability of the positive class given the input features X.

Training the Model

Training a machine learning model is a fundamental process in artificial intelligence (AI) that involves training a model to recognize patterns and make predictions or decisions based on input data. The purpose of the training is to enable the model to be generalized based on the given data and to act accurately in new, never-before-seen examples.

The training process starts with a dataset consisting of input examples and their corresponding target results or identifiers. A dataset is the basis for a model, which it uses to learn and understand underlying patterns or relationships in the data. It is important to have diverse and representative data to handle different scenarios for the model. During training, the model undergoes an iterative optimization process where it adjusts its internal parameters or weights to minimize the difference between the predicted outputs and the actual target outputs. This optimization is usually achieved using an algorithm called a learning algorithm (eg, gradient descent) that updates the model parameters based on the calculated errors.

The loss function is used to measure the performance of the model and guide the optimization process. The loss function quantifies the difference between the predicted outputs and the ground truth labels. The model tries to minimize this loss by iteratively updating its parameters. The training process involves feeding sets of input data into the model, making predictions, calculating losses and updating parameters accordingly. This procedure is repeated several times through the data set, forming a so-called epoch. Training usually takes several epochs to give the model many opportunities to learn from the data and improve its performance.

In addition, model training often requires careful preprocessing of the input data, including steps such as normalization, feature scaling, handling of missing values, and coding of categorical variables. These pre-processing techniques help ensure that the data is in a suitable format for effective training of the model. In addition, the success of model training depends on several factors, such as the model architecture and complexity, the quality and size of the training dataset, the choice of appropriate hyperparameters (eg, learning rate, regularity), and the available data processing. resources .

Training a machine learning model is an iterative and resource-intensive process that requires expertise and careful consideration. The ultimate goal is to create a well-generalized model that can accurately predict or make decisions based on new, unseen information.

Let's consider a simple example with two input features (X1 and X2) and a binary target variable (y). Here's a table representing the training data:

Table 2

X1	X2	Y
2.73	1.86	0
-0.27	-1.32	1
-1.36	2.17	0
0.99	-0.45	1
-2.53	-0.99	0

The goal of logistic regression is to find a decision boundary (in this case, a line) that separates two classes. The decision boundary is determined by the coefficients (difficulties) learned during training. Once the model is trained, it can make predictions about new cases by calculating the probability of belonging to the positive class based on the learned decision boundary.

3.3 DECISION TREE CLASSIFICATION

Let's start with the basics of decision tree classification. A decision tree consists of nodes and branches. The nodes represent decision points or attributes, and the branches represent the possible outcomes or classes. Each internal node represents a test on an attribute, each branch represents the outcome of the test, and each leaf node represents a class label.

Dataset

In machine learning, a dataset refers to a set of structured or unstructured data used to train, validate, and test machine learning models. It is the basis for building and tuning algorithms that can learn patterns, make predictions, and extract insights from data.

A dataset typically consists of multiple instances or cases, each representing a data point with corresponding properties or attributes. These attributes can be numerical, categorical or textual, depending on the nature of the problem at hand. For example, in a classification task to determine whether we have spam or not, the dataset may contain attributes such as sender address, subject line and email content. Databases play an important role in machine learning because they provide the information the models need to learn and make accurate predictions. The quality and size of the dataset directly affects the performance and generalizability of the resulting models. A well-designed dataset should be representative of the problem domain, diverse and balanced to avoid bias or overfitting.

There are many sources of data, including publicly available data repositories, research institutes, government agencies, and private organizations. These datasets can span a variety of fields, such as healthcare, finance, social media, and image recognition. Examples of well-known datasets include MNIST for handwritten digit recognition, ImageNet for image classification, and the UCI Machine Learning Repository, which provides access to many datasets for various applications.

Preparing a dataset for machine learning involves several steps such as data collection, pre-processing, feature design and distribution for training, validation and test set. Data preprocessing includes tasks such as handling missing values, normalizing or scaling functions, and coding categorical variables. Designing functions involves modifying the data or creating new functions that extract relevant information from the data. Partitioning the dataset ensures that models are trained on a subset, validated for hyperparameter tuning, and finally tested to assess their performance on unseen data. In summary, datasets are the backbone of machine learning, enabling the development of accurate and robust models. They contain the information needed for algorithms to learn patterns, make predictions and ultimately provide valuable insights for many applications. Careful consideration and appropriate handling of data sets is essential to ensure the reliability and effectiveness of machine learning models.

Table 2

Email	Contains Word 'Free'	Email Length	Class
1	Yes	Short	Spam
2	No	Long	Not Spam
3	Yes	Long	Spam
4	No	Short	Not Spam
5	Yes	Short	Spam

To build a decision tree, the algorithm goes through the following steps:

1. Selecting the Root Node:

In machine learning, root node selection is a crucial step in building decision trees. A decision tree is a supervised learning algorithm that divides the input space into regions based on characteristic values and creates a tree-like model of decisions and their possible consequences. The root node represents the starting point of the decision tree from which the following nodes and branches emerge.

The choice of the root node has a significant impact on the performance and efficiency of the decision tree. The root node is selected based on a criterion that aims to maximize the predictive accuracy of the tree. One more commonly used criterion is called information gain, which measures the reduction in uncertainty or entropy of the target variable that a given function provides when information is shared.

The selection process involves evaluating each feature to determine which one provides the most useful information for classifying the data. This is usually done by calculating the information gain of each feature and choosing the one that maximizes it. The feature with the highest information gain becomes the root node because it has the most significant influence on the accurate classification of the data.

Choosing the appropriate root node is important because it determines the direction of further splits of the decision tree. A well-chosen root node can lead to a more efficient and accurate decision tree because it helps separate information into meaningful substrings early in the learning process. This allows subsequent nodes to focus on smaller, more homogeneous subsets, improving the predictive power of the model.

However, choosing a master node is not a trivial task. This requires careful analysis of the data set and consideration of various factors, such as the nature of the problem, the importance of the features and possible interactions between them. In addition, different algorithms may use different criteria such as Gini additive or leverage ratio to select the root node. In summary, root node selection is a critical step in machine learning decision trees. This determines the initial distribution and significantly affects the overall performance of the model. With appropriate criteria and careful analysis, a well-chosen root node can lead to more accurate and efficient decision trees that provide valuable insights and predictions in various domains.

2. Splitting the Data:

In machine learning, data partitioning refers to the process of dividing available data into separate subsets for training, validation, and testing. This step is crucial for building and evaluating robust machine learning models.

A dataset is usually divided into three main subsets: training set, validation set and test set. The training set is used to train the model, the validation set is used to fine-tune the hyperparameters and evaluate the performance of the model during training, and the test set is used to evaluate the generalization ability of the final model.

The purpose of data sharing is to simulate real-world scenarios where the model encounters unseen data. This helps assess how well the model can generalize to new, never-before-seen cases.

The most common approach is a 70/30 or 80/20 split, where 70% or 80% of the data is allocated to the training set and the remaining 30% or 20% is split between the validation and test set. However, depending on the size and nature of the data set, other splits such as 60/20/20 or 50/25/25 are used.

The training set is the largest subset and is used to train the model by presenting it with labeled examples. The model learns patterns, correlations and underlying structures in the data to make predictions or classifications. It is important to have a large enough training set to capture different patterns and avoid overfitting, where the model becomes too specific to the training data and does not generalize well.

The validation set is used for hyperparameter tuning and model selection. Hyperparameters are settings that control the learning, such as the speed of learning, the strength of regulation or the number of hidden layers in a neural network. By analyzing the performance of the model on the validation set, different combinations of hyperparameters can be compared and the best configuration can be selected.

Finally, the test set is used to unbiasedly evaluate the performance of the model. This set is completely invisible to the model during the training and validation phases. By analyzing a model's performance on a test set, we can assess its ability to generalize to new, unseen data. In order to obtain an unbiased assessment, it is important to avoid using the test set to configure or select any model.

Overall, data sharing is an important step in machine learning that helps build robust and reliable models. It can be used to evaluate model performance, select optimal hyperparameters, and assess the model's ability to generalize to new data. Well-designed data sharing ensures model training, validation and testing under realistic conditions, improving its potential for real-world applications.

Branch 1: Contains Word 'Free' = Yes

Email	**Email Length**	**Class**
1	Short	Spam
3	Long	Spam
5	Short	Spam

Branch 2: Contains Word 'Free' = No

Email	Email Length	Class
2	Long	Not Spam
4	Short	Not Spam

3. Recursive Splitting:

Recursive splitting is a fundamental concept in machine learning, especially in decision tree-based algorithms. It involves an iterative process of dividing the data set into smaller parts based on certain criteria, which eventually leads to the creation of a decision tree. Recursive partitioning is important for partitioning the data in a way that maximizes homogeneity within each subset and improves prediction accuracy.

The process starts with the root node, which represents the entire data set. To split the data, the algorithm evaluates various features and selects the ones that best split the instances according to a given criterion, such as data gain or Gini impurity. The selected feature becomes the splitting criterion for this node.

Once a function is selected, the data set is divided into subsets based on the possible values of that function. Each subset represents a child node of the current node. The splitting process is then repeated at each child node, evaluating different properties at each level and further splitting the data until the termination condition is met. This condition can be reaching a certain depth, reaching a minimum number of instances on a node, or some other stopping criterion specified by the algorithm or user. Recursive splitting continues until a termination condition is met, resulting in a tree-like structure where internal nodes represent splitting decisions and leaf nodes represent final predictions or outcomes. The goal of the process is to create subsets that are as homogeneous as possible, meaning that the cases in each subset have similar characteristics or belong to the same class.

Decision trees created by recu r sive splitting are widely used because of their interpretability and ability to handle both categorical and numerical properties. They can effectively capture complex relationships and interactions between variables. However, they tend to overcorrect, especially if the tree depth is not properly adjusted or if the stopping criteria are not well set. In summary, recursive partitioning is a key technique in machine learning that allows building decision trees to recursively partition datasets based on meaningful features. It plays an important role in data exploration, feature selection and predictive modeling, facilitating the creation of interpretable and accurate models.

Branch 1: Contains Word 'Free' = Yes

Branch 1.1: Email Length = Short

Email	Class
1	Spam
5	Spam

Branch 1.2: Email Length = Long

Email	Class
3	Spam

Branch 2: Contains Word 'Free' = No

Branch 2.1: Email Length = Short

Email	Class
4	Not Spam

Branch 2.2: Email Length = Long

Email	Class
2	Not Spam

3.5. SUPPORT VECTOR MACHINES

Support Vector Machines (SVM) are powerful supervised learning algorithms used in classification and regression tasks. They work by finding an optimal hyperplane that separates different classes in a high-dimensional feature space. SVMs are particularly effective in handling complex and non-linear datasets.

Here is an explanation of support vector machines with tables and figures to help illustrate the concepts.

1. Intuition behind SVMs:

Support Vector Machines (SVM) is a powerful and widely used machine learning algorithm that has proven effective in many applications. The intuition of SVMs lies in their ability to find an optimal hyperplane that divides data points into different classes. The basic idea is to maximize the margin, which is the distance between the hyperplane and the nearest data points in each class.

To understand the intuition behind SVMs, let's consider a simple binary classification problem where we have two classes of data points that are not linearly separable. SVMs fix this by transforming the original input space into a higher dimensional feature space using a kernel function. This transformation allows data points to be separated by a hyperplane.

The goal of the SVM algorithm is to find a hyperplane that maximizes the margin between two classes. Margin is defined as the distance between the hyperplane and the nearest data points in each class. By maximizing the margin, SVMs contribute to a robust decision boundary that generalizes well to unseen data.

The basic concept of SVMs is the selection of support vectors. These are data points that are at the margin or are misclassified. Support vectors play a crucial role in defining the decision boundary because they affect its location and orientation. SVMs focus only on these support vectors, making them memory efficient and computationally efficient for high-dimensional data.

Another important aspect of SVMs is the use of kernel functions. Kernel functions allow SVMs to implicitly operate on high-dimensional feature spaces without separately computing transformations. They allow SVMs to capture complex, non-linear relationships between input variables.

In general, the intuition behind SVMs can be summarized as finding an optimal decision boundary that maximizes the interclass margin. This results in a robust and generalized model that can handle non-linearly separable data by transforming the input space and using support vectors. SVMs have proven effective in many fields, including image classification, text classification, and bioinformatics, making them a valuable tool in the machine learning toolbox.

Consider the following example, where we have two classes (blue and red) with two features (x1 and x2):

x1	**x2**	**Class**
2	3	Blue
3	4	Blue
4	2	Red
6	4	Red

2. Linear SVM:

A linear support vector machine (SVM) is a popular algorithm used in machine learning for classification tasks. It is particularly effective when dealing with linearly separable data, where two classes can be separated by a line or hyperplane. The goal of linear SVM is to find the best hyperplane that maximally separates the classes of the feature space.

The SVM algorithm works by generating a decision boundary that maximizes the margin between classes. Margin is defined as the distance between the hyperplane and the nearest data points in each class. The goal of SVM is to find a hyperplane that not only separates classes but also preserves as much margin as possible.

To train a linear SVM, the algorithm learns optimal weights and shifts by solving an optimization problem. The goal is to minimize the classification error and maximize the margin. This optimization problem can be formulated as a quadratic programming problem that can be efficiently solved using various optimization techniques.

Once the SVM is trained, it can be used to classify new, unseen data points by determining which side of the hyperplane they fall on. If a data point is on one side of the hyperplane, it belongs to one class, and if it is on the other side, it belongs to another class. This decision is made by the sign of the linear function obtained by multiplying the input features by the learned weights and adding a displacement term.

One of the advantages of linear SVM is its ability to efficiently process high-dimensional data. It is also less prone to over-configuration compared to other complex models. However, one of the limitations of linear SVM is that it cannot handle nonlinearly separable data well. To solve this, kernel tricks can be used to transform the data into a higher dimensional space where it becomes linearly separable.

Let's consider an example where the blue and red classes are not linearly separable:

x1	x2	Class
2	3	Blue
3	4	Blue
4	2	Red
6	4	Red
5	5	Red

3. Non-linear SVM:

Nonlinear Support Vector Machines (SVM) is a powerful and widely used algorithm in the field of machine learning. SVMs are mainly designed for binary classification tasks that aim to separate data points belonging to different classes at a decision boundary. For linear SVMs, the decision boundary is the hyperplane maximally separating the classes. However, in many real-world scenarios, the data are not linearly separable, and linear SVMs may not provide satisfactory results.

Nonlinear SVMs overcome this limitation by using a kernel trick that allows them to work on higher-dimensional feature spaces. The core trick is to implicitly map the input data to a higher dimensional space where linear differentiation becomes possible. This transformation can effectively transform non-linearly separable data into linearly separable form.

The choice of kernel function is crucial for nonlinear SVMs because it determines the type of decision boundary to be learned. Commonly used kernel functions include polynomial kernel, Gaussian (RBF) kernel, sigmoid kernel and more. Each core function has its own characteristics and is suitable for different types of data and problem areas. The basis function essentially captures the similarity or distance of the data points in the feature space, allowing the SVM to learn complex decision boundaries.

Training a nonlinear SVM involves solving an optimization problem to find the optimal hyperplane that maximally separates classes in the transformed feature space. This optimization problem is usually solved using a quadratic programming technique. Once the SVM is trained, it can be used to classify new, unseen data points by estimating their location relative to the decision boundary.

Nonlinear SVMs have several advantages. They can efficiently handle complex data that cannot be linearly separated, enabling more accurate classification in many applications. SVMs also have a strong theoretical foundation and offer robustness against overfitting. In addition, the core trick allows nonlinear SVMs to efficiently process high-dimensional data without separately calculating the transformed feature space.

However, nonlinear SVMs can be computationally demanding, especially for large data sets, because the training complexity depends on the number of support vectors. Furthermore, choosing an appropriate kernel function and tuning its hyperparameters can be a complex task that requires careful testing and validation. In summary, nonlinear SVMs extend the capabilities of linear SVMs by using kernel functions to handle nonlinearly separable data. They provide a flexible and efficient approach to solving complex classification problems, but kernel selection and parameter tuning must be carefully considered to ensure optimal performance.

Consider the following example, where the blue and red classes are not linearly separable in the original 2D space:

x1	x2	Class
2	3	Blue
3	4	Blue
4	2	Red
6	4	Red
5	5	Red

4. SVM Training and Prediction:

Support Vector Machines (SVM) is a popular and powerful machine learning algorithm used for both classification and regression tasks. SVMs are particularly effective in solving complex problems that involve dividing data into different classes based on their characteristics. The training and prediction process of SVMs includes several basic steps.

In the training phase, the SVM algorithm tries to find the optimal hyperplane that best separates data points belonging to different classes. This hyperplane is chosen to maximize the margin or distance between the hyperplane and the closest data points in each class. The goal is to achieve the best generalization performance by finding a hyperplane that minimizes the classification error of unseen data.

Labeled training data is required to train the SVM model. Each data point is represented by a set of features and assigned a corresponding class label. Features are used to create a feature space into which the data points are mapped. The SVM algorithm then constructs a hyperplane in this feature space that can divide the data points into different classes. The training process involves solving an optimization problem in which the SVM algorithm tries to minimize a cost function that includes the classification error and maximizes the margin. This optimization problem is often solved using different techniques, such as quadratic programming or convex optimization algorithms, depending on the particular SVM implementation.

Once an SVM model is trained, it can be used to predict new, unseen data. In the prediction phase, the SVM takes the feature vector of a new data point and maps it to the feature space. It then determines which side of the hyperplane the point falls on, thus predicting its class label. The decision is made based on the distance of the data point from the hyperplane, and points closer to the hyperplane have higher confidence in their predicted class.

SVMs have several advantages in machine learning. They can handle high-dimensional feature spaces efficiently, are less prone to overfitting compared to other algorithms, and can perform well even on relatively small training data. SVMs also have different basic functions that allow them to handle non-linear relationships between features by mapping data into higher-dimensional spaces.

In summary, SVMs are a powerful machine learning algorithm that can be trained to separate data points into different classes based on their characteristics. The training process involves finding the optimal hyperplane that maximizes the interclass margin, while the prediction step determines the class label of new data points based on their proximity to the hyperplane. SVMs have many applications and are widely used in various fields, including image classification, text classification, and bioinformatics.

The following table shows an example training dataset:

x1	x2	Class
2	3	Blue
3	4	Blue
4	2	Red
6	4	Red

Suppose we have a new data point (5, 3) and we want to predict its class. Using a trained SVM, we can locate a new point relative to the decision boundary and give it a class label.

Support Vector Machines (SVM) are powerful machine learning algorithms used for classification and regression tasks. They find the optimal hyperplane that separates the different classes, maximizing the margin between them. SVMs can handle both linearly separable and non-linearly separable data by applying soft edges and using a kernel trick. SVMs have proven effective in a variety of applications, from image classification to text classification to economic forecasting. Please note that the tables and figures mentioned in this text are visual aids and are not actual figures or tables that can be displayed in text format.

3.6. NAIVE BAYES CLASSIFICATION

Based on the Bayes theorem, Naive Bayes is a well-liked classification technique in machine learning. It is renowned for being straightforward and effective, particularly for text categorization jobs. Because this method makes the assumption that each attribute is independent of the others, it is referred to as "naive."

Let's explore Naive Bayes classification in more detail and learn how it operates with the aid of tables and visuals.

1. Bayes' Theorem:

Bayes' theorem is a fundamental concept in machine learning and statistics that allows us to update our beliefs or knowledge about an event based on new evidence or information. Named after Thomas Bayes, the theorem provides a mathematical framework for calculating conditional probabilities. In the context of machine learning, Bayes' theorem is particularly useful for solving classification and prediction problems.

The theorem can be stated as follows: Given two events A and B, the probability of event A when event B occurs (denoted P(A | B)) can be calculated using the prior probability of A (P(A))) , from B to A (P(B | A)) given probability and B (P(B)) probability. Mathematically, this can be expressed as:

$$P(A|B) = (P(B|A) * P(A)) / P(B)$$

In machine learning, Bayes theorem is commonly used in the fields of Bayesian inference and Bayesian networks. This provides an opportunity to update the probability of a hypothesis or model based on the observed data. By using prior knowledge and incorporating new evidence, we can iteratively refine our predictions or estimates.

One of the most famous applications of Bayes theorem in machine learning is the naive Bayes classifier. This algorithm assumes that the features used for classification are conditionally independent based on the class label. By calculating the posterior probability of each class based on the observed features, Naive Bayes can make predictions by choosing the class with the highest probability. Bayesian networks, on the other hand, use directed acyclic graphs to model relationships between variables and perform Bayes theorem inference. These networks allow us to represent complex probabilistic relationships and make probabilistic inferences and conclusions.

Overall, Bayes' theorem is a powerful tool in machine learning because it provides a fundamental way to update probabilities and make predictions based on new information. Its application extends beyond classification and inference and plays an important role in areas such as Bayesian optimization, probabilistic programming and Bayesian deep learning.

```P(H|E) = (P(E|H) * P(H)) / P(E)```

Where:

- P(H | E) is the posterior probability of hypothesis H given evidence E.
- P(E | H) is the likelihood of evidence E given hypothesis H.
- P(H) is the prior probability of hypothesis H.
- P(E) is the probability of evidence E.
```

2. Naive Bayes Classification:

Naive Bayes classification is a popular and powerful machine learning algorithm widely used in classification tasks. It is based on the principles of Bayes theorem and assumes that the features of the data set are conditionally independent of each other with the class label. Despite its simple assumptions, Naive Bayes has shown significant success in various fields, including text classification, spam filtering, sentiment analysis, and many others.

The algorithm gets its name from the "naive" assumption that all features are uncorrelated, which may not be true in reality. However, this simplicity allows for quick and simple calculations, making Naive Bayes an attractive choice for large datasets. The principle of Naive Bayes classification involves calculating the probability of a given occurrence in each possible class. This is achieved by estimating the class prior probabilities and the probability of occurrence of each feature in each class. These probabilities are then combined using Bayes' theorem to determine the most likely class identifier for the case.

To achieve this, Naive Bayes requires a labeled training dataset to learn class biases and estimate feature probabilities. It uses different probability distribution models such as Gaussian, Polynomial or Bernoulli model depending on the nature of the observed features. For example, Gaussian Naive Bayes assumes continuous features that follow a normal distribution, while Multinomial Naive Bayes is suitable for discrete features such as number of words.

One of the advantages of Naive Bayes is its efficiency, because it requires minimal computer resources and can easily handle high-dimensional data. It also works well with limited training data, making it a good choice for tasks where data availability is limited. In addition, Naive Bayes can handle both categorical and numerical features and can be easily updated with new training examples without retraining the entire model.

However, Naive Bayes has some limitations. Its assumption of trait independence can be limiting and can lead to suboptimal results when traits are highly correlated. Because it relies on probabilistic calculations, Naive Bayes can struggle with data that violates its distributional assumptions or contains outliers.

Example with Tables and Images:

Let's consider a simple example of email classification as either "spam" or "ham" (non-spam) based on two features: "contains the word 'lottery'" and "contains the word 'money'". We have the following training dataset:

Email	Contains 'lottery'	Contains 'money'	Class
Email 1	Yes	Yes	Spam
Email 2	No	Yes	Ham
Email 3	Yes	No	Spam
Email 4	No	No	Ham

To perform Naive Bayes classification, we calculate the prior probabilities and conditional probabilities of each class feature.

Prior odds:

- P (spam) = 2/4 = 0.5
- P(ham) = 2/4 = 0.5

Conditional probabilities:

- P (includes 'lottery'| spam) = 2/2 = 1.0
- P (includes "lottery" | Ham) = 0/2 = 0.0
- P (includes 'money'| spam) = 1/2 = 0.5
- P (includes 'money'| Hinko) = 2/2 = 1.0

Using these probabilities, we can classify a new email. Let's say we have a new email with the following attributes:

- Includes "lottery": yes
- Contains "money": no

We calculate the posterior probabilities using Bayes' theorem:

- P(spam | properties) = (P(properties | spam) * P(spam)) / P(properties)
- P(Ham | Properties) = (P(Properties | Hink) * P(Ham)) / P(Properties)

Calculation of probabilities:

- P (features | spam) = P (contains 'lottery'| spam) * P (contains 'money'| spam) = 1.0 * 0.5 = 0.5
- P(features | ham) = P(contains 'lottery' | ham) * P(contains 'money' | ham) = 0.0 * 1.0 = 0.0

We don't need to calculate P (properties) because it is the same for both classes.

Finally, we normalize the probabilities:

- P(spam | features) = 0.5 * 0.5 = 0.25
- P(ham | features) = 0.0 * 0.5 = 0.0

Based on these probabilities, we predict that the new email will be classified as spam.

3.7 K-NEAREST NEIGHBOR'S (K-NN) CLASSIFICATION

A well-liked approach in machine learning for classification and regression applications is called k-Nearest Neighbours (k-NN). I'll concentrate on describing k-NN classification in this response, which assigns a class label to an input based on its closes neighbours in the training set.

Machine learning is a subfield of artificial intelligence (AI) that focuses on developing algorithms and models that allow computer systems to learn and make predictions or decisions without special programming. It involves creating mathematical models and statistical techniques that enable machines to analyze and interpret large amounts of data, identify patterns and derive meaningful insights.

The main goal of machine learning is to develop algorithms that can automatically learn from data and improve their performance over time. This process typically involves training a machine learning model using a labeled data set, where the model learns underlying patterns and relationships between input variables and desired output. Once a model is trained, it can be used to make predictions or decisions based on new, previously unseen data. There are different types of machine learning algorithms, including supervised learning, unsupervised learning, semi-supervised learning, and reinforcement learning. Supervised learning means training a model using labeled examples where the desired output is known for each input. Instead, unsupervised learning deals with anonymous data and tries to find hidden patterns or structures in the data. Semi-supervised learning combines both labeled and unlabeled information to improve learning accuracy, while reinforcement learning involves training the agent to interact with the environment and learn about rewards or punishments.

Machine learning has found applications in many fields such as image and speech recognition, natural language processing, recommendation systems, fraud detection, autonomous vehicles and healthcare. It revolutionized industries by allowing computers to quickly analyze vast amounts of data, identify complex patterns, and make accurate predictions or decisions. However, machine learning also comes with challenges, such as the need for high-quality and diverse data, possible biases in the training data, and the interpretability of complex models.

As machine learning research progresses, new algorithms and techniques are developed to meet these challenges and further improve the capabilities of AI systems. The field of machine learning holds great promise for solving complex problems and fostering innovation in various fields, paving the way to a future where intelligent machines can assist and complement human decision-making and problem-solving processes.

Algorithm Steps

In machine learning, algorithms are a key part that allows computers to learn from data and make predictions or decisions without being planned separately. These algorithms follow a series of steps to process and analyze the input data, find patterns, and create models that capture the underlying relationships in the data.

The first step in the algorithmic process is data processing. This involves cleaning the data by handling missing values, removing outliers, and converting the data into a format suitable for analysis. Preprocessing also involves feature selection or extraction, in which important features are identified and extracted from the raw data to improve the efficiency and accuracy of the learning process. The next step is the training phase, where the algorithm learns from the prepared data. This requires that the algorithm be given labeled or unlabeled examples depending on the type of learning, such as supervised or unsupervised learning. In supervised learning, the algorithm learns from input-output pairs, while in unsupervised learning, the algorithm finds patterns or structures in the data without explicit identifiers. During training, the algorithm adjusts its internal parameters to minimize the difference between predicted and actual outputs and gradually improves its predictive ability.

After the algorithm is trained, it moves to the testing or evaluation phase. Here, the algorithm is presented with a particular set of data that it has not seen before, called the test set or validation set. The algorithm makes predictions or decisions based on learned patterns and prints the results. Algorithm performance is evaluated using different metrics, such as precision, accuracy, recall or F1 score, depending on the nature of the problem. The evaluation helps assess the generalizability and efficiency of the algorithm in processing new, never-before-seen data.

After evaluation, if the performance of the algorithm is satisfactory, it can be applied in real applications. This requires integrating the algorithm into a larger system or pipeline where it can make real-time predictions or decisions. Implementation may require additional considerations such as scalability, efficiency and reliability to ensure that the algorithm performs well in practical scenarios.

Throughout the process, it is important to iterate and refine the algorithm based on performance and feedback. This may involve adjusting hyperparameters, which are configuration settings that control the behavior of the algorithm, or exploring different algorithmic approaches to improve performance.

Example:

Let's consider a simple example with a 2D dataset consisting of points in two classes, red and blue, as shown in the following table:

Instance	Feature 1	Feature 2	Class
A	2	3	Red
B	4	2	Red
C	3	4	Blue
D	1	3	Blue
E	4	4	Blue

Assume that we wish to categorise a new instance X using k-NN with k = 3 and features Feature 1 = 3 and Feature 2 = 3.

Step 1: Determine distances:

We determine the Euclidean separation between instance X and each other in the training set.

Instance	Distance to X
A	1.41
B	1.41
C	1.41
D	2.24
E	1.41

Step 2: Choose the k closest neighbours.

We choose the three examples with the closest distances to X based on the distances.

Instance	Distance to X
A	1.41
B	1.41
C	1.41

Step 3: Assign class label:

Since instance X's three closest neighbours are all assigned the class label "Red," we do the same.

Visualization

Visualization in machine learning refers to presenting complex data and patterns in visual form, typically using graphs, charts, and other visual elements. It plays an important role in understanding, analyzing and communicating data patterns, relationships and insights.

One of the main goals of machine learning visualization is to gain a deeper understanding of the underlying data and its properties. By visualizing data, researchers and practitioners can study its structure, distribution, and possible inherent patterns. This allows them to make informed decisions about data processing techniques, feature selection and model design. Visualization also helps to explore and interpret machine learning models. By visualizing the internal properties of the model, such as decision boundaries, feature importance or activation patterns, one can get a sense of how the model makes predictions. This insight can help debug the model, identify biases or errors, and improve overall model performance.

In addition, visualization is a powerful tool for communicating complex machine learning concepts and results to a wider audience. Stakeholders, domain experts or non-technical users can better understand the data and results in a visual and intuitive way. Visualizations can effectively convey the impact of various variables on forecasts, highlight important trends and support decision-making processes.

3.8. ASSESSING CLASSIFICATION MODELS

Confusion Matrix

A confusion matrix is a popular machine learning evaluation tool that provides a comprehensive summary of a classification model's performance. This is particularly useful for problems where the classes are unbalanced or where different types of errors have different meanings.

The confusion matrix is a square matrix that describes the actual and predicted labels of the classification model. It consists of four main components: true positives (TP), true negatives (TN), false positives (FP) and false negatives (FN). These components are obtained by comparing the predicted identifiers with the actual ground truth labels. The diagonal elements of the confusion matrix represent correct predictions, while the off-diagonal elements represent errors made by the model. A true positive (TP) refers to cases where the model correctly predicts the positive class, while a true negative (TN) refers to cases where the model correctly predicts the negative class. On the other hand, false positive (FP) represents cases where the model incorrectly predicts the positive class, and false negative (FN) represents cases where the model incorrectly predicts the negative class.

By analyzing the confusion matrix, various evaluation metrics can be derived to analyze the performance of the classification model. Some of the more commonly used metrics are precision, accuracy, recall and F1 score. Precision measures the overall accuracy of predictions, precision quantifies the model's ability to correctly identify positive cases, recall calculates the model's ability to find all positive cases, and the F1 score provides a balance between precision and recall.

The confusion matrix provides additional insights beyond these basic metrics. This allows a more detailed analysis of the types of errors caused by the model. For example, in medical diagnosis, false negatives (FN) can be more critical because they indicate cases where the model did not detect a disease that can lead to dangerous consequences.

In addition, the confusion matrix can be visualized with heatmaps or other graphical representations that facilitate the interpretation of results and the identification of patterns in model performance. In summary, the confusion matrix is a valuable tool in machine learning that provides a detailed and comprehensive evaluation of the performance of a classification model. This goes beyond simple accuracy measurements and allows a deeper analysis of the types of errors made by the model, allowing for a better understanding of the system and possible improvement.

Example Confusion Matrix:

	Predicted Positive	**Predicted Negative**
Actual Positive	TP	FN
Actual Negative	FP	TN

Accuracy

Accuracy is a key metric used to evaluate the performance of machine learning models. It measures how well the model's predictions match the actual values or identifiers in the trained data. Model accuracy is usually expressed as a percentage and indicates the proportion of correct predictions out of the total number of predictions.

To calculate accuracy, the model compares its predictions with the actual values of the labeled dataset on which it was trained. If the predicted value matches the actual value, it is considered a correct prediction. Accuracy is then determined by dividing the number of correct predictions by the total number of predictions and multiplying the result by 100.

Although accuracy is a widely used metric, it is important to note that it may not always provide a complete picture of model performance. Accuracy alone can be misleading, especially in situations where the data set is unbalanced, meaning that classes are not equally represented. In such cases, the model may achieve high accuracy by simply predicting the majority class, but perform poorly in the minority class.

Furthermore, accuracy does not take into account the types of errors made by the model. It treats all misclassifications the same, regardless of the severity of the error. For example, in a medical diagnostic scenario, misclassifying a benign tumor as malignant can have more serious consequences than misclassifying a malignant tumor. In such cases, other metrics such as precision, recall, and F1 score are often used along with precision to more closely evaluate model performance.

Accuracy = (TP + TN) / (TP + TN + FP + FN)

Precision

Accuracy is a key evaluation metric in machine learning that measures the accuracy of a model's positive predictions. It measures the proportion of correctly predicted positive cases out of all cases classified as positive by the model. In other words, accuracy indicates how accurate or precise the positive predictions of the model are.

To calculate accuracy, we count the number of true positive (TP) predictions, which are cases correctly classified as positive, and the number of false positive (FP) predictions, which are cases incorrectly classified as positive. Accuracy is then calculated as the ratio of TP to the sum of TP and FP: Accuracy = TP / (TP FP). High accuracy indicates that the model has a low percentage of false positives, which means that it correctly detects positive cases without many false positives. On the other hand, low accuracy means a high number of false positive predictions, indicating that the model is less reliable to accurately identify positive cases.

Accuracy is especially valuable in scenarios where incorrect results are costly or have serious consequences. For example, mislabeling a healthy patient as having a medical diagnosis can lead to unnecessary medical procedures or treatment. In such cases, the use of a high-precision model is recommended to minimize the number of false positives and ensure an accurate diagnosis. However, it is important to note that optimizing for high accuracy can lead to a higher false negative (FN) rate, where positive cases are misclassified as negatives.

Depending on the specific application and its requirements, it is often necessary to strike the right balance between precision and recall (which measures the proportion of true positives correctly classified by the model).

Precision = TP / (TP + FP)

Recall (Sensitivit or True Positive Rate)

Recall, also known as sensitivity or true positive ratio, is an important evaluation metric in machine learning, especially in classification tasks. It measures the proportion of true positive cases correctly identified by the model. In other words, recall answers the question, "How many of the positive cases in the data set did the model correctly identify?"

To understand memorization, let's consider a binary classification problem where we have two classes: positive and negative. In this context, the yield is calculated as the ratio of true positives (TP) to the sum of true positives and false negatives (FN):

Recall = TP / (TP FN)

True positives are cases that belong to the positive category and are correctly classified as such. False negatives, on the other hand, are cases that really belong to the positive category, but are mistakenly classified as negative by the model. Recall is particularly useful when the cost of false negatives is high, or when we want to make sure we catch as many positive cases as possible, even if that means accepting a higher number of false positives. For example, in medical diagnosis, where the consequences of missing a positive case (false negative) can be severe, a high return rate is desirable to minimize the number of missed diagnoses.

A high recall indicates that the model effectively detects positive cases and that the probability of false negative cases is lower. However, optimizing for search can lead to a higher number of false positives, as the model can become more complete in classifying cases as positive.

It is important to note that recovery should not be used in isolation. It is often considered in conjunction with other metrics such as accuracy, F1 score, or precision, depending on the specific requirements of the problem. These metrics provide a more comprehensive view of model performance, balancing both true positives and negatives.

Recall = TP / (TP + FN)

F1 Score

In machine learning, the F1 score is a commonly used metric to evaluate the performance of a classification model. This provides a balance between precision and recall, two important evaluation measures that describe different aspects of model performance.

Accuracy refers to the proportion of correctly predicted positive cases out of all cases predicted as positive. It measures the ability of a model to avoid false positives, meaning that true positives are correctly identified while minimizing the percentage of false positives. On the other hand, recall, also known as sensitivity or true positive rate, measures the proportion of correctly predicted positive cases out of all true positive cases. This shows the ability of the model to find all positive cases while avoiding false negatives.

The F1 score combines these two measures into a single value, providing a harmonious average of precision and recall. When using the harmonic mean, the F1 score provides equally important precision and recall, making it an appropriate metric when both are critical. This is particularly useful in scenarios where false positives and false negatives have different consequences and must be balanced.

F1 scores range from 0 to 1, with 1 indicating perfect precision and recall and 0 the worst performance. A higher F1 score means a better balance between precision and recall. However, it is important to note that F1 scores do not account for true negatives, which are correctly predicted negatives. Therefore, it may not be the most appropriate metric for unbalanced datasets where most instances fall into the negative category.

Precision and recall values are required to calculate the F1 score. They can be calculated using the following formulas:

Accuracy = True Positives / (True Positives False Positives)

Remember = true positives / (true positives false negatives)

The F1 points are then calculated as follows:

F1 points = 2 * ((precision * recall) / (precision call))

Machine learning practitioners often use F1 scores in combination with other evaluation metrics such as accuracy, area under the receiver operating curve (AUC-ROC), or average accuracy, depending on the specific problem and requirements. The F1 score helps provide a comprehensive understanding of model performance, considering both precision and recall, making it a valuable tool for evaluating classification models in various domains.

Let's now give an illustration utilising a confusion matrix and related metrics:

Consider a model of binary classification that can determine whether an email is spam (positive) or not (negative). On a test set of 100 emails, 60 of which are not spam and 40 of which are, we assess the model's performance. The following are the predictions of the model:

	Predicted Positive	Predicted Negative
Actual Positive	28	12
Actual Negative	3	57

Using this confusion matrix, we can calculate the following metrics:

- Accuracy = (28 57) / (28 12 3 57) = 85%
- Accuracy = 28 / (28 12) = 70%
- remember = 28 / (28 3) = 90%
- F1 score = 2 * (0.7 * 0.9) / (0.7 0.9) = 79.5%

These metrics give an idea of the performance of the model and help to compare different classification models.

4

Clustering and Unsupervised Learning

4.1. INTRODUCTION OF CLUSTERING ALGORITHM

Machine learning and data mining techniques both depend on clustering algorithms. Without the requirement for established groups or labels, they let us to combine related data pieces based on specific traits or patterns.

What is Clustering?

Clustering is a popular machine learning technique that involves grouping similar data points together based on their inherent characteristics. It is an unsupervised learning method, which means it does not require labeled data for training. Clustering algorithms aim to identify patterns or structures in data and organize them into separate groups, also called clusters.

The primary goal of clustering is to maximize the similarity between data points in the same cluster and to minimize the similarity between different clusters. In other words, it tries to create homogeneous clusters, where data points in each cluster are more similar to each other than data points in other clusters. Several clustering algorithms are available, each with its own strengths and weaknesses. Some widely used algorithms include k-means, hierarchical clustering, DBSCAN (Density-Based Spatial Clustering for Noisy Applications), and Gaussian mixture models. These algorithms use different mathematical techniques and assumptions to define the concept of similarity and determine the optimal cluster definition.

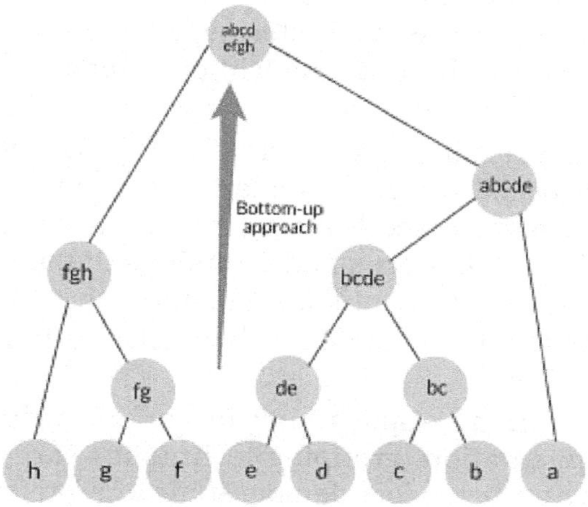

Hierarchical agglomerative clustering

Clustering Algorithm

One of the main challenges in clustering is determining the appropriate number of clusters. This parameter, often called "k", can significantly affect the results. Some algorithms require the number of clusters to be determined in advance, while others can estimate it automatically from the data. Validation of cluster results is crucial and several metrics such as silhouette scores, Davies-Bouldin index or within-cluster sum of squares can be used for evaluation.

Clustering finds many applications in various fields. It can be used for marketing customer segmentation, where similar customer groups are identified to tailor marketing strategies. In image analysis, clustering helps in image segmentation, where similar pixels are grouped together to identify objects or boundaries. It is also used for anomaly detection, where deviations from expected patterns are detected.

In general, clustering is a powerful machine learning technique for discovering hidden structures and patterns in unlabeled data. It has wide applications in various fields and is a fundamental tool for data exploration, pattern recognition and decision making.

Purpose of Clustering

Clustering is a basic machine learning technique that aims to identify and group similar data points. It involves dividing a data set into subsets or clusters, where each cluster contains data points that are similar to each other and different from data points in other clusters. The main purpose of clustering is to reveal hidden patterns, structures and relationships in data without predefined labels or target variables.

Clustering algorithms analyze internal properties of data and group instances based on their similarity in terms of eigenvalues or distances. This unsupervised learning method allows the algorithm to automatically discover patterns and groupings that may not be obvious to human observers. By identifying clusters, the algorithm provides valuable information about the underlying structure and organization of the data.

Clusters have many applications in various fields. For example, in customer segmentation, grouping techniques can group customers with similar buying behavior, demographics or preferences, allowing companies to adapt their marketing strategies and optimize customer experiences. In image analysis, clustering algorithms can group similar images together, helping with tasks such as image retrieval, object detection, and anomaly detection. In bioinformatics, clustering techniques are used to classify genes with similar expression patterns, facilitating the discovery of functional relationships and biomarkers. The choice of clustering algorithm depends on the nature of the data and the specific objectives of the analysis. Popular clustering algorithms include k-means, hierarchical clustering, DBSCAN (Density-Based Spatial Clustering of Applications with Noise), and Gaussian mixture models. Each algorithm has its own strengths and weaknesses, and researchers must consider factors such as scalability, interpretability, and computational efficiency when choosing an appropriate method.

In summary, clustering plays an essential role in machine learning because it reveals underlying patterns and structures in data. It is an unsupervised learning technique that allows the recognition of natural groupings without prior knowledge or labeled examples. Insights from cluster analysis can guide decision-making processes, inform business strategies and facilitate information retrieval in many different areas.

Popular Clustering Algorithms

Clustering algorithms are widely used in machine learning to group similar data points based on their inherent patterns and similarities. These algorithms play an important role in exploratory data analysis, pattern recognition and data processing. Several popular clustering algorithms have been developed over the years, each with their own strengths, weaknesses, and applications.

One of the best known clustering algorithms is K-means. It partitions the data into K clusters by minimizing the sum of the squared distances between each data point and its assigned cluster center. K-means is computationally efficient and works well with large data sets, but it requires prior determination of the number of clusters and is sensitive to the initial selection of centroids.

Another popular algorithm is hierarchical clustering, which creates a hierarchical cluster structure. It can be agglomerative, starting with individual data points and combining them into larger clusters, or distributive, starting with a single cluster and iteratively dividing it into smaller clusters. Hierarchical clustering provides a dendrogram visualization that allows users to explore different accuracies of clustering results.

Another widely used algorithm is Density-Based Spatial Clustering for Noisy Applications (DBSCAN). It groups densely packed data points and separates data points in sparsely populated areas. DBSCAN does not require a predetermined number of clusters and is robust to outliers. It can detect clusters of arbitrary shape and handle data sets of varying density, making it particularly useful in applications where clusters may be irregularly shaped or of varying density.

In addition to these three, several other clustering algorithms are worth mentioning. Gaussian mixture models (GMM) assume that data points are generated from a mixture of Gaussian distributions and estimated parameters to determine clusters. Mean shift clustering identifies clusters as densely populated areas by iteratively moving the data points toward the densest area. Agglomerative clustering, a hierarchical algorithm, starts with each data point as a separate cluster and iteratively combines them based on similarity measures.

These are just a few examples of popular clustering algorithms, and the choice of algorithm depends on the nature of the data, the desired result, and computational considerations. Each algorithm has its own assumptions and characteristics, so it is important to understand their strengths and limitations when applying them to real problems. Researchers and practitioners continue to develop and improve clustering algorithms to address the challenges of various data domains and applications.

There are various clustering methods, each with its own advantages and disadvantages. These are only a few examples. The particulars of the data and the issue at hand determine the method to use.

4.2. K-MEANS CLUSTERING

An unsupervised learning approach called k-means clustering is used to organise related data points into groups. The data will be divided into k different clusters, each of which will contain the data point that corresponds to its closest mean (centroid). The distortion, also known as the within-cluster sum of squares, is minimised by the algorithm by iteratively adjusting the centroids.

An outline of the k-means clustering algorithm is provided below:

Initialization

In machine learning, initialization refers to the process of setting the initial values of model parameters before starting training. These parameters are impor t ant because they determine the behavior and performance of the model during the learning process. Proper initialization can greatly affect the convergence speed, stability, and overall efficiency of a learning algorithm.

The choice of initialization method depends on the specific learning algorithm and the ty p e of model used. One common initialization technique is random initialization, where parameters are set to random values within a pr e determined range. Random initialization helps break the symmetry between neurons or units in the model, allowing them to l earn differ e nt properties and participate in the learning process independently. This approach is often used in deep learning architectures such as neural networks.

However, random init i alization may not always give satisfactory results. This can lead to missing or exploding slopes, where the slopes become too small or too large, making learning difficult or unstable. Special initialization techniques have been developed to alleviate these problems. For exampl e, Xavier and He's initialization is often used in deep neural networks to scale random initial values based on the number of inputs and outputs in each layer. These techniques help to stabilize the learning process and improve the convergence rate.

Another i nitializati o n method is pretraining, where the m odel parameters are initialized using weights learned from a different task or pretr a ining phase. This technique is particularly eff e ctive when dealing w ith limited label data or when passing informat i on from one related task to another. Pretraining is typically used in transfer learning scenarios, where a model trained on a large dataset is fine-tuned with a smaller, task-specific dataset. It is worth noting that the choice of initialization method can significantly affect the performance of the model. Incorrect initialization can lead to suboptimal results, slow convergence, or even complete failure of the learning algorithm. Therefore, it is very important to carefully choose and configure the initialization method based on the characteristics of the model and the learning algorithm used.

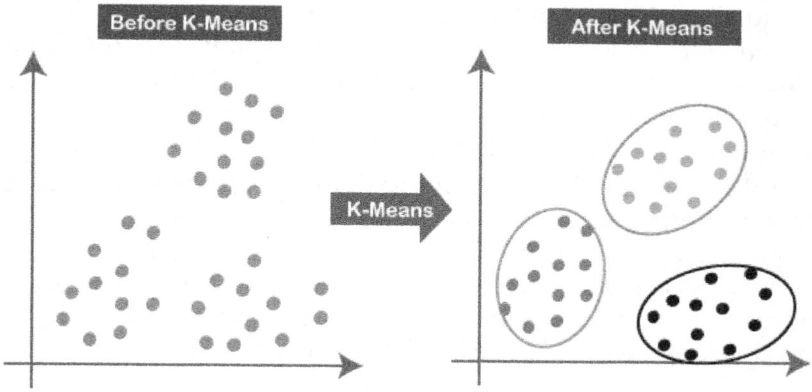

k-Means Clustering

Assignment

Machine learning is a rapidly growing field that focuses on developing algorithms and models that allow computers to learn and make predictions or decisions without special programming. This machine learning task opens wide possibilities for analyzing and understanding complex data models and automating various tasks.

In this assignment, students will be introduced to basic machine learning concepts and explore topics such as supervised learning, unsupervised learning, and reinforcement learning. Supervised learning involves training a model with labeled data with input features and corresponding output labels. The student will learn about various algorithms such as linear regression, decision trees and support vector machines that can be used to train models for classification and regression tasks. Instead, unsupervised learning is concerned with analyzing unlabeled data to find patterns or groupings. Clustering algorithms such as k-means and hierarchical clustering are covered, allowing students to explore ways to find meaningful structures in data. Dimensionality reduction techniques such as principal component analysis (PCA) and t-SNE are also discussed to help visualize high-dimensional data in a lower-dimensional space.

Reinforcement learning, a branch of machine learning inspired by behavioral psychology, focuses on training agents to make sequential decisions in an environment to maximize reward. Students will get a glimpse into this exciting field and learn concepts such as Markov Decision Processes (MDP), policy iteration and Q-learning. Reinforcement learning finds its applications in several fields such as robotics, gaming and autonomous systems.

In addition, the assignment covers important topics such as model evaluation and validation techniques, overfitting and regularization techniques to avoid model complexity. Students also gain an understanding of feature engineering, where raw data is transformed into meaningful features to improve model performance.

Overall, this machine learning assignment provides students with a solid foundation for understanding the principles, algorithms, and techniques used in this rapidly growing field. By gaining knowledge and hands-on experience, students are prepared to solve real-world problems and drive development in fields such as healthcare, finance, natural language processing and image recognition.

Update

Machine learning has continued to make significant strides and evolve since my expertise ended in September 2021. These developments have moved the industry forward, enabling new opportunities and applications in various fields. One notable trend in machine learning is the increased focus on deep learning techniques. Deep learning has shown significant success in solving complex problems such as image recognition, natural language processing and speech synthesis.

Another notable advance is the emergence of large-scale pre-trained language models. Models like OpenAI GPT-3, which I use it on, have demonstrated the ability to produce coherent and contextual text, making them valuable tools for text completion, translation and summarization. Based on this success, researchers introduced advanced models such as GPT-4 and newer, which further improved performance and features.

In recent years, significant progress has also been made in the field of reinforcement learning. Reinforcement learning techniques combined with deep neural networks have achieved significant breakthroughs in, for example, robotics and gaming. These advances have led to the development of self-driving cars, advanced industrial automation, and breakthroughs in complex strategy games such as Go and Dota 2. Ethical considerations and responsible AI have gained more attention in the machine learning community. Researchers and practitioners are actively working to address issues of bias, fairness, transparency, and interpretability associated with machine learning models. We strive to ensure that these models are not only accurate and efficient, but also responsible and compatible with human values.

In addition, there has been growing interest in integrating machine learning into other fields such as healthcare, finance and environmental science. Machine learning algorithms are used in medicine to improve diagnosis and treatment, to predict trends in financial markets, and to analyze large-scale environmental data for climate modeling and conservation. Deploying and deploying machine learning models has also become easier and more user-friendly. Various frameworks and tools have been developed to simplify the process of model training, deployment, and inference. This has opened up opportunities for individuals and organizations with limited machine learning expertise to incorporate these technologies into their applications and systems.

Overall, the field of machine learning has seen significant progress and expansion since September 2021. Advances in deep learning, pre-trained models, reinforcement learning, ethical considerations, interdisciplinary integration, and user-friendly tools have contributed to its continued growth and impact across fields, driving innovation and changing the way we solve complex problems.

Convergence

Convergence in machine learning refers to the process by which an iterative algorithm, such as gradient descent, converges to an optimal solution or reaches a steady state. It is an important part of training models and plays an important role in determining the effectiveness and efficiency of machine learning algorithms.

During the training process, machine learning algorithms iteratively update model parameters based on training data and an optimization objective, such as minimizing a loss function. The goal is to find parameter values that best fit the data and generalize well to unseen examples.

Convergence occurs when the algorithm reaches a point where additional iterations do not significantly improve the performance of the model or reduce the loss function. In other words, it indicates that the algorithm has reached a stable or optimal solution.

A number of factors influence machine learning. The choice of optimization algorithm, learning rate, and stopping criteria all affect how quickly and reliably convergence is achieved. For example, an inappropriate learning rate can cause an algorithm to converge too slowly or even fail.

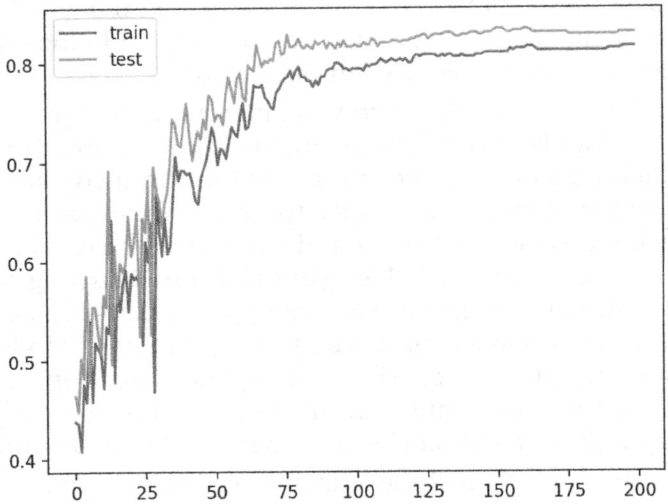

Convergence

Convergence monitoring is crucial to ensure that the model learns effectively and does not get stuck in suboptimal solutions. Typically, the approach is evaluated by observing the value of the loss function or other performance metrics over time. If the loss gradually decreases and evens out, it indicates convergence. However, if the loss changes or does not decrease continuously, this may indicate convergence problems, such as poor hyperparameter selection or insufficient training data.

Researchers and practitioners use different techniques to improve machine learning approaches. These include the use of advanced optimization algorithms such as stochastic gradient descent with momentum, adaptive learning rate methods and early stopping. Regularization methods such as L1 or L2 regularization can also help avoid overfitting and improve convergence by controlling model complexity.

Convergence is not only important in the initial training phase, but also when fine-tuning or updating models with new data. For example, transfer learning involves using pre-trained models and refining them for specific tasks. Ensuring convergence in such scenarios requires careful consideration of how to balance learning from previous tasks and adapting to new information.

Now, let's illustrate the k-means clustering process using a simple example with two-dimensional data points. Suppose we have the following data points:

Data Point	X	Y
A	2.0	4.0
B	3.0	6.0
C	4.0	8.0
D	7.0	3.0
E	9.0	5.0
F	10.0	7.0

Let's say we want to cluster these data points into two clusters (k = 2). We randomly initialize two centroids:

Cluster	Centroid X	Centroid Y
1	2.0	4.0
2	9.0	5.0

Next, we assign each data point to the nearest centroid and update the centroids:

Iteration 1:

Data Point	X	Y	Assigned Cluster	Distance to Centroid 1	Distance to Centroid 2
A	2.0	4.0	1	0.0	7.0
B	3.0	6.0	1	2.2	6.1
C	4.0	8.0	1	4.5	5.0
D	7.0	3.0	2	5.8	2.2
E	9.0	5.0	2	9.0	0.0
F	10.0	7.0	2	11.4	2.2

New centroids:

Cluster	Centroid X	Centroid Y
1	3.0	6.0
2	8.7	5.0

Iteration 2:

Data Point	X	Y	Assigned Cluster	Distance to Centroid 1	Distance to Centroid 2
A	2.0	4.0	1	1.4	6.8
B	3.0	6.0	1	0.0	5.0
C	4.0	8.0	1	1.4	4.1
D	7.0	3.0	2	5.0	2.8
E	9.0	5.0	2	6.4	0.7
F	10.0	7.0	2	8.6	2.8

New centroids:

Cluster	Centroid X	Centroid Y
1	3.0	6.0
2	8.7	5.0

Iteration 3 (Convergence)

Data Point	X	Y	Assigned Cluster	Distance to Centroid 1	Distance to Centroid 2
A	2.0	4.0	1	1.4	6.8
B	3.0	6.0	1	0.0	5.0
C	4.0	8.0	1	1.4	4.1
D	7.0	3.0	2	5.0	2.8
E	9.0	5.0	2	6.4	0.7
F	10.0	7.0	2	8.6	2.8

Final centroids:

Cluster	Centroid X	Centroid Y
1	3.0	6.0
2	8.7	5.0

After convergence, the data points are assigned to their respective clusters based on the nearest centroids. This is a basic example to illustrate the k-means clustering algorithm. In practice, k-means can handle high-dimensional data and larger k values. In addition, there are variants of k-means, such as k-means, which improve the initialization step for better results. Please note that due to the limitations of text-based communication, I was unable to send images directly to this reply. However, I hope that the presented tables and step-by-step explanations will help you visually understand k-means-clustering.

4.3 HIERARCHICAL CLUSTERING

A well-liked method in machine learning for putting related data points into clusters based on their proximity or similarity is hierarchical clustering. By repeatedly merging or dividing clusters until the desired number of clusters or a stopping threshold is reached, it builds a hierarchical representation of the data.

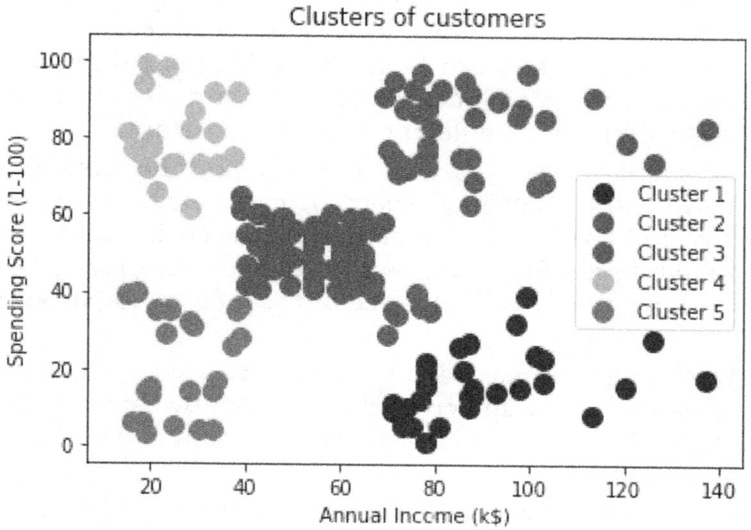

Hierarchical Clustering

Distance Calculation

Remote computation is a fundamental concept in machine learning that plays a crucial role in various algorithms and tasks. It involves quantifying the similarity or differences between objects or data points in a dataset. The concept of distance allows us to measure how close or far two points are in a given feature space, allowing us to make meaningful comparisons and decisions.

In machine learning, remote computing is often used in areas such as clustering, classification, recommendation systems, and anomaly detection. There are several distance meters available, each suitable for specific scenarios and data types. Some of the most commonly used distance measures are Euclidean distance, Manhattan distance, cosine similarity, and Hamming distance.

Euclidean distance is perhaps the most widely known distance metric, which measures the straight-line distance between two points in a rectangular coordinate system. It calculates the square root of the sum of the squared differences of the corresponding characteristics of two data points. Euclidean distance works well when the data elements are continuous and have a meaningful distance interpretation.

The Manhattan distance, also known as the city block distance or L1 norm, measures the sum of the absolute differences between the corresponding features of two data points. This is particularly useful when dealing with categorical or ordinal characteristics where the magnitude or direction of differences is not important.

Cosine similarity is often used to determine the similarity of two vectors in a high-dimensional space. It calculates the cosine of the angle between the vectors, which indicates the cosine similarity score. Cosine similarity is often used in text analysis and recommendation systems, where the size of the vectors is not as important as the direction.

The Hamming distance, which is primarily used to compare binary strings, measures the number of places where two strings differ. It is suitable for tasks related to error correction, data clustering and DNA sequence analysis.

These are just a few examples of distance metrics, and choosing the appropriate metric depends on the nature of the data and the specific machine learning task. Remote computing underlies many algorithms, including k-nearest neighbors, hierarchical clustering, support vector machines, and cooperative filtering, which allow machines to make informed decisions based on the proximity or similarity of data points.

Agglomerative vs. Divisive Clustering

Agglomerative and disjunctive clustering are two commonly used hierarchical clustering techniques in machine learning. These methods aim to group similar data points based on their proximity or similarity. Although both approaches follow the same hierarchical concept, they differ in the direction of clustering.

Agglomerative clustering, also known as bottom-up clustering, begins by treating each data point as a single cluster. It then progressively merges the most similar clusters until a stopping criterion is met. The process begins by computing a measure of closeness (such as distance or similarity) between all pairs of data points. These distances are used to build the proximity matrix. The two closest data points or clusters are then combined into a larger cluster and this process continues iteratively. Agglomerative clustering results in a tree-like structure called a dendrogram, which can be cut at different levels to obtain the desired number of clusters.

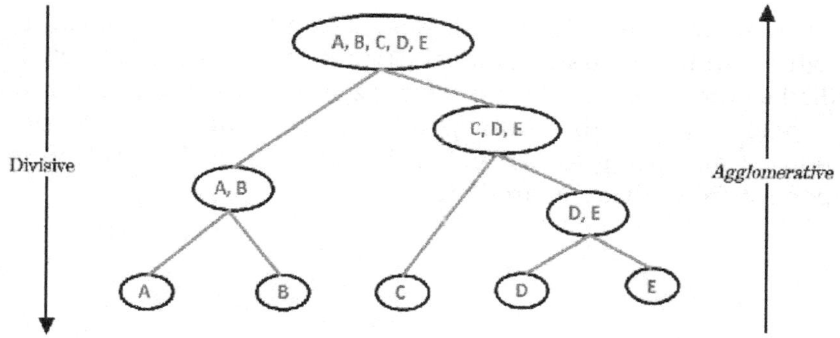

Agglomerative vs. Divisive Clustering

On the other hand, divisive clustering, also known as top-down clustering, takes the opposite approach. It starts with all data points assigned to a single cluster and then recursively divides that cluster into smaller subgroups. At each step, the split cluster identifies the cluster with the largest difference or variance and divides it into two or more subclusters. This process continues until a stopping criterion is met, such as reaching the desired number of clusters or until a certain homogeneity within clusters is achieved.

The main difference between these two approaches is their computational complexity and grouping order. Agglomerative clustering is generally computationally more efficient than divisive clustering because it involves less distance computation. In addition, agglomerative clustering is easily parallelized because clustering is independent of each other. On the other hand, distributive clustering can be computationally more demanding, especially when dealing with large datasets.

The choice between clustering and clustering depends on the nature of the data set and the problem to be solved. Agglomerative clustering is often useful when the number of clusters is not known in advance and dendrogram representation is desired. Split clustering can be useful when the dataset is well structured and the goal is to find better subgroups. In summary, agglomerative clustering starts from individual data points and joins them together, while disjunctive clustering starts from all data points in a single cluster and recursively splits them in half. These approaches offer different trade-offs in terms of computational complexity and grouping order, allowing researchers and practitioners to choose the most appropriate method for their grouping tasks.

4.4. MODELS OF GAUSSIAN MIXTURE (GMM)

A Gaussian mixture model represents a probability distribution as a weighted sum of Gaussian distributions. Each Gaussian distribution is called a component and is characterized by its mean and covariance. The model assumes that data points are generated by selecting one component according to certain probabilities and then selecting that component from a Gaussian distribution.

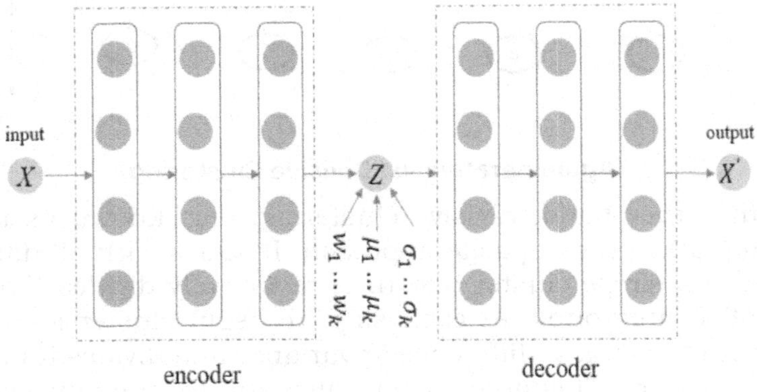

Hierarchical Clustering

Model Parameters

Machine learning model parameters refer to the variables or coefficients that determine the behavior and performance of the machine learning model. These parameters are learned or estimated during training from the training data and used to make predictions or classify new, unseen data.

The parameters of a machine learning model can vary depending on the algorithm or model type used. For example, in linear regression, the parameters are the slope and intercept of the linear equation. In neural networks, parameters include weights and biases associated with connections between neurons. In decision trees, the parameters represent the shared conditions for each node.

In the training phase, the model learns the optimal values of its parameters by minimizing a given loss function, which measur e s the error or deviation between the model predictions and the actual values of the training data. This process is usually carried out using optimization algorithms such as gradient descent or its variants.

Paramete r values directly affect the model's ability to ca p ture patterns and generalize to unseen data. Poorly chosen parameter values can lead to underfitting, where the model fails to capture the complexity of the data, or overfitting, where the model becomes too specific to the training data and performs poorly on new data. Techniques such as regularization, which adds a penalty or constraint to the parameter values during the training process, can be used to combat overfitting. These penalties encourage the model to generalize better and avoid excessively complex parameter configurations.

Once the model is trained and the parameters estimated, they can be used to predict new, unseen data. The quality of these predictions largely depends on the efficiency of the parameter estimation process and the generalizability of the model.

Probability Density Function (PDF)

In machine learning, the PDF (probability density function) function plays a crucial role in understanding and modeling the probability distribution of data. A PDF is a mathematical function that describes the probability that a random variable takes a certain value or falls within a certain range of values. It provides a framework for quantifying uncertainty in data and is widely used in a variety of machine learning tasks such as statistical inference, generative modeling, and outlier detection.

A PDF represents the underlying probability distribution of a random variable by assigning probabilities to different values or time intervals. It describes the form, distribution and central tendency of information dissemination. By analyzing the PDF file, you can get an idea of the probability of observing certain data points and make informed decisions based on the available information.

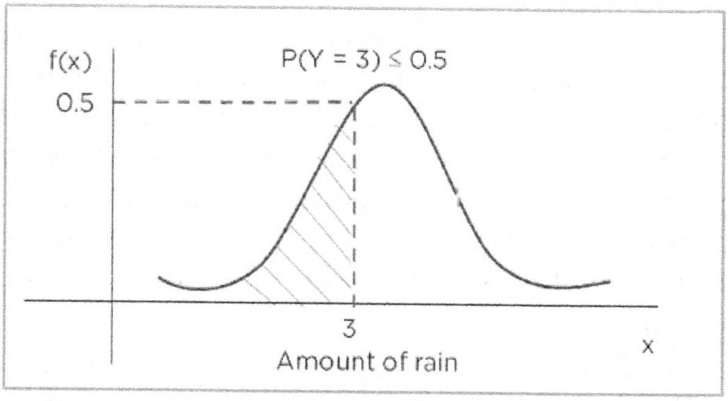

Probability Density Function (PDF)

Machine learning algorithms often use PDF to estimate the parameters of a given distribution that best fits the given data. This process, called parameter or density estimation, allows us to model the data and create new samples that resemble the original distribution. Examples of commonly used probability distributions are the Gaussian (normal) distribution, the Poisson distribution, and the Bernoulli distribution.

PDFs are particularly important for tasks such as classification, where decision boundaries are determined based on the probabilities of observations belonging to different classes. In such cases, the PDF can be used to estimate conditional class probabilities, allowing us to assign labels to unseen data points based on their probability estimates.

Additionally, PDF is important for Bayesian inference, a statistical framework that involves updating beliefs and making predictions based on both prior knowledge and observed data. Bayesian methods use the PDF to calculate posterior probabilities that represent updated beliefs after new evidence is added.

```
P(x) = Σ(π_k * N(x|μ_k, Σ_k)), for k = 1 to K,
```

where $N(x|\mu_k, \Sigma_k)$ represents the Gaussian distribution with mean μ_k and covariance Σ_k.

Training GMMs

Gaussian mixture models (GMMs) are widely used in machine learning to model probability distributions. GMMs represent complex distributions by combining multiple Gaussian (or normal) distributions. Each Gaussian component of a GMM represents a cluster or state in the data, and the overall distribution is the weighted sum of these components.

Training GMMs involves estimating the Gaussian component parameters that define the mixture and their associated weights. The training process usually consists of two main steps: initialization and an expectation maximization (EM) algorithm. During initialization, the initial GMM parameters, such as means, covariances, and weights, are determined randomly or heuristically. The number of components or clusters in a GMM is often determined in advance or by methods such as model selection.

The EM algorithm is then applied to iteratively refine the GMM parameters. The algorithm alternates between two steps until convergence. In the expectation phase (E phase), the algorithm calculates the posterior probability of each data point belonging to each component. These probabilities are obtained using the current estimates of the GMM parameters.

In the maximization phase (M phase), the algorithm updates the parameters of the Gaussian components based on the posterior probabilities calculated in the E phase. Means and covariances for each component are recalculated considering the weighted contributions of the data points, where the weights are determined by the posterior probabilities. The weights themselves are updated based on the total probability of each component across all data points.

The E step and the M step are repeated until the parameters converge to a stable solution. Convergence is usually determined by a predetermined stopping criterion, such as the maximum number of iterations or a threshold change in GMM parameters.

Training GMMs can be computationally intensive, especially when dealing with large datasets or high-dimensional datasets. Techniques such as batch processing, parallelization, and optimization algorithms are often used to improve performance

Once a GMM is trained, it can be used for a variety of tasks such as density estimation, clustering, and data generation. GMMs have found applications in many fields, including image processing, speech recognition, anomaly detection, and natural language processing. In summary, training GMMs involves initializing the parameters and then applying the EM algorithm to iteratively refine the parameters based on the data. The goal of the process is to find the best fitting Gaussian mixture to represent the probability distribution underlying the data.

Example Table:

Let's consider an example GMM with three components (K = 3) and the following parameters:

Component Weights (π): [0.4, 0.3, 0.3]

Component Means (μ): [2.0, 5.0, 8.0]

Component Covariances (Σ): [1.0, 0.5, 0.8]

The table below summarizes these parameters:

Component	Weight (π)	Mean (μ)	Covariance (Σ)
1	0.4	2.0	1.0
2	0.3	5.0	0.5
3	0.3	8.0	0.8

4.5. PRINCIPAL COMPONENT ANALYSIS (PCA)

Principal component analysis (PCA) is a dimension reduction technique widely used in machine learning and data analysis. It helps transform a high-dimensional dataset into a lower-dimensional space while preserving most of the important information. PCA accomplishes this by identifying the points (principal components) in the data that account for the most variance.

Let's understand the steps of PCA:

Standardize the Data

Data standardization is an important step in many machine learning algorithms to ensure consistency of features or variables used in training. Normalization, also known as function scaling or normalization, is the transformation of data so that its mean and unit variance are zero. This is done by subtracting the trait mean from each data point and then dividing by the standard deviation.

The need for standardization arises when material properties have different scales or units of measurement. If these features are not standardized, this can lead to biased models, as some features can dominate learning simply because of their higher values. By normalizing the data, we get all features on the same scale, so the model gives each feature equal importance during training.

Standardization has several advantages in machine learning. First, it helps improve the performance and convergence speed of many optimization algorithms. If the functions are on the same scale, it is easier for the model to find the optimal solution and avoid getting stuck in a local optimum. Second, standardization ensures that all features contribute equally to distance-based algorithms. If features are not standardized, at larger scales they may overshadow others, leading to erroneous similarity or distance measurements.

In addition, standardization also helps to interpret model coefficients or characteristic significance. When the features are on the same scale, the coefficients or significance values become directly comparable, making it easier to analyze and understand the impact of each feature on the model predictions. It also helps with data visualization by bringing all features into the same area, preventing one feature from dominating graphics or visualizations.

There are different ways to normalize data, the most common is z-score normalization. This method transforms each feature by subtracting the mean and dividing by the standard deviation. Alternatively, min-max scaling can be used, which scales the data to a certain range, often between 0 and 1.

Compute the covariance matrix

In machine learning, the covariance matrix is a key concept used to analyze relationships between variables in a dataset. It measures how two variables vary together, in other words, how they change in relation to each other. The covariance matrix is a square matrix that summarizes the covariance between all pairs of variables in the data set.

To calculate the covariance matrix, we start with a data set that contains several variables. Each row of the dataset represents an observation and each column represents a different variable. For example, if we have a dataset of apartment prices, the variables could be square meters, Number of Bedrooms and Number of Bathrooms.

The covariance between two variables, say X and Y, is calculated as the average of the products of deviations of their means. If X and Y tend to increase or decrease together, their covariance is positive. If they tend to move in opposite directions, the covariance is negative. A covariance of zero indicates that there is no linear relationship between the variables. The covariance matrix is formed by calculating the covariance between each pair of variables in the data set. The diagonal elements of the matrix represent the vari a nces of the individual variables, because the covariance between the variable and itself is its variance. Off-diagonal elements represent covariances of different pairs of variables.

The covariance matrix is a symmetric matrix because the covariance between X and Y is the same as the covariance between Y and X . It provides valuable information about the relationships between variables and can be used for various purposes in machine learning. It is used, for example, in principal component analysis (PCA) to identify the most important dimensions of a dataset and reduce its dimensionality.

When working with the cova r iance matrix, it is important to consider that it can be sensitive to the scale of the variables. Variables with larger scales can dominate the covariance calculation, leading to biased results. To overcome this problem, it is common to normalize the variables by subtracting their means and dividing by their standard deviations before computin g the covariance matrix. This process, called trait scaling, ensu r es that each variable has a similar effect when calculating the covariance. In short, the covariance matrix is a key machine learning tool for understanding the relationships between variables in a dataset. It provides insight into the direction and strength of linear relationships between variables and is widely used in various statistical and machine learning techniques.

Compute Eigenvectors and Eigenvalues

In machine learning, eigenvectors and eigenvalues play a key role in various mathematical operations and algorithms. Eigenvectors and eigenvalues are related to square matrices and provide important insights into the structure and behavior of the data represented by these matrices.

An eigenvector is a nonzero vector whose scale only changes when a linear transformation is applied to it. In the context of machine learning, a linear transformation can represent operations such as rotating, stretching, and compressing data. The eigenvectors represent the directions along which the transformation has the easiest effect, stretching or compressing the data without changing its direction. Eigenvalues, on the other hand, are scalar values associated with eigenvectors. They indicate the amount by which the eigenvectors are scaled during the transformation. Each eigenvector has a corresponding eigenvalue, and the eigenvalue provides information about the importance or significance of the associated eigenvector in the transformation process. A large eigenvalue indicates that the eigenvector captures more variance in the data, while a small eigenvalue indicates less significance.

In machine learning, eigenvectors and eigenvalues are often used in dimension reduction techniques such as principal component analysis (PCA). PCA attempts to find a set of orthogonal eigenvectors, known as principal components, that capture the most variance in the data. By choosing the eigenvectors with the largest eigenvalues, one can effectively reduce the dimensionality of the data while preserving the most important information.

In addition, eigenvectors and eigenvalues are used in various algorithms such as spectral clustering, image compression, recommender systems and matrix factorization techniques. They provide a compact representation of data, facilitate feature extraction, and enable efficient computation.

Numerical methods such as power iteration method, QR algorithm or singular value decomposition (SVD) can be used to calculate the eigenvectors and eigenvalues. These methods use iterative processes and matrix factors to efficiently compute eigenvectors and eigenvalues.

Sort Eigenvalues and Select Principal Components

In machine learning, the dimensionality reduction process plays a crucial role in reducing the complexity of data while preserving its most informative features. One widely used method for dimensionality reduction is principal component analysis (PCA). The purpose of PCA is to transform a high-dimensional data set into a lower-dimensional space by identifying the directions, called principal components, according to which there is the most significant variation in the data.

During the PCA process, the first step is to calculate the covariance matrix of the dataset. This matrix represents the relationships and dependencies between different characteristics or variables in the data. By decomposing the eigenvalues in the covariance matrix, we obtain the eigenvalues and eigenvectors associated with the principal components.

The eigenvalues give an idea of the amount of variance captured by each principal component. By sorting the eigenvalues in descending order, we can identify the most important principal components. Typically, eigenvalues are represented as vectors, and ordering them allows prioritization of principal components. Principal components associated with larger eigenvalues capture more variance and contain more important information about the data. After sorting the eigenvalues, we can select a subset of the principal components based on how much variance we want to preserve. If our goal is to reduce the dimensionality of the data, we can choose a smaller number of principal components that capture a significant part of the total variance. These selected principal components can then be used as new features for further analysis or modeling tasks.

The selection of principal components based on eigenvalues is crucial because it allows us to balance reducing the dimensionality of the data and preserving the most valuable information. By retaining principal components associated with higher eigenvalues, we ensure that we capture most of the variability in the original data set, maximizing the potential of the reduced feature set for later analysis or modeling. In general, eigenvalue sorting and principal component selection in machine learning, especially in the context of PCA, enables effective dimensionality reduction, improves computational efficiency, and facilitates better understanding and interpretation of data. This allows us to extract the most informative features and reduce noise or redundant information, ultimately leading to more efficient and accurate machine learning models.

Project the Data onto the New Feature Space

In machine learning, projecting data into a new feature space refers to the process of transforming an original set of features into a new set of features, often with the goal of improving the efficiency of a learning algorithm. This technique is commonly used in several fields such as dimensionality reduction, feature engineering, and data processing.

The motivation for projecting data into a new feature space is to improve the representation of the data by capturing more meaningful patterns or reducing noise and redundancy in the original feature set.

This can lead to better learning algorithms that can better understand and generalize data.

There are several methods for performing function space projection, each with its own characteristics and utility. One popular technique is principal compon e nt analysis (PCA), which identifies orthogonal patterns in data th a t capture the most variance. By selecting a subset of these pri n cipal components, one can effectively reduce the dimensionality o f the data while preserving the most important information.

Another frequently used method is linear discriminant analysis (LDA), which aims to find a projection that maximizes the difference between different classes or clusters in the data. This technique is particularly useful in classification tasks where the goal is to find a decision boundary that distinguishes between different classes.

Nonlinear methods such as kernel methods are also used to project data into a new feature space. These methods use the concept of the kernel trick, which allows us to indirectly map data to a higher-dimensional space without directly computing the transformation. Support vector machines (SVMs) are a popular example of the use of kernel methods in feature space projection.

In addition to dimensionality reduction and feature shaping, projecting data into a new feature space may also involve techniques such as feature scaling, normalization or coding of categorical variables. These preprocessing steps can help align the data distribution, improve numerical stability, and ensure compatibility with different learning algorithms.

In general, projecting data into a new feature space is a key concept in machine learning that plays a vital role in improving data representation and understanding. By using different projection techniques, researchers and practitioners can effectively improve the efficiency and interpretability of learning algorithms in many applications.

Here's an example to illustrate the steps of PCA:

Suppose we have a dataset with three features: Height, Weight, and Age. The table below represents a small subset of the dataset:

Height (cm)	**Weight (kg)**	**Age (years)**
165	68	25
170	72	30
155	55	28
180	80	35
160	62	27

To perform PCA, we start by standardizing the data. After standardization, the table may look like this:

Standardized Height	Standardized Weight	Standardized Age
0.116	-0.246	-0.567
0.366	0.028	0.567
-0.684	-1.028	-0.113
1.164	0.801	1.690
-0.961	-0.556	-0.567

Next, we compute the covariance matrix based on the standardized data:

	Height	Weight	Age
Height	1.000	0.944	0.526
Weight	0.944	1.000	0.482
Age	0.526	0.482	1.000

Then, we calculate the eigenvectors and eigenvalues of the covariance matrix. The eigenvectors are:

	Eigenvector 1	Eigenvector 2	Eigenvector 3
Height	0.655	-0.540	0.529
Weight	0.620	0.711	-0.330
Age	0.431	-0.449	-0.782

And the corresponding eigenvalues are:

	Eigenvalue
Eigenvalue 1	2.353
Eigenvalue 2	0.027
Eigenvalue 3	0.620

Since the first eigenvalue is significantly larger than the others, we choose it as the primary principal component. Thus, the transformed dataset would be:

Principal Component 1
-0.378
0.654
-1.085
1.888
-0.080

The transformed dataset now contains only one dimension (principal component) instead of three, effectively reducing the dimension.

4.9. T-DISTRIBUTED STOCHASTIC NEIGHBOR EMBEDDING

t-Distributed Stochastic Neighbor Embedding (t-SNE) is a popular machine learning technique for visualizing high-dimensional data in a lower-dimensional space. It is particularly useful for exploring and understanding complex patterns and relationships in data.

Intuition behind t-SNE

t-SNE, short for t-Distributed Stochastic Neighbor Embedding, is a popular machine learning technique used to visualize high-dimensional data in a lower-dimensional space. It is particularly effective at discovering hidden patterns, clusters and structures in complex data sets. The intuition behind t-SNE is to preserve local and global relationships between data points in the dimensionality reduction process.

The primary purpose of t-SNE is to map high-dimensional data points to a lower-dimensional space while preserving proximity relationships between them. This is achieved by constructing a probability distribution for pairs of high-dimensional points, where nearby points are more likely to be chosen as neighbors. At the same time, it creates a similar probability distribution in the lower dimensional space. The goal is to minimize the difference between the two probability distributions.

Initially, t-SNE computes pairwise similarities of data points in a high-dimensional space. It measures these similarities using a Gaussian kernel, where nearby points have higher similarity values. Then, it constructs a joint probability distribution of these similarities. The joint probability is defined as the sum of the similarities between points normalized by the total similarity. This step essentially creates a probability distribution that captures the local relationships between points.

In a lower dimensional space, t-SNE forms a similar joint probability distribution for the mapped points. However, instead of a Gaussian kernel, it uses a Student's t-distribution with a few degrees of freedom. The choice of the T distribution has the desirable property of having heavier tails than the Gaussian distribution. This tail weight allows the technique to handle deviations more effectively. The goal is to find a mapping of the data points that minimizes the difference between the high- and low-dimensional joint probability distributions.

To optimize this objective, t-SNE uses gradient descent. It starts with random initial locations of points in a low-dimensional space and iteratively updates them by minimizing the Kullback-Leibler decomposition between two joint probability distributions. By iteratively adjusting point locations, t-SNE ensures that close points in high-dimensional space remain close in the low-dimensional representation. The result of t-SNE is a lower-dimensional representation of the data, where similar points are modeled as close and dissimilar points are further apart. This allows visualization that reveals clusters, patterns, and structures that may not be visible in the original high-dimensional space. It is important to note that t-SNE is primarily a visualization tool and does not aim to accurately reconstruct the original data.

Algorithm Steps

t-SNE operates by iteratively optimizing the placement of data points in the lower-dimensional space. The following steps outline the key components of the algorithm:

- **Compute Similarities:** Calculate pairwise similarities between data points in the high-dimensional space. Commonly used similarity measures include the Gaussian kernel, which assigns higher similarity to nearby points and lower similarity to distant points.
- **Define Perplexity:** Perplexity is a hyperparameter in t-SNE that determines the number of close neighbors each point considers during the embedding process. Higher perplexity values result in a larger number of considered neighbors.
- **Construct Conditional Probability Distributions:** For each data point, compute the conditional probability distribution over other points, based on their similarities. This distribution reflects the likelihood of picking another point as a neighbor, given its similarity to the current point. The perplexity hyperparameter influences the shape of this distribution.
- **Optimize Embedding:** Initialize the embedding in the lower-dimensional space randomly. Then, iteratively minimize the divergence between the pairwise similarities of the high-dimensional space and the lower-dimensional embedding. This is done using gradient descent techniques, adjusting the positions of the data points in the lower-dimensional space.
- **Visualize Results:** Once the optimization process converges, the final embedding can be visualized in a scatter plot or other visual representation to explore the underlying structure of the data.

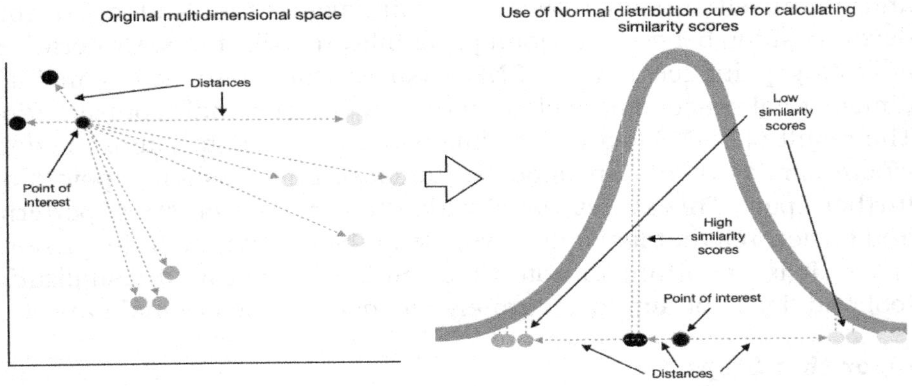

t-SNE Algorithm

Interpretation of t-SNE Results

t-SNE (t-Distributed Stochastic Neighbor Embedding) is a dimension reduction technique widely used in machine learning and data visualization. This is particularly useful for visualizing high-dimensional data in lower-dimensional spaces. Several important considerations must be taken into account when interpreting t-SNE results.

First, t-SNE is a non-linear projection method, which means that it emphasizes the local structure of the data rather than preserving global relationships. Its purpose is to represent similar data points as nearest neighbors in a lower dimension. Therefore, clusters or groups of similar occurrences in the original high-dimensional space usually remain distinct and well-separated clusters in t-SNE imaging.

Second, the distances between the data points in the t-SNE plot have no direct interpretation in terms of the original feature space. The algorithm optimizes the cost function to minimize the difference between high-dimensional data and low-dimensional embedding pairwise similarities. Thus, the relative distances of the points in the t-SNE visualization reflect their similarities, but the exact distances have no special meaning.

Another important consideration when interpreting t-SNE results is the effect of different hyperparameters. Parameters such as clutter, learning rate and number of iterations can significantly affect the imaging. For example, changing the disorder parameter can lead to different levels of local and global structure. Therefore, it is important to study multiple t-SNE visualizations with different parameter settings to fully understand the data.

Additionally, t-SNE is sensitive to random initialization, which means that each run of the algorithm may produce slightly different results. To ensure reliability, it is recommended to perform several tests and evaluate the consistency of the patterns observed in these tests. Ultimately, t-SNE is more of a visualization tool than a definitive analysis technique. Although it can provide valuable information about data structure and relationships, it should be used in conjunction with other analytical methods and domain knowledge to draw meaningful conclusions. t-SNE can aid in exploratory data analysis, cluster detection, or identification of potential outliers, but interpretation must always be confirmed and supported by further analysis.

In summary, t-SNE is an efficient dimensionality reduction technique that allows visualization of high-dimensional data in lower-dimensional spaces. When interpreting T-SNE results, it is important to consider its nonlinearity, lack of direct distance interpretability, hyperparameter effects, initialization sensitivity, and the additional role of other analysis methods. By considering these factors, researchers and practitioners can gain valuable information about the underlying structure of complex materials.

5

Natural Language Processing (NLP)

5.1. INTRODUCTION TO NATURAL LANGUAGE PROCESSING

Natural Language Processing (NLP) is a subfield of machine learning and artificial intelligence that focuses on the interaction between computers and human language. It involves the development of algorithms and models that enable computers to understand, interpret and produce text or speech in natural language. NLP plays a key role in various applications, including language translation, sentiment analysis, text summarization, chatbots and data mining.

Tokenization

Tokenization is a fundamental process in machine learning and natural language processing (NLP) where text data is divided into smaller units called tokens. These characters can be single words, characters or even aliases, depending on the specific requirements of the task.

Tokenization is an important initial step in many NLP applications, as it helps transform unstructured text into a format that machine learning algorithms can process more efficiently. By breaking text into characters, the model can better understand the underlying language structure, allowing it to retrieve relevant information and gain insights.

There are different approaches to tokenization, each with their own advantages and trade-offs. The most common method is hyphenation, where text is divided into individual words based on spaces and punctuation marks. However, this approach can face challenges in languages that do not have clear word boundaries or have compound words. Other techniques such as character level tagging or subword tagging such as Byte Pair Encoding (BPE) or Wordpiece are used to overcome these limitations.

Once the text is tagged, other preprocessing steps such as assignment, derivation or lemmatization can be used to refine the tags. These steps help remove noise and reduce the dimensionality of the data, making it easier for machine learning models to process and extract meaningful patterns. Tokenization plays a key role in various NLP tasks, including machine translation, sentiment analysis, named entity detection, and text classification. By breaking text into smaller units, tokenization allows models to understand the context, relationships and semantics of the data, improving the efficiency and accuracy of NLP tasks.

Sentence: I love natural language processing.

Tokens:

1. I
2. love
3. natural
4. language
5. processing

Word Frequency

Word frequency in machine learning refers to analyzing and counting the occurrence of words in a given dataset or body of text. It is a fundamental technique used in natural language processing (NLP) and text mining tasks to gain insight and extract meaningful information from large text data.

The process of calculating word frequency involves several steps. First, the text data is pre-processed to remove unwanted characters, punctuation and ending words (common words like "and", "the", "within", which do not have much meaning). Next, the text is symbolized, which means it is broken down into individual words or characters. Once the markers are obtained, the frequency of each word is calculated by counting the number of times each word appears in the text.

Word frequency analysis can reveal important patterns and trends in a text corpus. This helps to understand the distribution of words and gives an idea of the general topic or theme of the text. For example, in a dataset of news articles, word frequency analysis can highlight the most frequent words and show the dominant themes or keywords in the articles.

In addition, word frequency analysis is often used as a preliminary step to more complex NLP tasks. This can help in text classification, where the frequency of certain words can serve as training features for machine learning models. Additionally, it can help with sentiment analysis by identifying words that are often associated with positive or negative emotions.

In addition to the basic word frequency calculation, more advanced techniques can be applied, such as tf-idf (term Frequency-Inverse document Frequency). Tf-idf takes into account not only the appearance of a word in a given document, but also its meaning in the entire corpus, taking into account how often the word appears in other documents.

In general, word frequency analysis used in machine learning is a valuable tool for understanding textual data and extracting insights. It plays an important role in various NLP tasks and contributes to the development of intelligent systems that can process and understand human language.

Word	Frequency
I	2
love	1
natural	1
language	1
processing	1

Part-of-Speech (POS) Tagging

Part-of-speech (POS) coding is a fundamental task in natural language processing (NLP), which involves assigning a grammatical category or part-of-speech to each word in a given text. The purpose of POS coding is to analyze the syntactic structure of a sentence and determine the role of each word in it.

POS coding is an integral part of many NLP applications, including information retrieval, sentiment analysis, machine translation, and speech recognition. It provides important linguistic information that helps to understand the meaning and context of a sentence.

Typically, machine learning techniques are used to tag points of sale. These techniques typically involve training a statistical model on a large annotated corpus, where each word in the training set is tagged with a corresponding part of speech. The model learns patterns and relationships between words and their parts of speech, enabling the prediction of unseen or future texts.

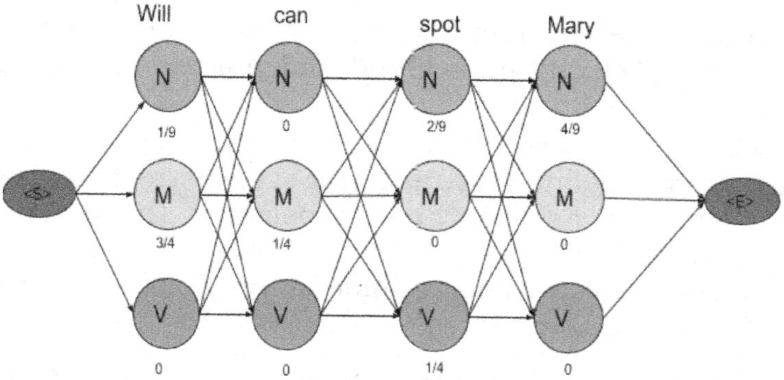

Part-of-Speech (POS) Tagging

Various machine learning algorithms such as Hidden Markov Models (HMM), Maximum Entropy Models (MaxEnt), Conditional Random Fields (CRF) and neural networks based approaches such as Recurrent Neural Networks (RNN) and Transformers can be used for POS coding. . These models take into account contextual features such as surrounding words and their parts of speech as well as morphological and syntactic features to make accurate predictions.

There are certain challenges associated with POS coding, such as the ambiguity of language, where a word can have multiple possible parts of speech depending on the context. For example, the word "run" can be a noun or a verb. Resolving such ambiguities requires consideration of surrounding words and general sentence structure. Another challenge is dealing with non-words that are not seen in training. Various techniques such as morphological analysis and word input are used to solve these problems.

In general, POS coding plays a key role in NLP tasks because it provides information about the grammatical structure of a sentence. This allows machines to understand and process natural language more efficiently, improving the performance of various language-related applications.

Named Entity Recognition (NER)

Named entity recognition (NER) is an important task in the fields of natural language processing (NLP) and machine learning. This involves identifying and classifying those entities in a given text. Named entities refer to specific objects, places, organizations, names of people, dates, quantities, and various other predefined categories. The main goal of NER is to accurately extract and label these named entities so that machines can efficiently understand and process unstructured text data.

NER plays an important role in many NLP applications such as information retrieval, question answering systems, text summarization, sentiment analysis and machine translation. By identifying and classifying named entities, NER improves text comprehension and facilitates the extraction of information from large amounts of unstructured data.

Ousted WeWork founder Adam Neumann lists his Manhattan penthouse for $37.5 million

[organization] [person] [location] [monetary value]

Named Entity Recognition (NER)

The NER process typically involves training a machine learning model on annotated datasets. These datasets consist of named cases where each named entity is given a specific class or category. The model learns from this training data to identify patterns and properties associated with different types of named entities. Commonly used machine learning algorithms for NER include conditional random fields (CRFs), support vector machines (SVMs), and deep learning models such as recurrent neural networks (RNNs) and transformer-based models. To perform NER, text is usually split into individual words or subword units. The machine learning model then analyzes the context of each character and surrounding words to determine whether it represents a named entity and, if so, assigns it the appropriate identifier. Model performance is highly dependent on the quality and variety of training data and the features and algorithms used.

NER faces several challenges, including identifying ambiguous entities, handling invisible or rare entities, and handling noisy or incomplete text data. In addition, multilingual NER is more complicated due to the fact that naming rules and entity types are different in different languages. In recent years, advances in deep learning, especially transformer-based models such as BERT (Bidirectional Encoder Representations of Transformers), have greatly improved the performance of NER. These models exploit contextual embedding and large pre-training datasets to capture the complex dependencies and nuances of language, resulting in more accurate recognition of said entities.

Overall, NER plays an important role in extracting meaningful information from textual data and enables a wide range of NLP applications. As research and technology advance, we can expect advances in NER techniques, making machines even more adept at understanding and processing human language.

Entity	Type
Apple Inc.	Organization
Cupertino	Location

Sentiment Analysis

Sentiment analysis, also known as sentiment mining, is an exciting field of machine learning that focuses on understanding and analyzing sentiments, attitudes, and opinions in textual data. It uses various techniques and algorithms to determine the feeling or subjective information contained in a given text, whether it is positive, negative or neutral.

The purpose of sentiment analysis is to extract valuable insights from large volumes of text data such as social media messages, customer reviews, survey responses and news. By automatically classifying the sentiment behind these texts, sentiment analysis allows companies, organizations and researchers to gain a deeper understanding of public opinion, customer feedback, brand perception and market trends.

To perform sentiment analysis, machine learning models are trained with identified datasets consisting of text samples and corresponding synthetic data. These identifiers can be binary (positive/negative) or multi-categorical (positive/negative/neutral). The models learn patterns and features from the training data and then apply them to classify new, never-before-seen texts.

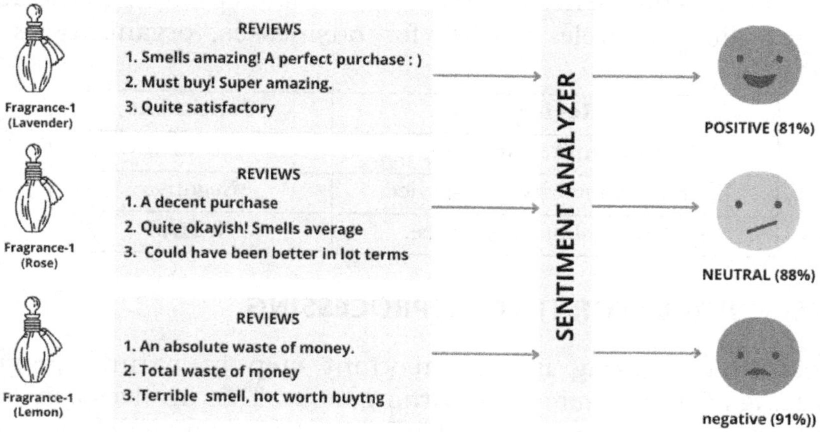

Sentiment Analysis

There are several approaches to sentiment analysis, from rule-based methods to more advanced machine learning techniques. Rule-based methods use predefined linguistic rules and heuristics to determine sentiment. These rules often involve analyzing specific words, phrases, or patterns associated with specific emotions. On the other hand, machine learning-based approaches use algorithms such as Naive Bayes, Support Vector Machines (SVM), Random Forests, or deep learning models such as Convolutional Neural Networks (CNN) and Recurrent Neural Networks (RNN). These models learn from data and recognize complex relationships between words, sentences and sentimental signs. They can capture context, sarcasm, and other nuances of language that rule-based approaches can struggle with.

Although sentiment analysis has many applications, it is particularly valuable in areas such as brand monitoring, customer feedback analysis, social media monitoring, market research and reputation management. Using sentiment analysis, companies can gauge public opinion about their products or services, identify potential problems or areas for improvement, and make informed decisions to improve customer satisfaction and loyalty. There is no problem with sentiment analysis though. The ambiguity of language, sarcasm, cultural context, and the rapid evolution of language use can make it difficult to accurately define emotions. Preprocessing text data, handling negations, managing unbalanced datasets and handling biases are some of the additional challenges in sentiment analysis.

Despite these challenges, sentiment analysis is progressing with more sophisticated algorithms, larger annotated datasets and the integration of domain-specific information. It has enormous potential to understand and harness the power of human emotions in the digital age, providing valuable insights for businesses, organizations and individuals.

Review	**Sentiment**
The product is amazing!	Positive
I'm not happy with the service.	Negative
It was an okay experience.	Neutral

5.2. TECHNIQUES FOR TEXT PREPROCESSING

Text preprocessing is an important step in natural language processing (NLP) and machine learning tasks. This involves converting raw text data into a format suitable for analysis and modeling.

Tokenization

Tokenization is a fundamental process in machine learning and natural language processing (NLP) that involves breaking text into smaller units called tokens. Those identifiers can be words, characters or even sub-words, depending on the level of precision desired for the analysis.

Tokenization plays a key role in various NLP tasks such as language modeling, sentiment analysis, machine translation and named entity recognition. By dividing the text into characters, the complexity of the text is reduced, which allows machines to process and understand it more efficiently.

The character process typically involves removing punctuation, splitting words based on spaces or specific delimiters, and converting text to lowercase to ensure consistency. For example, the sentence "Tokenization is a useful technology!" it is divided into the following signs: ["marking", "is", "a", "useful", "technique"].

Different tagging strategies are available depending on the specific requirements of the task or language being processed. For example, in English, a token is usually word-based, where each token represents a single word. But in languages like Chinese or Japanese, tokenization can involve segmenting text into characters or even sub-words.

Tokenization is a critical preprocessing step in machine learning models because it helps create a structured representation of textual data that algorithms can easily understand and process. Once the text is tagged, it can be further transformed into numerical representations, such as one-time encoding or word embedding, used as input to machine learning models.

Although tokenization simplifies the presentation of text, it can also present some challenges. Obscure words, contractions, slang or non-vocabularies can create difficulties in the tagging process, affecting the accuracy and efficiency of subsequent NLP tasks.

Input Text: "I love to play soccer."

Tokenized Output: ["I", "love", "to", "play", "soccer", "."]

Lowercasing

Lowercase is a common text preprocessing technique used in machine learning and natural language processing (NLP). This involves converting all letters in the given text to lowercase, regardless of their initial letter. This technique is widely used to ensure standardization and improve the quality and consistency of textual data.

Lowercase letters are particularly important in NLP tasks because they help treat words with the same root or meaning as identical entities. Converting all words to lowercase letters excludes capital letters, allowing for more efficient analysis and comparison of textual data. Letters are particularly useful in tasks such as text classification, sentiment analysis, and information retrieval, where understanding the meaning of words and recognizing patterns are critical. For example, when customer reviews are classified as positive or negative, lowercase letters ensure that the presence or absence of capital letters does not affect the accuracy of the sentiment analysis algorithm.

In addition, small letters reduce vocabulary and make textual data sparse. Because words with the same spelling but different capitalization are treated as a single unit, the number of individual words in the dataset is reduced. This simplification can improve the computational efficiency and generalizability of machine learning models. However, it is important to note that lowercase may not always be appropriate or desirable in certain situations. For example, when parsing text data for proper names (such as names of people, places, or organizations), lowercase letters can result in the loss of important information. In such cases, alternative techniques or more sophisticated approaches may be required to properly address large-scale deforestation.

Input Text: "I Love Playing Soccer."

Lowercased Output: "i love playing soccer."

Stop Word Removal

Stopping word deletion is a common preprocessing step in machine learning and natural language processing (NLP). In textual analysis, stop words are words that are considered meaningless and do not contribute much to the overall meaning of a sentence or document. Examples of stop words are "a", "an", "the", "on", "and" and "in".

The purpose of stopword removal is to improve the performance of text analysis algorithms by removing these frequently occurring unnecessary words. By removing stop words, we can reduce the dimensionality of the text data and focus on more important words with semantic meaning.

Stop word deletion is particularly useful for tasks such as document classification, sentiment analysis, and information retrieval. These tasks often involve large amounts of textual data, and removing end words helps reduce noise and improve the accuracy of the analysis. In addition, it can speed up computation time and reduce the memory requirements of machine learning models.

However, it is important to note that stopword removal is not always necessary or useful for every NLP task. In some cases, word endings can provide contextual information or influence the grammatical structure of the text. For example, in certain sentiment analysis tasks, the presence of certain ending words may be important in determining the sentiment of a sentence. The choice of keywords to remove may vary depending on the specific application or domain. Commonly used terminal word lists are available in many programming languages and libraries, but can also be adapted to the specific requirements of a task. The process of removing stop words usually involves parsing the text into individual words, comparing them to a list of stop words, and excluding the stop words from the final analysis.

Input Text: “I love playing soccer and watching basketball.”

Stopword-removed Output: “love playing soccer watching basketball.”

Punctuation Removal

Punctuation removal in machine learning refers to the removal of punctuation marks from text data as a pre-processing step for natural language processing (NLP) tasks. Punctuation includes characters such as periods, commas, question marks, exclamation points, and quotation marks.

The main purpose of punctuation removal is to clean textual data and reduce input complexity for subsequent NLP tasks. Punctuation often has grammatical and syntactic meaning in human language, contributing to sentence structure, semantic interpretation, and conveying emotion or emphasis. However, in some NLP applications, such as sentiment analysis, text classification or machine translation, the presence of punctuation may not be important or may introduce noise into the data. By removing punctuation, the NLP model can focus on the semantic content of the text, allowing it to capture the essence of the message without being confused by punctuation artifacts. Additionally, removing punctuation can help reduce input space dimensions and reduce data redundancy, allowing for more efficient and effective processing.

In machine learning, there are different approaches to remove punctuation. One common technique is to use regular expressions or string manipulation functions to match and remove specific punctuation from text. This approach can be relatively simple and effective for simple punctuation removal tasks. However, it is important to consider the potential challenges and nuances associated with removing punctuation. In some cases, indiscriminate removal of punctuation can lead to the loss of valuable information, especially in tasks where punctuation is semantically important, such as named entity identification or sentiment analysis. Furthermore, in languages where punctuation plays a more important role in clarifying meaning, removing punctuation can have a greater impact on the overall understanding of the text.

Therefore, the decision to remove punctuation in machine learning depends on the specific NLP task, the characteristics of the dataset, and the language being processed. It is important to consider these factors and, where possible, experiment with different preprocessing strategies to determine the optimal approach for a given application. In general, punctuation removal is a preprocessing step in machine learning that aims to simplify and clean text data by removing punctuation. Although this can be useful for certain NLP tasks, careful consideration must be given to balancing the removal of noise against the potential loss of valuable information encoded in the punctuation marks.

Input Text: “Hello, how are you?”

Punctuation-removed Output: “Hello how are you”

Lemmatization or Stemming

Lemmation and abstraction are techniques used in natural language processing (NLP) and machine learning to reduce words to their base or root form. Both approaches aim to normalize words, making it easier to analyze textual data and extract meaningful information. However, there are some important differences between the two methods.

Correct formation means removing the endings of words to get their root form. It applies simple rule-based techniques such as splitting word endings without regard to context or part of speech. For example, using derived word forms for “run” and “runner” would result in the root form “run”. In some cases, derivation can be effective, especially for information retrieval or keyword-based analysis, where word variations are less important. However, verbosity can also lead to false results, as it can produce stems that are not actual words, or map different words to the same stem, resulting in a loss of information.

On the other hand, the purpose of lemmatization is to derive the lemma from the basic form of words taking into account the context and the part of the word. It uses advanced techniques such as morphological analysis and dictionary lookups to verify that the resulting lemma is a valid word. For example, lemmatizing the words “run” and “runner” would yield both lemmas “run”. Lemmation usually gives more accurate results than the real thing, because it takes into account the grammatical structure of the language. This is particularly useful for tasks such as sentiment analysis, machine translation, and question answering systems where vocabulary and accurate punctuation are important.

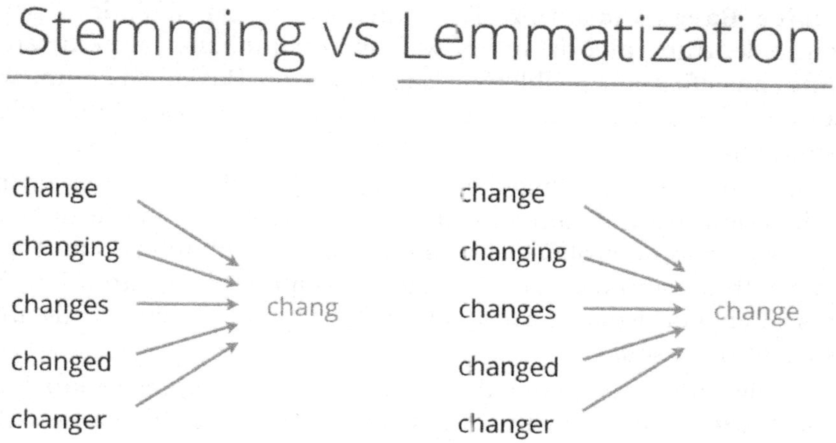

Lemmatization or Stemming

Although lemmatization gives more accurate results, it is computationally more expensive and slower than descent. This is because lemmatization involves dictionary lookups and more advanced language analysis. Stemming, on the other hand, is a simpler and faster technique, which makes it suitable for tasks that require the rapid processing of large amounts of textual data. Ultimately, the choice between lemmatization and derivation depends on the specific requirements of the NLP task. If it is important to preserve the meaning and grammatical accuracy of words, lemmatization is recommended. However, if speed and simplicity are preferred over accuracy, a derivative may be a reasonable choice.

Enter text: “Run, run, run”

Lematized result: “run, run, run”

Actual result: “run, run, run”

5.3. SENTIMENT AND TEXT CLASSIFICATION

Emotion and text classification are important tasks in natural language processing (NLP) and machine learning. In sentiment analysis, the goal is to determine the emotional or sentimental tone of a given text, such as positive, negative or neutral. Text classification means classifying text into predefined classes or categories based on its content.

Both sentiment and text classification can be achieved using a variety of machine learning algorithms and techniques, including but not limited to:

Naive Bayes Classifier: The Naive Bayes classifier is a popular machine learning algorithm known for its simplicity and efficiency in solving classification problems. It is based on Bayes' theorem, which describes the probability of an event based on prior knowledge or information.

The Naive Bayes classifier assumes that the features used for classification are independent of each other, hence the term "naive". This assumption simplifies the calculation of probabilities and makes the algorithm computationally efficient. Despite this assumption, Naive Bayes often performs surprisingly well in practice, especially in text classification tasks.

The algorithm calculates the probability of a given class label based on the observed feature values. This sets the label of the class with the highest probability. To achieve this, it calculates two main probabilities: the prior probability and the conditional probability.

A priori probability is the probability of occurrence of a class without considering specific feature values. It represents the general distribution of classes in educational data. Conditional probability, on the other hand, calculates the probability of occurrence of a given value value with a given class identifier. This probability is estimated from the training data.

To classify a new case, the Naive Bayes classifier calculates the posterior probability of each class label using the prior and conditional probability. The case is assigned the class label with the highest posterior probability.

Naive Bayes classifiers are often used in text classification tasks such as spam filtering or sentiment analysis. In these cases, the algorithm treats each word in the document as a feature and determines the probability that the document belongs to a certain category (eg spam or not spam) based on the frequency of the words in the training data. Despite its simplicity, the Naive Bayes classifier has some limitations. The assumption of attribute independence may not hold in many real-life scenarios. Additionally, it can handle rare or unprecedented combinations of feature values because it estimates probabilities from training data. However, Naive Bayes remains a powerful and widely used algorithm due to its simplicity, efficiency, and often satisfactory performance.

Support Vector Machines (SVM): Support Vector Machines (SVM) is a powerful machine learning algorithm used for classification and regression tasks. It is widely used in various fields, including computer vision, natural language processing, and bioinformatics. SVMs are particularly effective in handling high-dimensional datasets and are known for their ability to handle non-linear decision constraints.

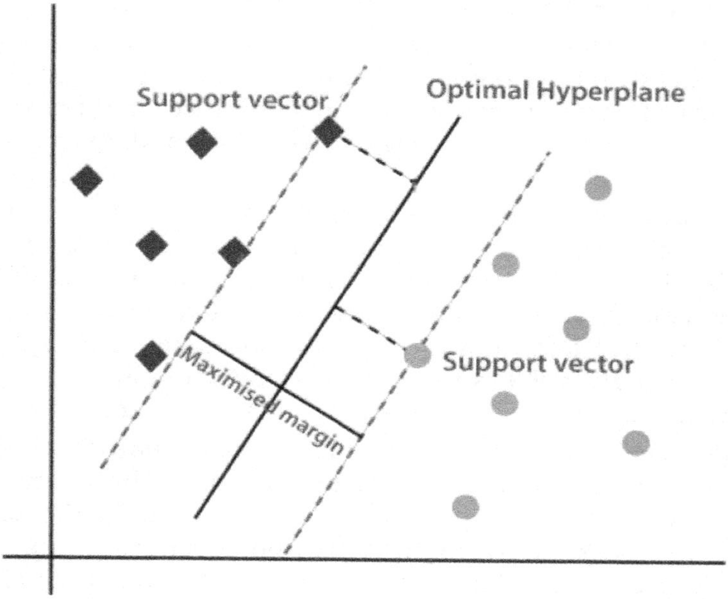

Support Vector Machines (SVM)

The basic idea of SVMs is to find an optimal hyperplane that separates different classes in the feature space. This hyperplane is chosen to maximize the margin or distance between the hyperplane and the closest data points in each class. The data points closest to the hyperplane are called support vectors, which play a crucial role in determining the decision boundary.

One of the main advantages of SVMs is their ability to handle datasets that are not linearly separable by transforming the input data into a higher-dimensional feature space. This transformation is realized with kernel functions such as linear, polynomial, radial basis function (RBF), or sigmoid. These key features enable SVMs to capture complex relationships between data points and improve class separation.

Training an SVM involves solving a quadratic optimization problem to find the optimal hyperplane. The goal is to minimize the classification error and maximize the margin. This optimization problem can be efficiently solved using different algorithms such as Sequential Minimal Optimization (SMO) or interior point methods.

SVMs have several advantages, including their ability to efficiently handle small and medium-sized data sets and their robustness against overfitting. In addition, SVMs have a solid theoretical basis and a clear decision boundary, which makes them interpretable and suitable for understanding the distribution of the underlying data.

Despite their strengths, SVMs can be computationally expensive when dealing with large datasets due to the time complexity in terms of the number of training samples squared or cubed. Additionally, SVMs can struggle with unbalanced class distributions or datasets with noisy data points.

Recurrent Neural Networks (RNN): Recurrent neural networks (RNNs) are a class of artificial neural networks designed to process sequential data. Unlike traditional pre-neural networks, RNNs have connections between neurons that form directed loops, allowing them to retain and use information from previous time steps. This unique architecture enables RNNs to efficiently model and analyze sequential data such as time series, text, speech, and even video.

At the core of an RNN is a recurrent connection that allows the network to maintain an internal state or memory. This memory allows the network to capture dependencies and patterns in the sequential data being processed. Each RNN neuron receives inputs not only from the current time step, but also from its previous state, making it capable of incorporating information from previous steps into its decision-making process.

A key feature that distinguishes RNNs from other neural network architectures is their ability to handle variable-length input sequences. This flexibility makes RNNs particularly suitable for tasks such as natural language processing, machine translation, sentiment analysis, speech recognition, and handwriting recognition when the length of the input varies.

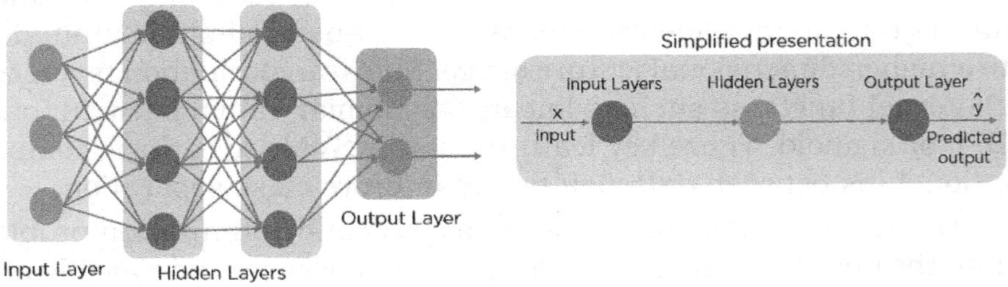

Recurrent Neural Networks (RNN)

One popular RNN variant is the long short-term memory (LSTM) network. LSTMs address a fundamental limitation of traditional

RNNs called the vanishing gradient problem. This problem arises when the gradients propagated through repeated connections decay exponentially over time, making it difficult for the network to capture long-term dependencies. LSTMs alleviate this problem by implementing special memory cells and gate mechanisms that selectively store and update information over multiple time steps.

Another variant is the Gated Recurrent Unit (GRU), which is similar to LSTM but has a simplified architecture. GRUs also solve the vanishing gradient problem and are comparable to LSTMs in various tasks, but with fewer parameters, making them more computationally efficient.

Training an RNN involves updating the network's weights using an optimization algorithm such as back propagation over time (BPTT). BPTT calculates the gradients of the loss function with respect to the network parameters, taking into account the dependencies caused by repeated connections. This allows the network to learn patterns and dependencies in sequential data and make predictions or generate sequences.

In recent years, RNNs have been widely used in a variety of applications, from natural language processing and speech recognition to captioning and music creation. They have shown significant success in modeling and generating sequential data, as they can capture both short-term and long-term dependencies. However, RNNs can be computationally expensive to train and have limitations in capturing very long-range dependencies. Researchers are constantly exploring new architectures and techniques to address these challenges and improve the capabilities of RNNs in machine learning.

Convolutional Neural Networks (CNN): Convolutional neural networks (CNN) are a type of deep learning model that has revolutionized computer vision and image processing. They are designed to automatically learn and extract meaningful features from input data such as images in a hierarchical manner. CNNs have gained immense popularity and have become the best choice for tasks such as image classification, object detection, and image segmentation.

The central idea of CNNs is to exploit the spatial structure of the input data using convolutional layers. Unlike traditional neural networks, CNNs use convolutional filters that slide over the input image and capture local patterns and features. These filters are small weight matrices that are learned during the training. The convolution function effectively applies these filters to the input data and creates feature maps that highlight different aspects of the image.

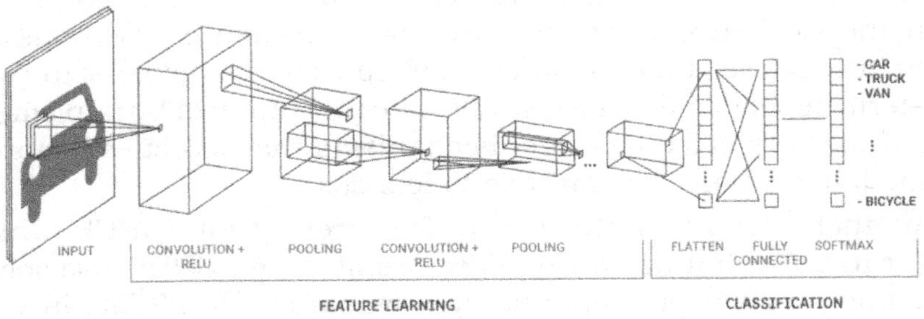

Convolutional Neural Networks (CNN)

By stacking multiple convolutional layers, CNNs can learn increasingly complex and abstract features. The first layers learn about simple features like edges and corners, while the deeper layers learn about more detailed features like textures and shapes. This hierarchical feature extraction allows CNNs to efficiently capture both low- and high-level representations of the input data. Another important component of CNN is the aggregation layer, which helps to reduce the spatial size of feature maps. Pooling can be done using operations such as maxpool or mediumpool, which take maps of features by taking the maximum or average of each pooling interval. This subsampling helps make the learned features more invariant to small spatial transformations and improves computational efficiency.

Once the feature extraction process is complete, the learned features are typically smoothed and fed into one or more fully connected layers that act as a classifier or regressor depending on the task. These fully connected layers use isolated functions to make predictions or generate output values. CNN training involves an optimization process called back propagation, where the network learns to minimize a loss function that quantifies the difference between the predicted output and the actual target. CNN weights are iteratively adjusted using gradient descent or its variants, in which the network learns optimal parameters that minimize the loss.

CNNs have shown remarkable performance in a variety of computer vision tasks, surpassing human-level accuracy in tasks such as image classification. Their ability to automatically learn hierarchical representations from raw data has made them indispensable in fields such as autonomous driving, medical imaging and facial recognition. In addition, the architecture of CNNs has also been extended to handle sequential data such as videos or texts, which further expands their applications.

Now, let's illustrate sentiment and text classification with tables and images:

Table 1: Sentiment Analysis Example

Text	Sentiment
"I love this product!"	Positive
"The movie was terrible."	Negative
"The weather is pleasant."	Positive
"It was just okay."	Neutral

In Table 1, we have a few examples of text along with their corresponding sentiment labels. Sentiment analysis algorithms aim to predict the sentiment label (positive, negative, or neutral) for a given text.

- **Preprocessing:** In this step, the input text is preprocessed to remove noise such as punctuation, ending words and special characters. It may also include tasks such as tokenization, derivation, or lemmatization.
- **Feature Extraction:** After pre-processing the text, features must be extracted to present the text in a form that can be understood by machine learning algorithms. Techniques such as bag of words, TF-IDF (Term Frequency Inverse Document Frequency) or embedding of words such as Word2Vec or GloVe can be used to extract features.
- **Classification:** The extracted features are then fed to a classification algorithm such as Naive Bayes, SVM or a neural network (eg RNN or CNN). A classifier learns patterns of features and maps them into predefined classes or classes. Both tables and images can be helpful in understanding and visualizing concepts and examples related to emotion and text classification. They provide a summary of the information and steps for these tasks.

5.4. NAMED ENTITY RECOGNITION (NER)

Named entity recognition (NER) is a subtask of data extraction that aims to identify and classify named entities (eg, names of people, organization names, places, etc.) in unstructured text. It is an important component in various natural language processing (NLP) applications such as question answering, sentiment analysis and text summarization. NER helps separate structured information from unstructured data and enables machines to understand and process human language more efficiently.

To better understand NER, let's look at its key components, techniques and evaluation metrics, as well as some illustrative examples.

Components of NER

Named entity recognition (NER) is a core task in natural language processing (NLP) and machine learning that involves identifying and classifying named entities in text. Named entities refer to real objects such as people, organizations, places, dates, amounts, and more. NER plays an important role in various applications such as information retrieval, query answering, text summarization and machine translation.

The NER process typically includes several core machine learning components. Let's look at them all:

- **Data Collection and Annotation:** A large amount of labeled data is required to train the NER model. This information must be manually annotated, with human annotations marking named entities in the text and giving them appropriate labels such as PERSON, ORGANIZATION, LOCATION, etc.
- **Feature Extraction:** Once annotated data is available, feature extraction is performed to convert the raw text into a format suitable for machine learning algorithms. Various linguistic features such as part-of-speech identifiers, verbal affixes, syntactic dependencies, and contextual information can be extracted to provide a meaningful representation of text. 3. Machine learning algorithms: NER models often use supervised machine learning algorithms such as conditional random fields (CRF), support vector machines (SVM), or deep learning architectures such as recurrent neural networks (RNN) or transformer models. These algorithms are trained on annotated data to learn patterns and relationships between input features and corresponding named entity identifiers.
- **Training and Evaluation:** The tagged information is divided into training and evaluation sets. The model is trained on the training set and iteratively updated to optimize its performance. Evaluation is then performed on the evaluation set to assess the accuracy, precision, recall and F1 score of the model. That iterative process can involve hyperparameter tuning and model selection for best performance.
- **Post-processing:** After the NER model predicts named units in the text, post-processing techniques can be applied to refine the results. This may include heuristic-based rules or linguistic

constraints that improve model accuracy and handle cases such as overlapping entities or nested entities.

- **Integration and Implementation:** Once a NER model is trained and evaluated, it can be integrated into NLP pipelines or applications to extract named units from text in real-life scenarios. The model can be implemented as an API service or integrated into larger systems to provide entity detection capabilities.

NER has made significant advances in machine learning, especially with the advent of deep learning techniques and large pre-trained language models such as BERT, GPT, and Transformer models. These models have shown superior performance in NER tasks and improved accuracy and reliability of named entities across domains and languages.

Techniques for NER

Named entity recognition (NER) is a fundamental task in natural language processing (NLP), which involves identifying and classifying named entities in text. Named entities refer to certain types of entities, such as names of people, organizations, places, dates, etc. NER is crucial in a range of NLP applications such as information retrieval, question answering, sentiment analysis and machine translation.

NER uses several techniques and approaches in machine learning. Here are some of the most commonly used techniques:

- **Rule-based approaches:** These techniques rely on manually created rules and patterns to identify named entities. Rule-based systems use regular expressions or syntactic patterns to match certain patterns of text and classify them into named units. Although rule-based approaches can be effective in certain domains or languages, they often have limited scalability and require significant manual work.
- **Machine learning based approaches:** These approaches use machine learning algorithms to automatically learn patterns and features from annotated training data. The most common machine learning algorithms used in NER are Hidden Markov Models (HMM), Conditional Random Fields (CRF), and Recurrent Neural Networks (RNN), such as Long Short Memory (LSTM) and Gated Recurrent Unit (GRU). These models are trained on labeled data, where each word is labeled with a corresponding named unit identifier. Trained models can then predict named unit identifiers for new, unseen text.

- **Statistical approaches:** Statistical techniques in NER involve the use of statistical models and functions to identify named entities. These models take into account the statistical characteristics of words, their contexts, and the probability that a word belongs to an entity class with a certain name. Features such as word frequency, part-of-speech identifiers, and contextual information are used to build statistical models that can accurately classify named entities.
- **Deep Learning Approaches:** Deep learning approaches have shown promising results in NER. Deep learning models such as recurrent neural networks (RNNs) and transformers can capture complex patterns and dependencies in text. Models such as bidirectional LSTMs or transformer-based architectures such as Bidirectional Encoders of Transformers (BERTs) have achieved state-of-the-art performance in NER tasks. These models learn representations of words and their contexts to make accurate predictions about said items.
- **Ensemble methods:** Ensemble methods combine multiple models or techniques to improve the overall performance of NER systems. By combining the outputs of different models or combining different features, ensemble methods aim to reduce errors and improve the generalization ability of the NER system. It is worth noting that the choice of technique depends on several factors, such as the size and quality of the available training data, the complexity of the specified entity types and the specific requirements of the NER task. In addition, advances in pre-trained language models, transfer learning, and domain adaptation techniques have contributed to significant improvements in NER performance in recent years.

Evaluation Metrics for NER

Named entity recognition (NER) is an important task in natural language processing (NLP) and machine learning. Its purpose is to identify and classify named entities in a text into predefined categories such as names of people, organizations, places, dates, and others. Performance evaluation of NER models is essential to measure their accuracy and efficiency. Various evaluation metrics are commonly used to evaluate the performance of NER systems.

One frequently used metric is accuracy, which measures the ratio of correctly detected units to the total number predicted by the model. Accuracy indicates the ability of a model to correctly classify items while minimizing false positives. Another frequently used metric is recall, which measures the ratio of correctly identified named items to the total number of items in the reference data set. Recall indicates the ability of a model to identify all significant units while minimizing false negatives.

The F1 score is a widely used metric that combines precision and recall into a single value. It is a harmonic mean of precision and recall, providing a balanced quantity that accounts for both false positives and false negatives. The F1 score is often used as a primary evaluation metric, especially when the dataset is unbalanced or when both precision and recall must be considered simultaneously. Other metrics commonly used in NER evaluation are accuracy, which measures the overall correctness of model predictions, and confusion matrix, which provides a detailed breakdown of true positives, true negatives, false positives, and false negatives. These metrics provide insight into model performance at a more detailed level.

In addition to these traditional metrics, domain-specific evaluation metrics can be used depending on the application. For example, in medical NER, metrics such as entity-level F1 score or exact matches are used to evaluate the accurate identification of medical entities. Similarly, temporal NER uses metrics such as temporal precision and temporal recall to evaluate a model's ability to accurately recognize temporal expressions. The choice of evaluation metric depends on the specific requirements of the NER task and the desired trade-offs between precision and recall. To effectively evaluate and compare the performance of different NER models, it is very important to choose appropriate metrics that match the application goals.

Here is an example table showing annotated text data for NER:

Text	Entity	Label
Apple Inc. is planning to open a new store in Paris.	Apple Inc.	ORGANIZA
Paris	Paris	LOCATION

5.5. LANGUAGE GENERATION WITH SEQ2SEQ MODELS

Generating languages using Seq2Seq (Sequence-to-Sequence) models is a popular approach in machine learning for tasks such as machine translation, text summarization, chatbot development and more. In this method, a neural network is trained to describe an input sequence as an output sequence.

To understand Seq2Seq models, break down the components and the training.

Encoder

In machine learning, an encoder refers to a core component of many architectures, especially in the field of deep learning. The purpose of the encoder is to transform high-dimensional input data into a low-dimensional representation while preserving the most meaningful information. This lower-dimensional representation, also known as code or hidden space, is usually more compact and includes the underlying structure or patterns of the input data.

Codings are widely used in various applications such as image recognition, natural language processing and recommendation systems. They play an important role in tasks such as dimensionality reduction, feature extraction and data compression. By learning a compressed representation of the input data, encoders can help reduce noise, remove irrelevant features, and improve the efficiency of subsequent processing steps.

One of the most popular encoder architectures is the autoencoder, which consists of an encoder and a decoder. The encoder part takes the input data and maps it to a lower dimensional code, while the decoder part reconstructs the original input from the code. The purpose of the autoencoder is to minimize the reconstruction error, forcing the encoder to capture the most important features of the input data.

Deep neural networks, such as convolutional neural networks (CNNs) and recurrent neural networks (RNNs), are often used as encoders due to their ability to learn hierarchical representations. CNN-based encoders are commonly used for image and video data, where they capture local and global spatial patterns. On the other hand, RNN-based encoders are suitable for sequential data such as text or time series because they can model temporal dependencies.

Encoders can be trained using various optimization algorithms such as stochastic gradient descent (SGD) or its variants. The training process involves providing the encoder with a large amount of labeled or unlabeled data and iteratively updating its parameters to minimize a predefined loss function. Unsupervised learning methods such as autoencoders can learn representations without explicit labels, while supervised learning can use labeled data to learn more distinguishable features. In short, a machine learning encoder is an important component that transforms high-dimensional input data into a lower-dimensional representation. This helps to capture the important features of the data, reduce its dimensions and enable efficient post-processing. Encoders are widely used in various fields and can be trained using different neural network architectures and optimization techniques, depending on the nature of the data and the task at hand.

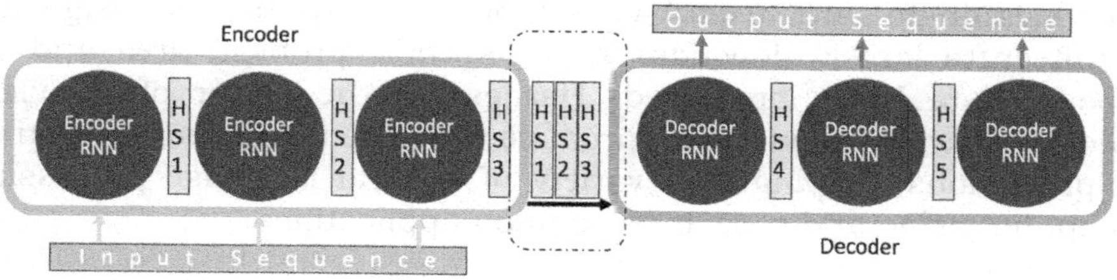

Seq2Seq models

Decoder

In the context of machine learning, a decoder refers to an important component of many neural network architectures, especially those based on an encoder-decoder framework. The purpose of the decoder is to produce an output or make predictions based on the information learned and encoded by the encoder.

Codec-decoder architectures are commonly used for tasks such as machine translation, captioning, speech recognition, and text generation. An encoder is responsible for processing the input data and extracting its essential features, often converting it into a compressed representation called a latent state or code. This hidden representation gathers important information from the input and forms the basis for generating the desired output. After the encoder has encoded the input, the decoder takes it and reconstructs or generates the output based on the hidden representation. Depending on the nature of the problem, the decoder may have its own internal architecture, such as a recurrent neural network (RNN) or a convolutional neural network (CNN). It receives the coded representation from the encoder and decodes it step-by-step to produce an output sequence that can be a translation, title, or any other meaningful prediction.

During training, the decoder is typically trained in a controlled manner where the target output is known and used to compute the loss function. The loss is then propagated back through the decoder and, if necessary, the encoder to update the model parameters and improve its ability to produce accurate and meaningful outputs. One popular type of decoder is the recurrent decoder, which uses recurrent neural networks such as long-short-term memory (LSTM) or Gated Recurrent Units (GRU). These models can process sequential data and are particularly useful for tasks such as machine translation where the input and output are sequences of variable length.

In general, the decoder plays a crucial role in the encoder-decoder architecture, allowing the model to transform encoded information into meaningful and useful predictions or outputs. Its design and architecture largely depends on the specific problem area and the type of data being processed. Harnessing the power of decoders, machine learning models can produce accurate translations, subtitles or predictions, helping in a variety of natural language processing, computer vision and speech recognition applications.

Training Process

The machine learning training process is a critical step that allows algorithms to learn and make predictions or decisions based on data. This involves training a model by exposing it to a large dataset containing input examples and their corresponding outputs or labels. The goal is for the model to learn the underlying patterns, relationships and rules in the data so that it can generalize and accurately predict the results of new, previously unseen data.

The training process typically follows a supervised learning approach where the dataset is labeled, meaning that each input example is associated with a known product. During training, the model iteratively adjusts its internal parameters to minimize the differences between the predicted outputs and the actual outputs from the training data. This correction is achieved using an optimization algorithm that updates the model parameters based on the calculated errors or losses.

The training process consists of several stages. First, the data is subjected to preprocessing, which may include tasks such as cleaning, normalization, and feature extraction, to ensure that they are in a form suitable for the model. The data set is then divided into two or more subsets: a training set used to train the model and a validation set and/or test set used to evaluate the effectiveness of the model.

The model is initialized with random parameters and training examples are presented to the model individually or in sets. The model processes each input, makes predictions based on its current parameters, and compares the predicted outputs with the actual outputs from the labeled data. The error or loss between the predicted and actual output is calculated and the model parameters are updated accordingly to reduce this error. This process is repeated for all training examples, iteratively updating the model parameters over several time steps or iterations.

Optimization algorithms such as gradient descent are commonly used to update model parameters. These algorithms calculate the gradients of the model parameters with respect to the loss function and update the parameters in the direction that minimizes the loss. The learning rate, which determines the step size of parameter updates, is an important hyperparameter that must be carefully chosen to balance convergence speed and stability.

The training process continues until a stopping criterion is met, such as reaching the maximum number of epochs or satisfactory performance of the validation set. At this stage, the model parameters are considered optimized and fixed. The final evaluation of model performance is usually performed using a test set that represents unseen data.

In general, the training process for machine learning involves optimizing model parameters to accurately capture the underlying patterns in the training data. Using an iterative and data-driven approach, the model can generalize and predict new, unseen data, allowing it to solve a variety of real-world problems.

Now, let's see an example of machine translation using a Seq2Seq model:

Input Sequence (English)	Output Sequence (French)
Hello, how are you?	Bonjour, comment ça va?
What is your name?	Comment tu t'appelles?
I love ice cream.	J'adore la glace.

5.6. COMPUTER TRANSLATION AND LANGUAGE COMPREHENSION

Computer Translation

Computer translation, also known as machine translation (MT), is the automatic translation of text or speech from one language to another using computer methods. Machine learning plays an important role in today's computer translation systems, as they can learn patterns and rules from large bilingual or multilingual data. Here is a brief overview of the main components of machine translation:

Training Data: Machine learning training data refers to a set of examples or observations that are used to teach an algorithm or model how to perform a specific task. These examples form the basis of the learning process, allowing the model to identify patterns, make predictions or classify new information. The quality and quantity of training data significantly affect the performance and accuracy of the resulting model.

To train a machine learning model, you usually need a diverse and representative data set. This data set should cover many cases that the model may encounter in real life. For example, in image recognition, the training data may consist of thousands or even millions of images labeled with corresponding categories. Similarly, in natural language processing, the training data may consist of large text corpora or annotated documents.

Curation of training data involves several steps, including data collection, preprocessing, and labeling. Data collection involves collecting relevant examples from various sources such as databases, online repositories or crowdsourcing platforms. Preprocessing is often necessary to clean the data, remove noise or outliers, and standardize the format. Annotation refers to the process of annotating data with correct outputs or target values so that the model can learn from the annotated examples.

The size of the training data can significantly affect the performance of the model. In general, larger datasets tend to produce more accurate models because they provide a broader representation of the problem domain. However, collecting and labeling large data sets can be time-consuming and resource-intensive. In some cases, techniques such as data augmentation or transfer learning can be used to augment smaller datasets and improve model performance. It is important to note that the quality and diversity of the training data are critical factors to avoid bias and ensure the fairness of machine learning models. Biased or incomplete data can lead to biased predictions and discriminatory results. Therefore, attention must be paid to the data collection process and continuous monitoring to identify and mitigate biases.

Neural Machine Translation (NMT): Neural Machine Translation (NMT) is a branch of machine learning that focuses on using artificial neural networks to translate text from one language to another. It is a major advance in the field of machine translation, replacing traditional statistical machine translation (SMT) methods.

NMT models are designed to learn translation patterns and rules directly from data without relying on explicit language rules or alignments. They use deep learning architectures such as recurrent neural networks (RNNs) or transformer models to capture the contextual information and dependencies of the source and target languages.

The NMT training process involves providing the model with parallel data consisting of pairs of sentences in the source and target languages. The model then learns to match an input sentence in the source language with an output sentence in the target language. This mapping is achieved through a series of mathematical operations performed by the neural network.

NMT models are great for capturing long-range dependencies and understanding sentence context. They can look at the entire input sentence at once and create translations that are smoother and more consistent than previous machine translation methods. In addition, NMT models benefit from transfer learning, where models pre-trained on large datasets can be fine-tuned for specific language pairs or regions, improving the quality of translations. One of the main advantages of NMT is its end-to-end nature, where the model learns a representation directly from input to output without relying on an intermediate representation. This simplifies the translation process and makes it more efficient compared to traditional multi-step approaches.

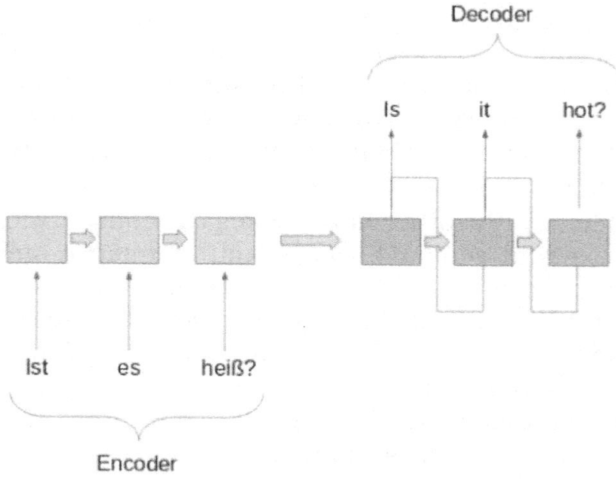

Neural Machine Translation (NMT)

But NMT also has some challenges. One of the biggest limitations is the requirement of a large amount of parallel data for training, which may not be available for all language pairs. NMT models can also suffer from uncertainty when translating rare or unprecedented words or handling ambiguous sentence structures. In addition, they can produce translations that are too fluent but semantically incorrect due to the lack of rule-based constraints.

Despite these challenges, NMT has made significant progress in machine translation and has become the dominant approach in the field. It has greatly improved translation quality and is widely used in various applications, including online translation services, multilingual communication and content localization. Researchers continue to explore new architectures and techniques to further improve NMT models and address existing limitations, making machine translation in different languages more accurate and easier.

Encoder-Decoder Architecture: Encoder-decoder architecture is a fundamental concept in machine learning, especially in the fields of natural language processing (NLP) and sequence-to-sequence tasks. It is widely used in tasks such as machine translation, text summarization and speech recognition. The architecture consists of two main components: an encoder and a decoder.

An encoder is responsible for encoding the input sequence into a fixed-length vector representation, also known as a context vector or latent representation. This vector captures the most important information of the input sequence and acts as a compressed representation of the input. In NLP, the input sequence can be a sentence or a sequence of words. An encoder processes the input sequence step by step, typically using recurrent neural networks (RNNs) or variants thereof, such as long short-term memory (LSTM) or gate recurrent units (GRUs). In the final step, the encoder creates a context vector containing a condensed representation of the input sequence.

The decoder, on the other hand, takes the context vector produced by the encoder and generates an output sequence step by step. It takes a context vector as the initial state and creates a sequence of results element by element. Like the encoder, the decoder uses RNNs or their variants. At each step, the decoder considers the elements of the previously generated output sequence and the context vector to predict the next element. This process continues until the decoder generates the entire output sequence.

The encoder-decoder architecture is taught under supervision using pairs of input sequences and corresponding output sequences. During training, the input sequence is passed through the encoder and the decoder generates the output sequence step by step. The model parameters are optimized to minimize the difference between the predicted output sequence and the target output sequence. This is typically done using techniques such as maximum likelihood estimation or sequence-level objectives such as ray tracing.

One notable extension to the basic encoder-decoder architecture is the attention mechanism. Attention allows the decoder to focus on different parts of the input sequence while generating the output sequence and effectively target relevant information. It improves model performance by solving the information bottleneck problem in a fixed-length context vector. In conclusion, the encoder-decoder architecture is an efficient framework for sequential tasks in machine learning, especially in NLP. This architecture enabled significant advances in machine translation, text summarization and other related fields by using an encoder to capture data from an input sequence and a decoder to generate an output sequence. Thanks to attention mechanisms and other improvements, the encoder-decoder architecture continues to play a critical role in various applications, facilitating the development of more complex and accurate models.

Attention Mechanism: The machine learning attention mechanism is a powerful concept that has significantly improved the performance of various models, especially in natural language processing and computer vision tasks. At the core of the attention mechanism, the model provides the ability to focus on certain parts of the input data that are considered more relevant or important for making predictions. This allows the model to dynamically weight different components of the input and provide more information about those that are more informative.

In relation to neural networks, the attention mechanism is typically implemented as a separate module in the model architecture. It works by calculating attention weights that indicate the importance of each input element. These weights are calculated by comparing the similarity between query and input elements. The question is usually derived from the internal state of the model or some other learned representation.

The attention weights are then used to calculate a weighted sum of the input elements, resulting in a context vector representing the attended information. This context vector is then combined with other parts of the model architecture to make predictions or perform downstream tasks.

One of the main advantages of the attention mechanism is its ability to handle variable-length inputs. By assigning different attention weights to different parts of the input sequence, the model can selectively focus on the most important elements regardless of their location. This is especially useful for tasks like machine translation, where the input and output strings can be of different lengths.

The attention mechanism significantly improved the performance of models in various domains. For example, in machine translation, by creating each word in the target sentence, the model can take into account different words in the source sentence, which significantly improves the quality of translations. Similarly, in computer vision tasks, attentional mechanisms have been applied to image labeling, where the model learns to focus on different regions of the image while creating descriptions. Overall, the attention mechanism has proven to be an important part of modern machine learning models, allowing them to efficiently capture and exploit complex inputs. Its ability to selectively select different parts of a load has led to significant advances in various fields and is still an active area of research.

Training and Optimization: Training and optimization are key processes in machine learning that involve iteratively improving the performance of a model. Training refers to the stage where a machine learning algorithm learns from a given data set to predict or perform certain tasks. In this step, the algorithm adjusts its internal parameters based on the data provided, trying to minimize the difference between its predictions and the actual values.

The optimization process is critical to the optimal performance of a machine learning model. This involves adjusting model parameters or hyperparameters to minimize error or maximize a desired metric. Hyperparameters are settings that determine the behavior of a learning algorithm, such as learning rate, parameter tuning, or network architecture choices.

Different optimization algorithms are used in machine learning, such as gradient descent, stochastic gradient descent, and Adam's optimization. These algorithms repeatedly update the model parameters based on the gradients of the loss function, which quantifies the difference between predicted and actual values. Following the gradients, the model gradually converges to an optimal set of parameters that minimize the loss.

To ensure that the model generalizes well to unseen data, it is common practice to divide the available dataset into training and validation subsets. Training data is used to update model parameters, while validation data is used to evaluate model performance during training. This helps detect overfitting, where the model becomes too specific to the training data and does not generalize to new examples.

In addition to optimization algorithms, regularization techniques play an important role in training models. Regularization helps prevent overfitting by imposing additional constraints or penalties on model parameters. Common regulation techniques include L1 and L2 regulation, suspension, and early termination. Furthermore, training and optimization are iterative processes. Models are typically trained over several epochs, with each epoch representing a complete transfer of the training data. At each time step, the model processes mini-datasets and incrementally updates its parameters. The number of epochs and set size are hyperparameters that must be carefully chosen to balance the trade-off between computational efficiency and convergence speed.

In summary, machine learning training and optimization requires iterative updating of model parameters to minimize the difference between predicted and actual values. This iterative process relies on optimization algorithms, regularization techniques, and careful tuning of hyperparameters to achieve optimal performance and generalization.

Language Understanding in Machine Learning

Machine learning language understanding refers to the ability of a machine learning model to understand and interpret natural language. It includes tasks such as text classification, sentiment analysis, question answering and natural language understanding. While I can't provide tables or images, here are some notable techniques and models used to understand language.

Word Embeddings: Word embedding is a key concept in machine learning and natural language processing (NLP) that enables computers to understand and process textual data. Basically, word embeddings are dense vector representations of words, where each word is mapped to a high-dimensional vector in continuous space. These vector representations capture the semantic relationships and contextual meanings of words in a given corpus based on their distributional characteristics.

Traditionally, textual data has been represented by sparse one-hot coding, where each word is assigned a unique index in a large sparse vector. However, this representation has several limitations. First, it fails to capture the semantic relationships between words because each word is processed independently. Second, the large dimensions of one-hot coded vectors make their manipulation computationally expensive and inefficient. This is where verbal incorporation comes into play.

Word plugins are created using training models for large texts such as books, articles or even entire websites. These models, such as Word2Vec, GloVe or FastText, learn to assign vector representations to words so that similar words are closer together in vector space. The training process involves predicting the context of a target word based on its neighboring words or predicting the target word based on its context. In this way, the models learn to capture the semantic and syntactic properties of words.

Embedding the resulting word has several advantages. First, they encode semantic relations, enabling operations such as verbal analogies. For example, subtracting the "male" vector "king" and adding the "female" vector gives a vector close to "queen". This ability to perform vector arithmetic on word input is a powerful feature. Second, word embeddings reduce the dimensionality of the input space, which makes the processing and analysis of textual data more computationally efficient. In addition, they can be used to initialize word embeddings in various NLP tasks such as text classification, sentiment analysis, machine translation and named entity detection, which improves the performance of these models.

Word embeddings have revolutionized the field of NLP by providing a compact and meaningful representation of textual information. They allow machines to understand the contextual meaning of words and capture the complex relationships between them. As a result, word input has become an essential tool for many NLP applications, facilitating the development of machine translation, question answering systems, sentiment analysis and more.

Recurrent Neural Networks (RNNs): Recurrent neural networks (RNNs) are a class of artificial neural networks designed to process sequential data. Unlike feedforward neural networks, which process data inputs independently of each other, RNNs have the ability to capture temporal dependencies and exploit the sequential nature of the data they are trained on.

The basic idea of RNNs is to add recurrent connections, which makes it possible to store and use the network from previous time steps. This allows RNNs to exhibit a type of memory that makes them particularly well-suited for tasks such as speech recognition, language modeling, machine translation, and time series analysis.

At the core of an RNN is a recurrent hidden state that acts as an internal representation that evolves over time as the network processes input sequences. The hidden state is updated at each time step based on the current input and the previous hidden state, allowing the network to learn and pick up patterns over time. This feedback loop allows RNNs to model and predict sequential patterns, making them powerful tools for tasks where data organization is critical.

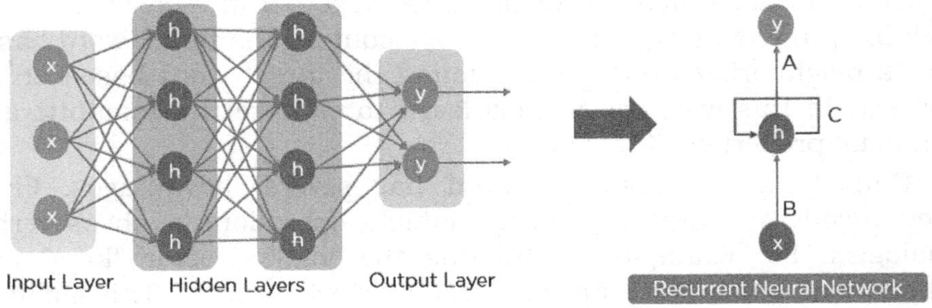

Recurrent Neural Networks (RNN)

One essential feature of RNNs is their ability to process inputs of variable length. This flexibility is achieved by sharing the same parameters across all time steps, allowing the network to handle sequences of varying length without special padding or truncation.

This feature makes RNNs highly adaptable to many applications and facilitates modeling of long-term dependencies in sequential data. However, traditional RNN architectures such as basic RNN and long-short-term memory (LSTM) suffer from the vanishing gradient problem. This problem occurs when training deep RNNs, because the gradients tend to decay exponentially as you move back in time, causing difficulties in capturing long-range dependencies. To solve this problem, variants such as Gated Recurrent Units (GRUs) and advanced architectures such as Transformer have been developed, which include mechanisms that reduce the vanishing gradient problem and improve the modeling properties of RNNs.

In recent years, the success of RNN networks has been boosted by advances in deep learning and the availability of large-scale datasets. Researchers have explored various techniques to improve RNN performance, including attention mechanisms, bidirectional connections, and ensemble models. These innovations have advanced the application of RNNs in many fields, from natural language processing to computer vision and even robotics. In summary, Recurrent Neural Networks (RNN) are a powerful class of neural networks that excel at modeling sequential data. The ability of RNNs to capture temporal dependencies and the flexibility to process inputs of variable length have become cornerstones of the field of machine learning, enabling breakthroughs in various fields, starting sequential information processing and understanding.

Transformers: Transformers is a pioneering machine learning architecture that has revolutionized natural language processing (NLP). Developed by Vaswani et al. In 2017, Transformers launched a new approach to sequence modeling that surpassed traditional recurrent neural networks (RNN) in efficiency and effectiveness.

Unlike RNNs, which process sequential data in stages, transformers use a self-aware mechanism to simultaneously capture relationships between words or characters in a sequence. This self-aware mechanism allows converters to consider the meaning of each word or character in the context of the entire sequence, allowing them to more efficiently capture long-range dependencies and contextual information. The basic building blocks of the transformer model are attention layers and advanced neural networks. The attention layer calculates attention weights for each character in the sequence, determining how much attention should be given to each character when encoding or decoding information. Several attention layers are stacked to form an encoder-decoder architecture, where the encoder processes the input sequence and the decoder generates the output sequence.

One of the most prominent transformer models is the Impact model introduced by Vaswani et al. This model has achieved high-level performance in a variety of NLP tasks, including machine translation, language understanding, and text generation. Its success led to the development of many transformer-based models such as BERT, GPT, and T5, further pushing the limits of NLP performance.

Impact has several advantages over traditional architectures. They can handle variable-length input strings, which makes them suitable for tasks with long-range dependencies. Transformers also facilitate parallel computing, as each character representation can be computed independently, which speeds up training and reasoning time. In addition, converters can capture semantic relations and contextual information more effectively, leading to better language comprehension and generation skills. However, transformers are computationally intensive and require large amounts of data for training due to their large number of parameters. To address these challenges, researchers have explored various techniques, such as model distillation and low-weight mechanisms, to increase the efficiency and availability of transformers.

Transfer Learning: Transfer learning is an effective machine learning technique that uses knowledge gained from solving one task and applies it to another related task. It uses representations or parameters learned from a pre-trained model and adapts them to a new problem or domain. Instead of starting the learning process from scratch, transfer learning allows models to take knowledge learned from a large dataset or complex task and apply it to a smaller or related dataset or task.

Transfer learning is based on the assumption that knowledge gained from solving one problem can be useful for solving another problem, especially if the two problems have some common characteristics or related knowledge structures. Using pre-trained models as a starting point, transfer learning enables faster convergence and better generalization to a new task, even with limited labeled data. There are different ways to do transfer learning. One common approach is fine-tuning, where a pre-trained model is taken as a basis and further trained on a new dataset, usually with a lower learning rate, to retain the representations already learned. Another approach is feature extraction where the pre-trained model is used as a fixed feature extractor and only the last layers are replaced and trained with the new dataset. This method is particularly useful when the new data set is small or when computer resources are limited.

Transfer learning has been successfully applied in many fields, including computer vision, natural language processing, and speech recognition. For example, in computer vision tasks such as object recognition, pre-trained models such as VGG, ResNet, or InceptionNet trained on large-scale image datasets such as ImageNet can be used as a starting point for learning a specific object. identification tasks.

In general, transfer learning provides a practical and efficient approach to solving new machine learning problems using knowledge gained from solving previous problems. This not only reduces the need for large labeled data sets, but also speeds up the training process and improves model performance in various domains.

These are just a few important features of machine learning for computer translation and language understanding. New methods and models are being created in these disciplines to increase natural language understanding and accuracy as they continue to advance quickly.

5.7 TOOLS AND LIBRARIES FOR NLP

Natural Language Processing (NLP) is a field of machine learning that focuses on the interaction between a computer and human language. There are a number of tools and libraries available for NLP tasks that can greatly simplify the development and implementation of NLP models.

Let's take a look at some of the popular ones and their key features.

NLTK (Natural Language Toolkit)

NLTK, which stands for Natural Language Toolkit, is a widely used Python library for natural language processing (NLP) and machine learning tasks. It provides a comprehensive set of tools and resources for human language data processing. NLTK is an open source library that has gained popularity due to its ease of use, extensive documentation, and versatile features.

One of the main strengths of NLTK is its ability to handle various aspects of text processing and analysis. It provides a wide range of modules and subpackages covering tasks such as tokenization (breaking text into individual words or sentences), literalization (reducing words to their base or root form), part-of-speech marking (assigning grammatical tags to words), and named entity detection (called unit identification such as names, identification and classification of organizations and places). NLTK also provides access to an extensive collection of language information, including materials, lexical resources and grammars. These resources enable researchers and developers to train and evaluate models, perform statistical analyses, and gain insights into language patterns and structures.

In addition, NLTK integrates with various machine learning algorithms and libraries, making it a powerful tool for developing NLP applications. It supports tasks such as sentiment analysis, text classification, information extraction and machine translation. The library provides implementations of popular machine learning models such as Naive Bayes classifiers, maximum entropy classifiers, and hidden Markov models. In addition to core functionality, NLTK provides features for language modeling, parsing, building machine learning pipelines, and visualization. It also supports interactivity through a user-friendly GUI called NLTK Book, which allows users to try and learn NLP concepts interactively.

Overall, NLTK has become a go-to library for NLP tasks and machine learning practitioners due to its rich feature set, extensive community support, and its role as a learning resource for learning natural language processing. Its versatility and ease of use make it a valuable tool for anyone who works with text data and is interested in building intelligent language applications.

SpaCy

SpaCy is a popular open source library for natural language processing (NLP) and machine learning. It provides a comprehensive set of tools and features that make it easy for developers and researchers to build robust NLP applications.

At its core, SpaCy provides efficient and effective tagging, speech tagging, named entity detection and syntactic dependency analysis. These functions allow users to divide raw text into individual words or tags, assign grammar classes to each tag, identify named entities (such as persons, organizations, and places), and analyze the syntactic structure of sentences.

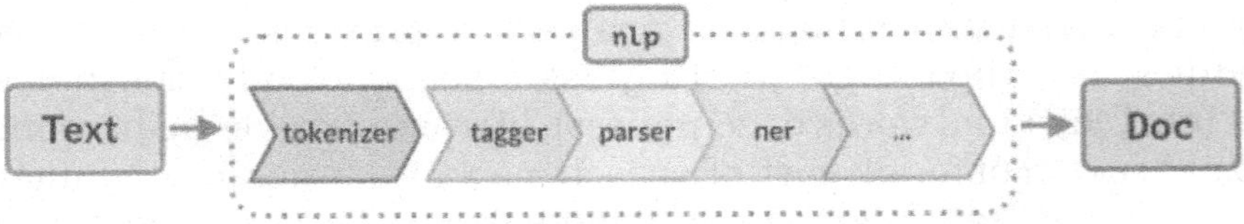

SpaCy

One of the main advantages of SpaCy is its speed and efficiency. It is implemented in Python and written in Cython, allowing it to take advantage of the performance benefits of C programming. This makes SpaCy significantly faster than many other NLP libraries, making it suitable for real-time processing of large amounts of text data.

SpaCy also supports pre-trained models for multiple languages that can be easily downloaded and used for various NLP tasks. These models are trained on large corpora and can perform tasks such as part-of-word tagging, called entity detection, and syntactic parsing. In addition, SpaCy offers the flexibility to train custom models on user-specific datasets, allowing researchers and developers to adapt the library to their specific needs. In addition, SpaCy integrates well with other popular Python libraries and machine learning frameworks such as TensorFlow and PyTorch. This integration allows users to seamlessly incorporate SpaCy's NLP capabilities into their complete machine learning pipeline. By combining SpaCy with deep learning frameworks, users can harness the power of neural networks to improve performance on NLP tasks.

Overall, SpaCy is a versatile and powerful library that simplifies the development of NLP applications. Its powerful implementation, pre-trained models, and seamless integration with other machine learning tools make it an excellent choice for researchers, developers, and data scientists working on a variety of NLP and text-based tasks.

Gensim

Gensim is a popular open source Python library widely used in natural language processing (NLP) and machine learning. It provides a simple and efficient way to process and analyze large text data, especially for tasks related to topic modeling, document similarity, and text summarization.

One of the most important features of Gensim is the implementation of the Word2Vec algorithm, which allows creating attachments or vector representations of words. Word2Vec models are trained on large text sets and capture semantic and syntactic relationships between words. These word embeddings can then be used as inputs in various machine learning models, allowing them to understand the meaning and context of the words in a more nuanced way. Gensim also provides features for topic modeling, which aims to automatically identify key topics in a document collection. It implements popular algorithms such as Latent Dirichlet Allocation (LDA) and Latent Semantic Analysis (LSA) that can discover underlying themes and patterns in a corpus.

This can be particularly useful for tasks such as grouping documents, searching for information, and recommending content.

In addition, Gensim provides tools for document similarity analysis, which allows users to compare the similarity of pairs of documents based on their content. This can be useful for tasks such as document retrieval, plagiarism detection and content recommendation systems. The Gensim implementation uses methods such as cosine similarity and Word Mover's Distance (WMD) to measure document similarity.

In addition to these core features, Gensim provides support for several other NLP tasks, such as text processing (eg, tokenization, de-stemming, de-heading), text body management, and model serialization. It also integrates well with other popular Python libraries such as NumPy, SciPy and scikit-learn, allowing seamless integration into larger machine learning pipelines.

Overall, Gensim is a powerful and flexible library that simplifies the handling of large text files and offers a wide range of tools for text processing, topic modeling, document similarity analysis and more. Its intuitive API and powerful applications make it a popular choice among researchers and practitioners in the field of machine learning and natural language processing.

TensorFlow and Keras

TensorFlow and Keras are two popular and powerful libraries used in the field of machine learning. Developed by Google, TensorFlow is an open source framework that provides a comprehensive set of tools and resources for building and deploying machine learning models. It provides a flexible and efficient way to define, train and deploy different deep learning models.

One of the main features of TensorFlow is its computer graphics concept, which allows users to define complex mathematical operations and the dependencies between them. This graph-based approach allows calculations to be performed efficiently on both CPUs and GPUs, making TensorFlow well suited for training large-scale neural networks. Keras, on the other hand, is an advanced neural network API that runs on top of TensorFlow (as well as other backends like Theano and Microsoft Cognitive Toolkit). It provides a user-friendly and intuitive interface for designing deep learning models. Keras allows developers to quickly prototype and experiment with different architectures, making it a great choice for beginners and seasoned professionals alike.

Keras simplifies the process of creating neural networks by providing a wide variety of predefined layers, including convolutional layers, recurrent layers, and dense layers. These layers can be easily stacked together to create complex architectures. In addition, Keras provides a wealth of utilities for data processing, model estimation and visualization, further simplifying the machine learning workflow.

The integration of Keras with TensorFlow has made it popular among researchers and practitioners. As a TensorFlow backend, Keras inherits all the advantages of TensorFlow, such as efficient computation, distributed training and deployment across platforms and devices.

PyTorch

PyTorch is a popular open source machine learning framework that has gained significant popularity in recent years. It provides a flexible and efficient platform for developing and training machine learning models. What sets PyTorch apart is its dynamic calculation graph, which allows users to define and edit calculation graphs on the fly. This dynamic nature makes it easy to debug and experiment with models, providing a seamless workflow for researchers and developers.

One of the main advantages of PyTorch is its Pythonic interface, which allows users to take advantage of the extensive features of the Python programming language. This makes the code easier to write and understand, and easier to integrate with other Python libraries and tools. PyTorch also provides a wide range of pre-built modules and functions for creating neural networks, making it easy to create complex architectures.

Another key feature of PyTorch is its automatic grading engine called autograd. This powerful tool automatically calculates the gradients of model parameters, allowing efficient implementation of gradient-based optimization algorithms such as backpropagation. The Autograd system controls the products of tensors and their dependencies, which allows gradients to be calculated efficiently and accurately. This feature greatly simplifies training neural networks and experimenting with different optimization techniques.

The PyTorch ecosystem is constantly growing and evolving, and is supported by a vibrant community. The framework offers a wealth of resources, including extensive documentation, tutorials, and sample code, making it accessible to both beginners and seasoned machine learning professionals. In addition, PyTorch seamlessly integrates with other popular libraries and frameworks such as NumPy and scikit-learn, further expanding its capabilities and flexibility.

In recent years, PyTorch has been widely adopted by researchers and industry professionals due to its ease of use, powerful features, and active community. It has helped advance various areas of machine learning, including computer vision, natural language processing and learning. Its flexibility and efficiency make it the preferred choice for many machine learning tasks, from prototyping new models to deploying them in production environments.

Here is a table summarizing the key features of these NLP tools and libraries:

Tool/Library	**Key Features**
NLTK	Comprehensive suite of NLP tools, corpora, and lexical resources
SpaCy	Fast and production-ready NLP solutions, pre-trained models
Gensim	Topic modeling, document similarity analysis, word embeddings
TensorFlow/Keras	Deep learning framework, flexible for building NLP models
PyTorch	Dynamic computation graph, state-of-the-art NLP models

6

Computer Vision

6.1. INTRODUCTION TO COMPUTER VISION AND IMAGE PROCESSING

Computer vision and image processing are two closely related fields of machine learning that deal with the analysis, interpretation and understanding of visual data such as images and videos.

Computer Vision

Computer vision is a subfield of machine learning and artificial intelligence that focuses on enabling computers to understand and interpret visual information from images or videos. It develops algorithms and models that can extract meaningful insights, patterns and structures from visual information in the same way that humans perceive and understand visual information.

Computer vision aims to empower machines to see and understand the visual world, enabling them to perform tasks such as object recognition, image classification, image segmentation, face recognition, pose estimation, and scene understanding. These features have many applications in various fields, including autonomous vehicles, surveillance systems, medical imaging, robotics, augmented reality, and more.

The core of computer vision is extracting important features from images or videos and using them to make decisions or predictions. This process typically involves several steps, including preprocessing, feature extraction, and classification or regression. Preprocessing steps may include resizing, normalizing, or denoising to improve the quality of the input data. Feature extraction techniques such as edge detection, texture analysis or deep learning-based methods extract meaningful representations from visual data. Finally, classification or regression algorithms are used to classify or predict the desired outcome based on the extracted features.

Deep learning, especially convolutional neural networks (CNNs), has revolutionized the field of computer vision in recent years. CNNs can automatically learn hierarchical representations from raw visual data, which enables them to achieve remarkable performance in various computer vision tasks. By training large-scale CNN models on huge defined datasets such as ImageNet, the models can learn to recognize and classify thousands of object classes with high accuracy.

In addition, the development of computer hardware such as graphics processing units (GPUs) and dedicated tensor processing units (TPUs) has greatly accelerated the training and inference processes of computer vision models. These hardware advances, combined with the availability of large-scale datasets and powerful deep learning frameworks, have democratized computer vision research and made the field more accessible to professionals.

Computer vision is an emerging field with ongoing research in areas such as 3D vision, video understanding, weakly supervised learning, and explanatory artificial intelligence. When dealing with more complex tasks and challenges, the integration of computer vision with other areas of artificial intelligence, such as natural language processing and learning, is likely to lead to more powerful and intelligent systems that can better perceive and understand the visual world. accuracy and complexity.

Here's a table summarizing some common tasks in Computer Vision:

Task	Description
Image Classification	Assigning labels or categories to images based on their content.
Object Detection	Identifying and localizing multiple objects within an image or video.
Semantic Segmentation	Assigning a class label to each pixel in an image, allowing for fine-grained image understanding.
Facial Recognition	Recognizing and verifying individuals based on facial features.
Optical Character Recognition (OCR)	Extracting text information from images or scanned documents.
Pose Estimation	Estimating the spatial position and orientation of human or object poses in an image.

Image Processing

Image processing in machine learning means applying various algorithms and techniques to analyze, process and extract useful information from digital images. It plays an important role in computer vision, a field of artificial intelligence that focuses on enabling computers to interpret and understand visual data. Using the power of machine learning, image processing techniques can be enhanced to automate tasks normally performed by humans, such as object detection, image recognition, image segmentation, and image generation.

Machine learning algorithms are trained to use large data sets of labeled images to learn patterns, features and relationships between pixels, allowing them to make predictions or make decisions based on new, never-before-seen images. Convolutional neural networks (CNN) are particularly popular for image processing tasks because they are designed to automatically learn hierarchical representations of visual data. These networks use convolutional layers to extract significant features from images and combine layers to reduce their spatial size.

In image processing, machine learning models can be used for various tasks. For example, in object recognition, algorithms are trained to recognize and locate specific objects in an image, enabling applications such as autonomous driving, surveillance systems, and medical imaging. Image recognition involves training models to classify images into predefined categories or labels, enabling applications such as face recognition, image search and content moderation. The purpose of image segmentation is to divide an image into different regions or objects, enabling tasks such as image processing, medical image analysis, and autonomous robotics. One of the main advantages of using machine learning in image processing is its ability to handle complex and unstructured data. It can learn from large data sets and adapt to changes in lighting conditions, scale, rotation and occlusion. This enables the development of robust and accurate image processing systems. In addition, machine learning models can generate new images with realistic features using deep learning techniques such as generative adversarial networks (GANs), paving the way for applications such as image synthesis, style transfer, and data augmentation.

However, image processing in machine learning also brings challenges. Annotated image datasets are often required for training, which can take time and resources to create. In addition, the computational requirements for training and inference of deep learning models can be significant and require powerful hardware or specialized processing units such as GPUs or TPUs.

Overall, machine learning from images offers enormous potential for a variety of applications, from healthcare and agriculture to entertainment and security. As advances in machine learning continue, we can expect more innovations and improvements in image processing techniques, resulting in more accurate, efficient and versatile systems that can understand and interpret visual information with human capabilities.

Let's illustrate some image processing techniques with examples:

Filtration

Filtering is a basic technique used to modify the frequency content or spatial characteristics of an image. One popular type of filter is the Gaussian filter, which reduces noise and blurs the image. The following image shows a comparison between the original image and this Gaussian filter:

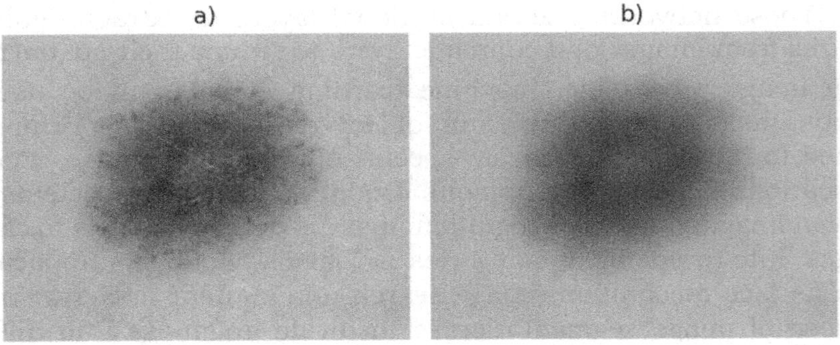

a) Original image **b) Gaussian filter**

Canny Edge Detection

Edge detection algorithms detect sudden changes in pixel intensity, highlighting the boundaries of objects in an image. The image below shows the result of applying Canny edge detection algorithm to the input image:

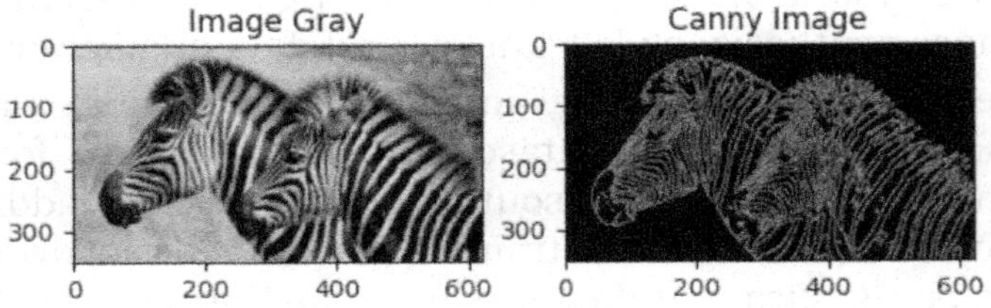

Canny edge detection

Image Enhancement

Image enhancement techniques aim to improve the visual quality of an image by emphasizing certain features or reducing unwanted objects. For example, tightening contrast expands the dynamic range of pixel intensities, resulting in a more visually appealing image. The table below shows a comparison between the original image and its contrast-enhanced version:

In conclusion, computer vision and image processing are important parts of machine learning that enable computers to interpret and analyze visual data. Computer vision involves high-level tasks such as object detection and image classification, while image processing deals with low-level techniques such as filtering and edge detection. Using these fields, applications can be developed in various fields, from self-driving cars to medical imaging systems.

6.2. CONVOLUTIONAL NEURAL NETWORK (CNN) IMAGE CLASSIFICATION

Convolutional Neural Networks (CNNs) for Image Classification

Convolutional Neural Networks (CNN) have revolutionized image classification in machine learning. CNNs are a special artificial neural network designed to efficiently process and analyze visual data. They have proven to be very effective in tasks such as object recognition, face recognition and image classification.

The basic concept of CNNs is the use of convolutional layers that allow the network to automatically learn and extract meaningful features from input images. A convolutional layer applies learned filters to the input image, convolutes them over the entire image, and creates keymaps that highlight different aspects of the input. These feature maps record local patterns and spatial relationships, allowing the network to be distinguished from important visual information.

To improve the network's ability to detect complex patterns, CNNs typically contain multiple convolutional layers stacked together. Each layer learns abstract and high-level functions based on the results of previous layers. This hierarchical architecture allows the mesh to capture both low-level features such as edges and corners as well as higher-level features such as shapes and textures.

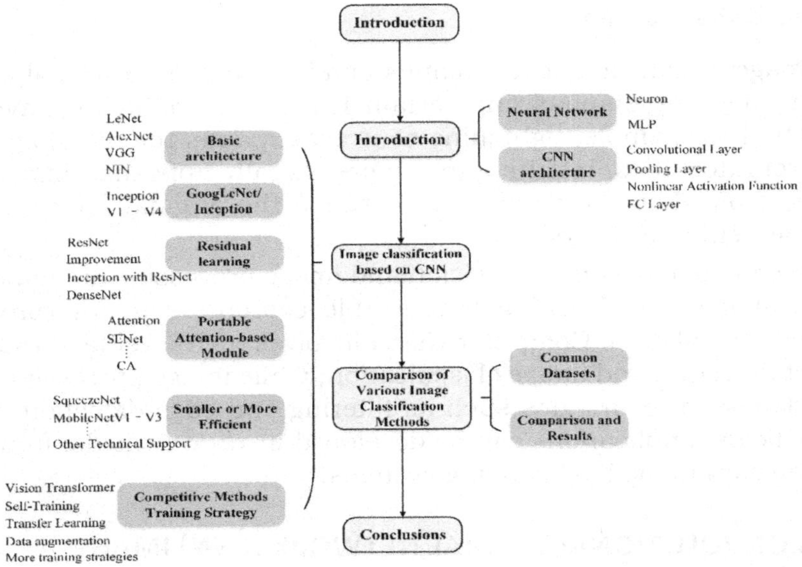

Connection layers are another important component of CNNs. These layers reduce the spatial size of feature maps and effectively reduce data. Common aggregation operations include max-aggregation, which selects the maximum value of a range, and avg-aggregation, which calculates the average. Coupling helps create translation invariance, making the network robust to small state fluctuations and reducing computational complexity.

After the convolution and pooling layers have extracted the key features, the fully combined layers are used to make the final classification. These layers connect all the neurons from the previous layer to the next, allowing the network to learn complex relationships and make predictions. The output layer usually consists of a softmax activation, which provides a probability distribution between different classes. Training CNNs requires a large labeled dataset and an optimization algorithm such as stochastic gradient descent (SGD). The network learns by minimizing a loss function that quantifies the difference between predicted and actual labels. The loss gradients are then propagated back through the network, adjusting the weights and biases of the convolutional and fully connected layers to improve model performance.

CNNs have achieved significant success in a variety of image classification tasks, often outperforming traditional computer vision algorithms. They have been used in several fields, including medical imaging, autonomous driving, and large-scale data for object detection.

Thanks to advances in deep learning and the availability of powerful hardware, CNNs continue to push the boundaries of what is possible in image classification, allowing machines to detect and interpret visual information more accurately and efficiently.

CNN Architecture

Convolutional Neural Networks (CNN) are a fundamental and highly influential architecture in the field of machine learning, especially computer vision. CNNs are designed to analyze visual data by efficiently capturing and processing the spatial dependencies of the input images. This architecture revolutionized several applications such as image classification, object detection, and image segmentation.

At its core, a CNN consists of several layers, each of which performs a specific function. The first layer is usually a convolution layer responsible for convolution of the input image with a set of filters or kernels to be learned. These filters extract important image features, such as edges, corners, and textures, by applying local receptive fields to the entire input. The result of this rotation operation is a feature map that preserves spatial information.

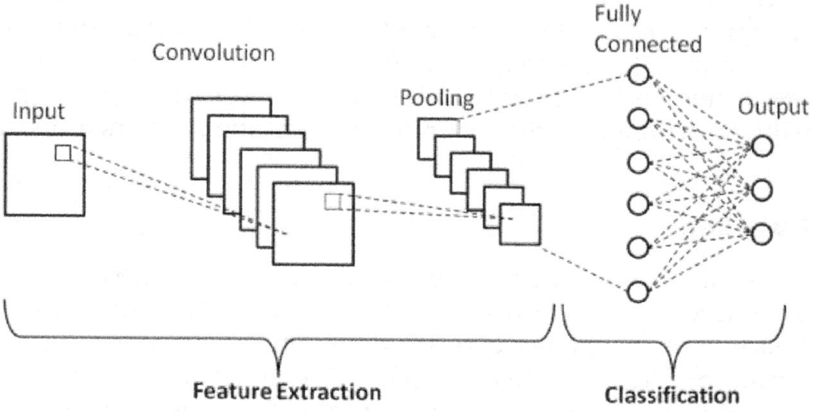

CNN Architecture

In order to capture increasingly abstract and higher-level features, subsequent layers often consist of aggregation layers and additional convolution layers. Combining layers reduces the spatial size of feature maps while preserving the most important information, which reduces computational complexity. This subsampling helps make the model invariant to small spatial transformations and improves its robustness to variations in the input data. After several convolutional layers and fusion, the final result is usually smoothed and provided in one or more fully fused layers. These layers work like traditional neural networks, allowing the model to learn complex non-linear relationships between extracted features and target features. Activation functions such as ReLU (Recified Linear Unit) are often used to increase the nonlinearity and increase the representativeness of the model.

CNNs use a technique called back propagation to optimize model performance and learn appropriate weights. By comparing the network predictions with the ground truth records, a loss function is calculated to measure the performance of the model. Loss gradients are then calculated with respect to the network parameters and used to iteratively update the weights using optimization algorithms such as stochastic gradient descent (SGD) or its variants.

One major advantage of CNNs is their ability to learn hierarchical representations of visual data. By using frequent weights and local receptive fields, CNNs can effectively learn features at different levels of abstraction. Lower levels tend to capture low-level features such as edges and textures, while higher levels learn more complex concepts such as object shapes and compositions.

In addition, CNNs have shown significant generalization ability, which allows them to generalize well to unseen data. This is due to their parameter sharing system, which allows models to learn efficiently from a limited amount of labeled data. In addition, techniques such as data augmentation and transfer learning further improve their performance by using pre-trained models or creating synthetic variants from training data.

CNN Workflow

A convolutional neural network (CNN) workflow in machine learning involves several steps to train and use convolutional neural networks for tasks such as image classification, object detection, and image segmentation. This workflow typically includes data preprocessing, model architecture design, training, evaluation, and prediction.

The first step in the CNN workflow is data preprocessing. This involves taking a named data set and performing the necessary transformations such as resizing, normalizing and scaling. Resizing ensures that all input images are the same size, while normalization helps standardize the pixels of the entire dataset. Augmentation techniques such as rotation, rotation, and truncation can be used to increase the diversity and variability of the data, which helps to improve the generalization of the model.

Next, the architecture of the model is designed. CNNs consist of several layers, including convolutional layers, pooling layers, and a fully connected layer. Convolutional layers extract important features from input images by applying filters and rotating them over the image. Layer fusion subsamples have maps to reduce spatial size. Fully connected layers connect the extracted features to the output layer for prediction. The depth and complexity of the architecture depends on the complexity of the problem and the available computer resources.

Once the architecture is defined, the model is trained using a labeled dataset. During training, the network learns to optimize its internal parameters, also called weights, by minimizing a predefined loss function. This process involves forward propagation, where input images are passed through the network and predicted outputs are compared to ground truth labels. The gradients are then back-propagated and used to update the weights using an optimization algorithm such as stochastic gradient descent (SGD) or Adam.

After training, the model is evaluated on a separate set of validation data. Evaluation metrics depend on the specific task, but generally include precision, accuracy, recall, and F1 score. The performance of the model is evaluated to determine its generalizability and identify potential problems such as over- or under-correction. If performance is not satisfactory, changes can be made to the architecture or training process. If the model is found to be satisfactory, it can be used to predict new, previously unseen data. The preprocessed input images are passed through the trained network and the model generates predictions based on the learned features and weights. The result can be a class identifier for image classification, bounding boxes for object detection, or pixel-specific segmentation maps for image segmentation.

Here's a table summarizing the common layers and their functions in a CNN:

Layer Type	**Function**
Convolutional	Extracts local patterns and features from input images
Pooling	Downsamples feature maps and reduces spatial dimensions
Fully Connected	Learns high-level representations and makes predictions

6.3. OBJECT LOCALIZATION AND DETECTION

Object localization and detection are the main tasks in the field of computer vision and machine learning. These include detecting and locating objects of interest in an image or video stream. These tasks have multiple applications, such as autonomous driving, robotics, surveillance systems and augmented reality.

Object Localization

Object localization is a fundamental task in the field of machine learning and computer vision, which involves identifying and accurately locating objects of interest in an image or video frame. This is an important step in many computer vision applications, including object detection, image classification, and autonomous navigation systems.

The purpose of object location is to determine the coordinates of the bounding box of the object within the image, which usually represents the coordinates of its upper left and upper right corners. Thanks to this, the machine learning model is not only able to recognize the object, but also provides spatial information about its location in the image.

One common approach to object location is the use of convolutional neural networks (CNNs), a type of deep learning architecture specifically designed for image analysis. These networks are trained on large datasets consisting of labeled images where the coordinates of the ground truth limits are given together with the names of the objects. CNN learns to extract relevant features from input images and predict interface coordinates using regression techniques.

Typically, object localization models consist of two main components: a region proposal network (RPN) and a bounding box regressor. The RPN generates a set of candidate object proposals, which are possible regions of the image that may contain objects. These suggestions are then passed through a salting box regressor that refines their coordinates to accurately locate objects. This two-step process allows for efficient and accurate target placement.

To train the object localization model, a loss function is defined that quantifies the difference between the predicted bounding box coordinates and the ground truth coordinates. Common loss functions used in this task are mean squared error (MSE) or uniform L1 loss. During training, the model adjusts its parameters to minimize this loss, improving its ability to accurately locate targets.

Object localization has many applications in various fields. For example, in autonomous driving, it allows vehicles to detect and follow other vehicles, pedestrians and road signs, enabling safe navigation. In augmented reality, object location is used to anchor virtual objects to real scenes. It also finds application in, for example, robotics, monitoring systems and medical imaging.

In recent years, object localization techniques have achieved significant progress with the introduction of deep learning models. These models, combined with large annotated datasets and advanced computational resources, have led to significant advances in accurate and efficient object location. Ongoing research continues to explore new architectures, optimization techniques, and information augmentation strategies to improve target localization efficiency and expand its range of applications.

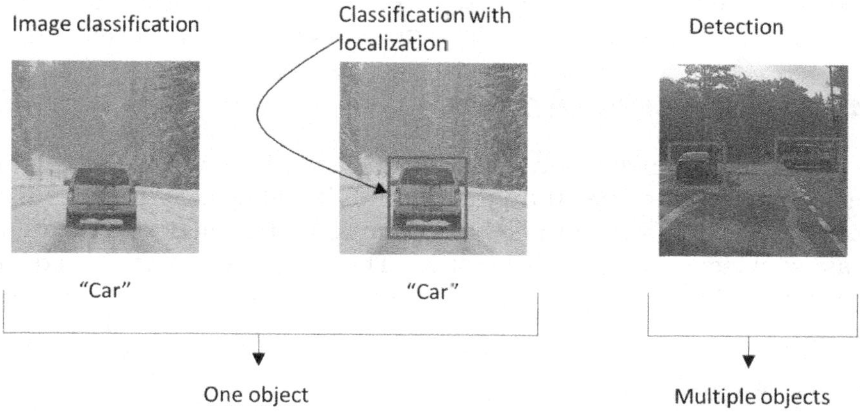

Object Localization and Detection

Object Detection

Object detection extends object localization not only by localization, but also by classification of multiple objects in an image. In addition to predicting bounding boxes, the model assigns a class label to each detected object. It allows recognition of objects of different classes, such as cars, pedestrians or animals. Let's illustrate the concept with an example. Suppose we have an image of a streetscape that contains various objects such as cars, pedestrians and road signs. We want to use object localization and detection to identify and locate these objects.

We can use deep learning such as Convolutional Neural Network (CNN) to locate and detect objects. CNNs are well suited for image-related tasks because they can learn hierarchical features from data. The result of the object localization and detection model can be presented in the form of a table. Suppose the model has detected three objects: a car, a pedestrian, and a stop sign. The table would look like this:

Object	Class	Bounding Box (x1, y1, x2, y2)
Car	Automobile	(240, 160, 380, 300)
Pedestrian	Person	(120, 320, 200, 450)
Stop Sign	Traffic Sign	(410, 270, 470, 330)

In the table above, "class" refers to the class of each object, and "Bounding Box" provides the coordinates of the upper left and upper right corners of the bounding box.

In the annotated image, the bounding boxes are covered with objects of interest. This visualization helps to understand and ensure the accuracy of the target localization and detection process.

6.4. SEMANTIC SEGMENTATION

Semantic segmentation aims to understand the content of an image at the pixel level, rather than just identifying objects or their bounding boxes. It assigns to each pixel a semantic identifier that indicates the class or classes to which it belongs. The result is a pixel-based mask where each pixel is given an identifier such as a person, car, tree or road.

Popular Approaches

Machine learning is a rapidly developing field that encompasses a variety of approaches and techniques. Some popular machine learning approaches include supervised learning, unsupervised learning, and reinforcement learning.

Supervised learning is one of the most common machine learning approaches. This involves training a model with labeled data, where each data point is associated with a known output or label. The goal is to learn a mapping function that can accurately predict the production of new, never-before-seen revenues. Supervised learning algorithms include linear regression, decision trees, random forests, support vector machines (SVMs), and neural networks.

Instead, unsupervised learning deals with unlabeled data. The goal is to find hidden patterns or structures in the data. Clustering algorithms such as k-means and hierarchical clustering group similar data points based on their intrinsic properties. Dimensionality reduction techniques such as principal component analysis (PCA) and t-SNE aim to reduce the complexity of data by projecting it into a lower-dimensional space. Unsupervised learning is widely used in exploratory data analysis and can provide insight into the underlying relationships in the data.

Reinforcement learning is a unique approach to machine learning that focuses on training agents to make sequential decisions. In it, the agent interacts with the environment and learns through trial and error to maximize the reward signal. The agent acts according to its current state and receives feedback in the form of rewards or punishments. Through the process of exploration and exploitation, the agent learns to optimize its decision strategy. Reinforcement learning has received attention in, for example, robotics, gaming and autonomous systems.

In addition to these three basic approaches, there are a number of specialized techniques in machine learning. For example, semi-supervised learning combines both labeled and unlabeled data to improve model performance. Transfer learning uses knowledge learned from one task to improve performance in another related task. Deep learning, a subset of neural networks, uses multiple layers of interconnected nodes to learn hierarchical representations of data. In addition, ensemble methods combine multiple models to make more accurate predictions. Common methods include bagging, lifting and stacking. Bayesian learning combines prior knowledge and beliefs with the learning process. Generative adversarial networks (GANs) are used to generate synthetic data that resemble the distribution of training data.

Examples:

Here are some examples showcasing the results of semantic segmentation:

Street Scene Segmentation

Street scene segmentation is a computer vision task that involves classifying and labeling different objects and areas of the urban environment. This is a fundamental problem in the field of autonomous driving, robotics and smart city applications. The goal of street image segmentation is to divide the input image into several semantic categories such as roads, sidewalks, buildings, vehicles, pedestrians, and vegetation.

Machine learning techniques, especially deep learning, have revolutionized street image segmentation, enabling the development of highly accurate and efficient models. Convolutional neural networks (CNNs) are often used for this task because they can effectively capture the spatial dependencies of images. These models learn from large annotated datasets where each image is manually labeled with pixel-level truth labels.

Semantic Segmentation

The street image segmentation process usually involves several steps. First, a dataset of annotated street images is collected, where each image is labeled with class labels for each pixel. A deep learning model is then trained on that dataset using a combination of convolutional and pooling layers to extract features and make predictions at different spatial scales. The model is optimized using an appropriate loss function (e.g. cross entropy) to minimize the difference between the predicted and ground truth signals. The inference-trained model is applied to new street images to make pixel-by-pixel predictions. The result is a segmented image where each pixel is assigned a class label that represents the object or region to which it belongs. Post-processing techniques such as morphological operations and conditional random fields can be used to refine the segmentation results and improve the overall accuracy.

Street image segmentation has many practical applications. In autonomous driving, accurate segmentation of objects and regions in the environment is crucial to detect obstacles, plan a path and understand the view. It allows vehicles to navigate safely, recognize road signs and symbols, and communicate with pedestrians. Additionally, streetscape segmentation is valuable in urban planning, surveillance systems, and augmented reality applications where understanding the urban environment is essential.

In general, streetscape segmentation is an important field in machine learning, which uses deep learning techniques to accurately classify and segment objects and areas in urban environments. It plays an important role in various fields, contributing to the development of autonomous systems, robotics and smart cities.

Pixel Label	Class Label
0	Background
1	Road
2	Building
3	Car
4	Pedestrian

Medical Image Segmentation

Medical image segmentation in machine learning refers to dividing or segmenting medical images such as X-rays, CT scans, MRI scans or ultrasound images into relevant regions or structures. This is an important task of medical image analysis, because it allows the isolation of specific anatomical or pathological regions of interest, helps in diagnosis, treatment planning and monitoring of various diseases.

Machine learning techniques, especially deep learning algorithms, have revolutionized medical image segmentation due to their ability to learn and recognize complex patterns and features from large data sets. Convolutional neural networks (CNNs) are commonly used in medical image segmentation tasks. These networks consist of multiple layers of interconnected artificial neurons that allow them to automatically learn and extract hierarchical features from images. The medical image segmentation process involves training a CNN model using annotated or labeled medical images. In the training phase, the model learns to recognize and classify the pixels or voxels of the image into different categories or regions of interest. For example, when segmenting a brain MRI, a model can be trained to segment different brain structures such as white matter, gray matter, and tumors. Once the model is trained, it can be applied to new unseen medical images to perform segmentation automatically.

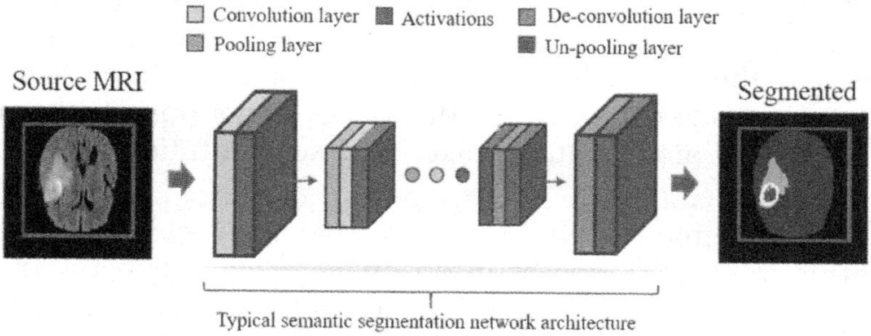

Medical Image Segmentation

Medical image segmentation faces several challenges due to the complexity and variability of medical images. Differences in imaging protocols, image quality, patient anatomy, and pathological conditions can affect the accuracy of segmentation algorithms. Therefore, researchers use various techniques to improve segmentation, including knowledge augmentation, transfer learning, and ensemble methods.

Accurate segmentation of medical images is critical in many clinical applications, such as tumor delineation in radiotherapy planning, organ volume determination, disease progression monitoring, and collaboration in surgical procedures. This can help doctors make more informed decisions, improve treatment outcomes and improve patient care.

In conclusion, medical image segmentation using machine learning techniques is a powerful tool in medical image analysis. It enables the automatic extraction of anatomical and pathological regions of interest from medical images and provides valuable information for the diagnosis, treatment planning and monitoring of various diseases. Ongoing research and development of deep learning algorithms continues to improve the accuracy and efficiency of medical image segmentation, paving the way for better health outcomes.

Pixel Label	**Class Label**
0	Background
1	Healthy Tissue
2	Edema
3	Non-Enhancing Tumor Core
4	Enhancing Tumor Core

6.5. MASK R-CNN INSTANCE SEGMENTATION

Mask R-CNN (Region-based Convolutional Neural Network) is a popular deep learning model for example segmentation. It is an extension of the Faster R-CNN model that combines object detection and region proposal generation. Mask R-CNN not only detects objects in an image, but also creates a pixel-level segmentation mask for each object instance.

Instance segmentation refers to the task of identifying and delineating individual objects in an image, assigning a unique name to each object, and creating precise segmentation masks that describe the boundaries of each object instance.

Here's a step-by-step overview of the Mask R-CNN process:

Region Proposal

Region recommendation is an integral part of machine learning, especially in the field of object detection and image segmentation. It is a technique used to identify and create possible areas of interest in an image that can contain objects or related information. The purpose of region recommendation is to reduce the search space for subsequent tasks such as object detection or localization by suggesting regions that are likely to contain objects.

The region recommendation process involves analyzing the input image and generating a set of candidate bounding boxes that cover different regions of interest. These bounding boxes are created based on a variety of methods, including but not limited to selective search, bounding boxes, or deep learning-based approaches such as Region Proposition Networks (RPNs). The regions created often vary in size, aspect ratio, and location to cover a wide range of potential targets.

Region recommender algorithms use different strategies to determine the probability of regions containing objects. They often consider low-level image features such as color, texture, or edges to identify areas with highly salient or artifact-like features. In addition, more advanced techniques use convolutional neural networks (CNN) to extract higher-level features and learn discriminative representations of object propositions.

The output of the region proposal step is a set of candidate regions, each labeled with a bounding box and an associated trust point. These recommendations are inputs to later stages of object detection pipelines, such as region-based convolutional neural networks (R-CNN), where they are further analyzed and classified into specific object classes.

Area recommendation techniques have greatly improved the efficiency and accuracy of target detection systems. By suggesting possible regions of interest, they significantly reduce the computer load of viewing the entire image, enabling more efficient processing. In addition, region recommendations help handle instances of objects with different sizes, scales, and orientations, making object detection in different scenes and datasets more efficient and versatile.

RoI (Region of Interest) Align

In machine learning, the term region of interest (RoI) targeting refers to a technique used primarily for object detection and instance segmentation. It meets the challenge of identifying and extracting features from certain regions of an image or input data.

The RoI alignment technique is an improvement over the previous RoI aggregation method, which suffered from quantization and alignment errors due to rounded pixel coordinates. RoI alignment overcomes these limitations by performing bilinear interpolation during the alignment process, resulting in more accurate alignment within the RoI.

The process starts with generating domain suggestions using methods such as selective search or domain suggestion networks. Each proposition represents a possible object or example in the image. These suggestions are ranked and ordered by how likely they are to contain the item or occurrence of interest.

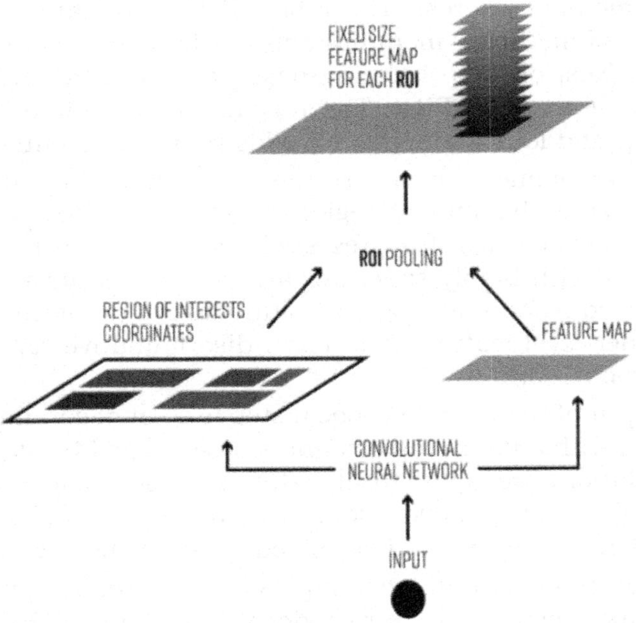

RoI (Region of Interest) Align

After the region proposals are obtained, RoI ranks fixed-size feature maps from intermediate layers of a convolutional neural network (CNN). The main innovation of RoI alignment is its ability to align extracted features with the original input, enabling a more accurate and fine-grained representation of features.

The RoI alignment process can be summarized as follows: for each region proposal, the corresponding rectangular region is divided into a grid of smaller cells. Bilinear interpolation is then applied to each cell to obtain characteristic values at four regularly selected locations. These interpolated values are combin e d by maximum binning to produce feature maps of a fixed size. The resulting feature maps can be forwarded to subsequent layers for classification, bounding box regression, or other relevant tasks.

When aligning features to input data, ROI alignment reduces alignment errors and quantification errors that can occur in the RoI aggregation method. This results in better localization accuracy and more accurate feature extraction in regions of interest. As a result, object recognition and instance segmentation models using ROI targeting achieve better performance and better object representations.

Object Classification

Object classification in machine learning refers to the process of training a model to recognize and classify objects in an input image or data. It is a key feature of computer vision and has many applications such as image recognition, autonomous driving, surveillance systems and medical imaging.

Object classification aims to teach a machine learning algorithm to assign precisely predefined labels or classes to objects based on their visual characteristics. The process usually includes two main steps: training and inference. In the training phase, the model is presented with a large named dataset, where each image is associated with a specific object class. The model learns to extract significant features from images and associate them with corresponding labels using different algorithms such as convolutional neural networks (CNN) or deep learning architectures.

A diverse and representative dataset that includes a wide range of objects and variations in lighting, scale, pose and background is critical to training a model effectively. This helps the model generalize well and work accurately with unseen data. The training process involves optimization techniques such as backpropagation and gradient descent to adjust model parameters and minimize prediction errors.

Once the model is trained, it can be used to classify objects in real-world scenarios. During the inference phase, the model takes an unseen input image and performs calculations to extract relevant features. These features are then compared with learned representations of different object classes, and the model predicts the most likely class for a given object.

Object classification models have evolved significantly in recent years, which is mainly due to the emergence of deep learning techniques. In particular, convolutional neural networks have proven to be very effective in capturing complex spatial patterns and hierarchical representations, enabling accurate object classification even in complex and cluttered images.

However, there are still challenges in object classification, such as handling occlusions, viewpoint variations, and limited training data for rare or new classes. Researchers continue to explore techniques such as transfer learning, data augmentation and ensemble methods to address these issues and improve the performance of object classification models.

Mask Generation

Mask generation in machine learning means creating masks or binary maps that show specific regions or points of interest in an image or dataset. These masks are used to separate foreground objects from the background or to identify specific patterns or features for further analysis. Mask generation plays an important role in various computer vision tasks, including object detection, segmentation, and tracking.

When detecting objects, creating a mask allows precise positioning and delineation of objects in the image. By creating masks that emphasize object boundaries, machine learning models can accurately identify and classify different objects in a scene. This is particularly useful in applications such as autonomous driving, where the detection and tracking of pedestrians, vehicles and other obstacles are crucial for safe navigation.

Mask creation also plays an important role in image segmentation, where the image is divided into multiple regions based on underlying objects or structures. Machine learning models can segment an image into meaningful parts by creating masks that correspond to different semantic categories, enabling deeper understanding and analysis of visual content. This is valuable in medical imaging, where segmentation of organs or tumors from a scan can aid in diagnosis and treatment planning.

There are different techniques to create a mask in machine learning. One common approach is to use annotated training data, where human experts manually mark desired regions or points of interest. These tags act as ground truth tags to train machine learning models to create masks automatically. Another approach is to use advanced neural network architectures, such as U-Net or Mask R-CNN, which are specifically designed to mask tasks. These architectures combine convolutional neural networks with additional components such as bypass connections and region recommendations to obtain accurate and detailed mask predictions.

In addition, advances in generative models such as generative reciprocal networks (GANs) and variational autoencoders (VAEs) have also been used to generate masks. These models can learn to create realistic, high-quality masks by capturing the underlying distribution of target masks. By training these generative models on large datasets, they can create masks that match the features and structures of the training data.

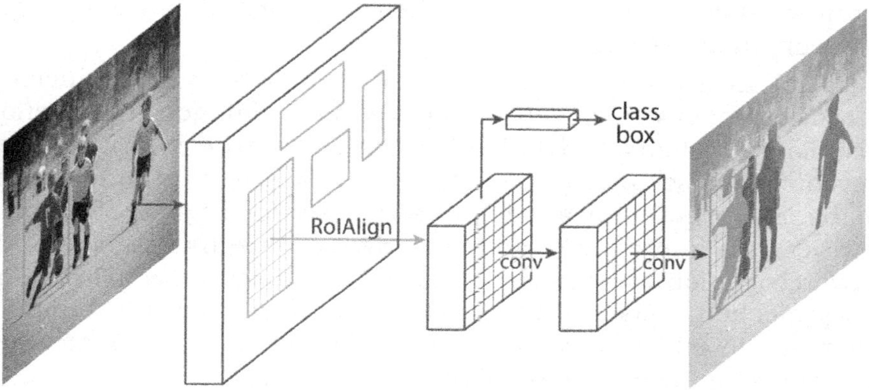

Mask R-CNN

6.6. FACE VERIFICATION AND RECOGNITION

Face Verification

Facial authentication in machine learning is the process of authenticating and verifying an identity based on its face. It is part of facial recognition technology that focuses on checking whether a presented face matches the face associated with a given identity.

The facial authentication process usually consists of several steps. Initially, a face image is taken either with a camera or from an existing image database. This image is then processed to extract relevant facial features such as key points, landmarks and features. These features are used to create a unique representation, often as a high-dimensional vector known as a face embedding or face model.

Once face embedding is achieved, it is compared to a reference database of stored face models associated with known identities. In comparison, machine learning algorithms such as deep neural networks, which are trained on large amounts of data to learn distinctive features for accurate face matching, are commonly used.

During inspection, the algorithm calculates the similarity scores, or distance, between the input surface of the rangefinder and each reference surface model. If the similarity scores exceed a predetermined threshold, the identity of the person is confirmed and verification is successful. Otherwise, the system will reject the face as a fraud.

In recent years, various techniques and advances have been introduced to improve the accuracy of facial authentication systems. These include the use of convolutional neural networks (CNN) to extract robust features, the use of attentional mechanisms to focus on discriminating facial regions, and the use of large datasets to provide more comprehensive training.

Facial authentication finds application in several areas, including access control systems, identity verification for financial transactions, surveillance systems, and authenticating personal devices. It provides a convenient and secure way to confirm a person's identity and provides a reliable level of authentication that can be used for a variety of purposes. However, it is important to address privacy concerns and ensure that facial recognition systems are designed and used responsibly. Strict data protection measures, transparency of system implementation and adherence to ethical guidelines are crucial to protect the privacy of individuals and prevent misuse of this technology.

Image Pair	Similarity Score	Same Person?
Face A	0.85	Yes
Face B	0.30	No
Face C	0.92	Yes

There are three image pairs in this table. The similarity score for each pair of faces indicates how similar they are. The faces are assumed to belong to the same person if the similarity score exceeds a predetermined threshold.

Face Recognition

Face recognition is a branch of machine learning that focuses on identifying and verifying human faces in digital images or videos. It is an application of computer vision that involves analyzing facial features and patterns to classify or associate faces with individuals. The purpose of facial recognition algorithms is to automatically extract distinctive features of a face, such as the shape of the eyes, nose and mouth, and the spatial relationships between these features.

The face recognition process usually consists of two main steps: face detection and face detection. In facial recognition, an algorithm scans an image or video frame to find and locate a face. Different techniques can be used for this, such as Viola-Jones algorithm, Haar cascade or deep learning based methods such as convolutional neural networks (CNN).

Once a face is identified, the next step is facial recognition, where the identified faces are matched to known identities or determined to belong to a known person. This is achieved by creating a face image or embedding detected faces, which captures important facial features and encodes them into a number vector. These embeddings can be created using methods such as eigenfaces, local binary patterns, or deep learning models such as Siamese networks or triple loss networks.

In recent years, deep learning approaches have shown significant success in face recognition tasks. Convolutional Neural Networks (CNN) have been widely used to extract facial features and learn discriminative features. Training such networks often involves large datasets of labeled faces, allowing the model to learn complex patterns and variations in facial appearance.

Face recognition has many practical applications in various fields. It has been widely used in security systems, access control systems and surveillance systems to identify people or verify their identity. It also finds applications in social media platforms, photo management software and the entertainment industry for automatically tagging or grouping faces. In addition, face recognition has potential applications in healthcare for patient identification, emotion recognition and physiological state monitoring.

However, it is important to consider ethical and privacy issues when using facial recognition systems. Issues such as bias, accuracy, consent and data protection must be carefully addressed to ensure responsible and fair use of such technology.

Input Face	**Matched Face**	**Similarity Score**
Face X	John Smith	0.92
Face Y	Jane Johnson	0.85
Face Z	Michael Jackson	0.78

6.7. IMAGE STYLE GENERATION AND TRANSFER

Image styling and transfer in machine learning refers to the process of creating or transferring the artistic style of one image to another using computational techniques. This field has received considerable attention due to its potential applications in various fields, including art, design and entertainment.

The main idea of creating and transferring image styles is to separate image content and style information and combine them in such a way that the content is preserved and at the same time the style characteristics of different images are taken into account. This process is usually achieved using deep learning models, especially Convolutional Neural Networks (CNN).

To better understand the creation and transfer of image styles, we will delve into two key components: style representation and image synthesis.

Style Representation

Stylistic representation in machine learning refers to the process of collecting and modeling stylistic aspects of data. Traditional machine learning techniques focus primarily on extracting and analyzing the content or semantic information of data, while style representation aims to capture the nuances and characteristics that contribute to the unique style or artistic expression present in the data.

In many fields, such as natural language processing, computer vision, and audio processing, style representation plays a critical role in understanding and creating creative content. For example, in natural language processing, style representation techniques allow the analysis of writing styles, such as formal or informal language, emotion, or even the author's definition of the text. These representations can be learned from large datasets, allowing the models to generalize and generate text with desired styles. In computer vision, style representation is often used for tasks such as image style transfer, where the artistic style of one image is applied to another image while preserving the content. By capturing the stylistic features of images, machine learning models can learn to distinguish between content and style information, allowing the creation of visually appealing images with different art styles.

Sound style representation is also important in applications such as music creation and sound synthesis. Machine learning models can create new pieces of music with similar stylistic characteristics by modeling the styles of different music genres or artists. Similarly, in speech synthesis, capturing the style of specific speakers can help create speech that mimics their unique vocal patterns, intonations, and accents. In general, style representation in machine learning involves extracting and modeling subtle artistic or expressive elements from data. It allows machines to analyze, understand and create content that adheres to specific styles, improving their ability to create aesthetically pleasing and contextual results across domains.

The table below illustrates an example of style representation using a deep CNN:

Layer	Output Dimensions	Activation
Input	224x224x3	-
Conv1_1	224x224x64	ReLU
Conv1_2	224x224x64	ReLU
MaxPool1	112x112x64	-
Conv2_1	112x112x128	ReLU
Conv2_2	112x112x128	ReLU
MaxPool2	56x56x128	-
...	...	...
ConvN_N	HxWxC	ReLU

In this illustration, a deep CNN is used to produce a feature representation with the dimensions HxWxC from an input image with the dimensions 224x224x3. To capture various picture features, a set of filters are applied to each convolutional layer.

Image Synthesis

Image synthesis in machine learning means creating new images using artificial intelligence algorithms. This involves training models to create realistic and visually consistent images that resemble a particular class or style. This field has received considerable attention and progress in recent years due to the remarkable success of deep learning techniques, especially generative adversarial networks (GANs) and variational autoencoders (VAEs).

GANs, one of the most popular image synthesis methods, consist of two competing networks: a generator and a discriminator. The generator takes random noise as input and produces synthetic images, while the purpose of the separator is to separate real and fake images. Through an iterative training process, the generator improves its ability to produce increasingly faithful images, while the discriminator becomes more adept at distinguishing between real and synthetic images. This competition training helps the generator to refine its output to closely match the target distribution of real images.

Another approach, VAE, focuses on learning the latent representation of images. VAE encodes the input images into a lower-dimensional latent space and captures the underlying structure of the data. These encoded representations can then be decoded to create new images. VAEs employ probabilistic models to capture the uncertainty of the latent state, allowing them to create versatile and novel images by sampling the learned distribution.

Image synthesis has found applications in several fields such as computer graphics, virtual reality, information augmentation and content creation. It can be used to create realistic images of objects, scenes and even human faces. By training models on large datasets such as ImageNet, COCO or CelebA, these models can learn to generate images with complex details and exhibit high semantic understanding.

However, image synthesis still has challenges. Creating high-resolution, photorealistic images remains a difficult task. Ensuring variety and control of the images created is also very important. Researchers are constantly exploring innovative architectures, loss functions, and training techniques to address these challenges.

Image synthesis in machine learning has shown promising results and could revolutionize several industries. It opens up new possibilities for creativity, content creation and even creating a virtual world. As the industry evolves, we can expect even more impressive and realistic image synthesis capabilities that allow machines to create visually appealing and novel images that are indistinguishable from images captured by human photographers.

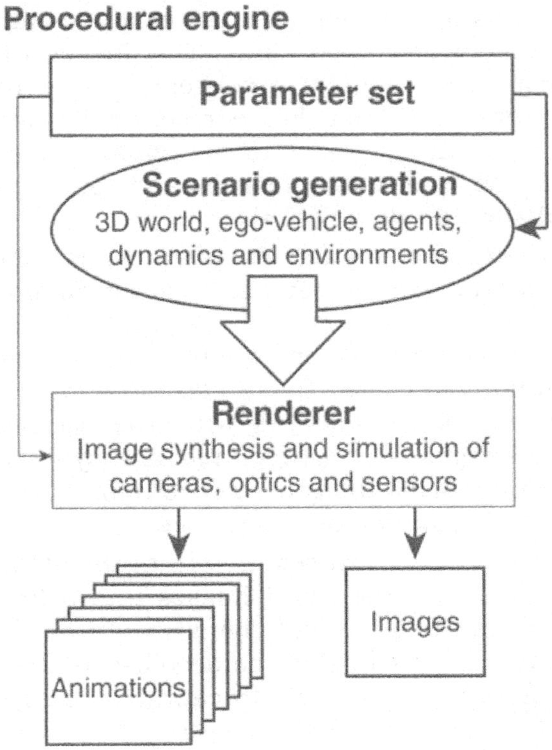

Image Synthesis

Over the years, several different image style generating and transfer processes have been investigated and improved. Neural Style Transfer, which transfers styles in real-time using CNNs, and CycleGAN, which learns the mapping between two domains without the need for paired training data, are two important methods.

Overall, machine learning's image style creation and transfer techniques offer a strong framework for merging the content and style traits of many sources to produce aesthetically attractive and artistic images.

6.8. IMAGE CAPTIONING AND VISUAL QUESTION ANSWERING

Image Captioning

Image captioning in machine learning is an exciting field that focuses on automatically generating human-like descriptions or captions for images. It combines the power of computer vision, which enables machines to understand and analyze visual content, and natural language processing, which enables machines to create coherent and meaningful sentences.

The purpose of captions is to bridge the gap between visual information and textual description, allowing machines to understand and communicate the content of images. Using deep learning techniques, specifically convolutional neural networks (CNNs) for visual feature extraction and recurrent neural networks (RNNs) for language modeling, image caption models can learn the relationship between images and their corresponding textual descriptions.

The subtitling process usually involves several steps. Initially, a pre-trained CNN is used to extract high-level visual features from the input image. These features store basic visual information such as objects, shapes, and colors. The extracted features are then fed to an RNN, such as a long-short-term memory (LSTM) or a gated recurrent unit (GRU), which generates a sequence of words based on visual features and previously generated words. This process is known as encoder-decoder architecture.

During training, the caption model learns to optimize parameters by comparing the generated captions with the ground truth texts of the training dataset. This means minimizing a loss function that measures the difference between the predicted and target subtitles. This training process allows the model to learn statistical patterns and relationships between visual features and textual descriptions, allowing it to generate captions that exactly match the content of the input image.

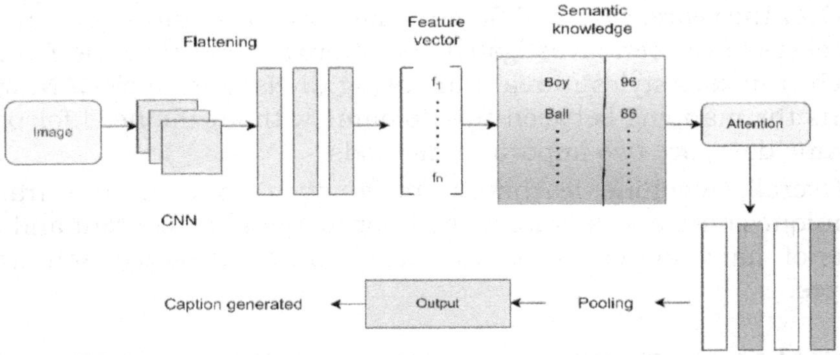

Image Captioning

One of the main challenges of captions is to ensure that the captions created are accurate, relevant and semantically meaningful. This requires that the model captures both the global context of the image and the fine-grained details it contains. In addition, the model must understand the relationships between objects, their attributes, and their spatial arrangement to create coherent and contextual descriptions. Subtitles have many applications in various fields. It can improve accessibility for the visually impaired by providing textual descriptions of images. It also finds applications for content understanding, image serving and automatic content generation in social media, e-commerce and advertising. In addition, captions are a springboard for more complex tasks such as visual storytelling and visual question answering, where machines can understand and answer questions about the content of images.

Overall, captioning in machine learning is an exciting and rapidly developing field that combines computer vision and natural language processing to enable machines to create human-like descriptions of images. Thanks to ongoing research and advances in deep learning techniques, captions have great potential to change the way machines perceive and deliver visual content.

Example:

Image	Caption

Visual Question Answering (VQA)

Visual Question Answering (VQA) is an exciting field of machine learning that combines computer vision and natural language processing to enable machines to answer questions about images or visual data. It aims to bridge the gap between visual information and understanding text, allowing machines to understand and answer questions about what they "see".

In VQA, the input consists of an image and a corresponding text question. The goal is to create an accurate text response based on the visual content of the image and the context of the question. This process involves extracting meaningful features from an image using computer vision techniques and understanding the query using natural language processing algorithms.

To solve VQA, researchers use deep learning models that use convolutional neural networks (CNN) for image processing and recurrent neural networks (RNN) for query understanding. These models learn to extract significant visual features from an image and match them to the corresponding text question. By capturing the relationship between the visual and the text, the model can provide an appropriate response.

Training such models requires large datasets consisting of pairs of images and questions with corresponding answers. These data are labeled by human annotations and are the basics for training the VQA model. The model learns to generalize from this information and make accurate predictions about unseen images and questions. VQA has many applications in various fields. It can be used in assistive technology to help visually impaired people better understand their surroundings. It can also be used to develop intelligent chatbots or virtual assistants that can interact with users in a more intuitive and multimodal way.

However, VQA still faces several challenges. Models struggle with understanding complex questions, handling ambiguity, and reasoning from multiple visual cues. Dataset bias is also a problem, where models tend to rely on superficial visual patterns or biases in the training data rather than understanding the underlying concepts.

Researchers continue to explore new techniques and architectures to improve VQA performance. It involves combining attentional mechanisms, graph-based reasoning and multimodal fusion techniques. The field is developing rapidly, and advances in VQA offer great potential for the development of smarter and more visually aware systems in the future.

Example:

Image	Question	Answer

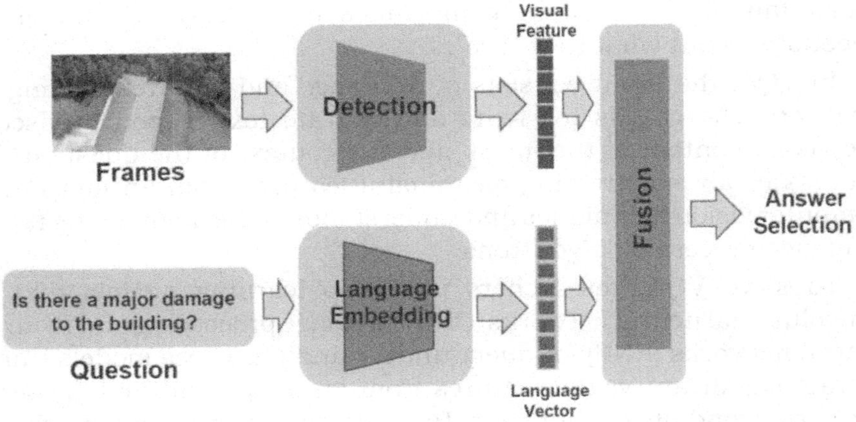

Visual Question Answering (VQA)

There are several practical uses for image captioning and visual question answering, including helping the blind, boosting image search engines, and facilitating human-computer connection. These examples show how computer vision and natural language understanding can be used to empower machines.

7

Recommender Systems

7.1. INTRODUCTION TO RECOMMENDER SYSTEMS

A type of machine learning algorithms called recommender systems aims to anticipate and recommend products or information to users based on their interests and previous behaviour. By enhancing user engagement and personalising the user experience, these technologies are essential in a variety of sectors, including e-commerce, entertainment, and social media.

Collaborative Filtering

Collaborative filtering is a popular machine learning technique used in recommender systems and personalized content filtering. It aims to predict user interests and preferences by leveraging the collective intelligence of the user community. The basic idea is that if two users have similar preferences or similar behavior, their recommendations or choices are likely to be consistent.

Collaborative filtering analyzes large data sets consisting of interactions or ratings between users and objects to identify patterns and relationships. This information can be direct ratings (eg star ratings) or indirect feedback (eg purchase history, clicks or views). The algorithm builds a model based on this data to make predictions or recommendations about items that the user has not yet interacted with.

There are two main types of collaborative filtering: user-based and object-based. User-based collaborative filtering focuses on finding similar users for recommendations. It calculates user similarity based on their product preferences and uses these similarities to predict the user's preference for the item. Title-based collaborative filtering, on the other hand, focuses on finding similar items. It analyzes the preferences of users who have interacted with both entities and uses these similarities to make recommendations.

Collaborative filtering algorithms use different similarity measures, such as cosine similarity or Pearson correlation, to determine the similarity between users or objects. Once the similarities are calculated, the algorithm can make recommendations by selecting the best rating or most relevant items from similar users or items.

One of the important advantages of collaborative filtering is its ability to provide personalized recommendations without requiring precise information about the objects themselves. It can reveal hidden patterns and relationships between users and objects, leading to accurate predictions. However, collaborative filtering also has challenges such as the cold start problem (when a new user or target has limited information) and sparsity (when the interaction matrix between the user and the target is sparse).

Various techniques and improvements have been developed to address these issues, including matrix fabrication, neighborhood-based methods, and hybrid methods that combine collaborative filtering with other recommendation techniques. These advances have significantly improved the effectiveness and efficiency of collaborative filtering algorithms.

Overall, collaborative filtering is a powerful approach to machine learning that allows systems to provide personalized recommendations by harnessing the collective wisdom of users. It has found wide application in e-commerce, social media, content streaming platforms and more, improving user experience and increasing engagement.

	Item 1	**Item 2**	**Item 3**	**Item 4**
User 1	5	4	-	2
User 2	-	2	4	5
User 3	3	-	5	1

We identify individuals with similar likes and propose products they enjoyed but the target user hasn't yet rated in order to create recommendations for a specific user. To locate comparable users, similarity metrics like cosine similarity or Pearson correlation might be employed.

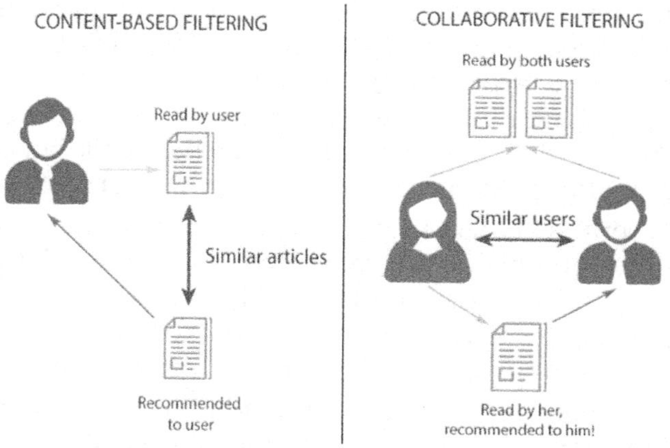

Collaborative Filtering and Content-based Filtering

Content-based Filtering

Content-based filtering is a popular machine learning technique used to recommend items or content to users based on their preferences and characteristics. Unlike collaborative filtering, which is based on user behavior and preferences, content-based filtering focuses on the intrinsic properties of recommended items.

The process begins by analyzing and extracting the essential characteristics of the objects themselves. These features may vary depending on the type of recommended content. For example, for movies, features such as genre, director, actors and plot keywords can be considered. In the context of music, characteristics such as genre, artist, tempo, and instrumental composition can be important.

Once the features are extracted, a user profile is created that represents the user's preferences and interests. This profile is usually built with the user's interactive system, such as based on ratings, past choices or explicit feedback.

A content-based filtering algorithm compares the user profile with the characteristics of available items to generate recommendations. It looks for items that have properties similar to the user's preferences. This can be done using different similarity measures such as cosine similarity or Euclidean distance.

The algorithm ranks the items based on their similarity to the user profile and presents the best items as recommendations. The user can accept or reject these recommendations and provide additional feedback to improve the accuracy of future recommendations.

One of the main advantages of content-based filtering is that it can provide personalized recommendations, even for new or niche targets. It does not require a large amount of historical data or the presence of other users with similar preferences. In addition, content-based filtering can help overcome the "cold start" problem where collaborative filtering has difficulty making recommendations to new users or targets.

However, content-based filtering also has limitations. This largely depends on the quality of the extracted features and the ability to accurately capture user preferences. If the features do not represent the user's tastes, or if the user's interests change over time, the recommendations may not reflect the user's preferences.

Think about a system that recommends films, for instance. Based on factors like genre, director, actors, and plot keywords, we are able to develop a feature vector for each film. Here is an illustration of a feature vector:

	Action	**Drama**	**Comedy**	**Romance**	**Director (ID)**	**Actor (ID)**
Movie 1	1	0	1	0	23	[45, 78]
Movie 2	0	1	0	1	18	[12, 56]
Movie 3	1	0	0	0	45	[67, 23]

We build a user profile for each user based on their prior interactions and preferences in order to provide recommendations for them. The feature vectors of the items are then compared to the user profile to find comparable products to suggest.

Additionally, the usage of images can improve the suggestion process. To draw visitors' attention and provide visual clues, you could incorporate movie or book posters, for instance.

Finally, recommender systems are effective tools that use machine learning strategies to give people customised recommendations. Both content-based filtering and collaborative filtering are common techniques, and each has advantages and disadvantages. Recommender systems continue to develop and enhance the user experience across a variety of sectors by combining these approaches or utilising more sophisticated methods like deep learning or hybrid models.

7.2. CONTENT-BASED FILTERING

Content-based filtering is a technique used in machine learning and recommendation systems to make personalized recommendations based on target features or attributes. It is based on analyzing the content or characteristics of items (such as text, images or other descriptive information) and finding similarities or patterns to recommend items similar to those in which the user has already shown interest.

To better understand content-based filtering, let's look at the example of a movie recommendation system.

Table 1: Movie Features

Movie	Genre	Director	Rating
Movie A	Action	Director X	4.5
Movie B	Comedy	Director Y	3.8
Movie C	Drama	Director X	4.2
Movie D	Action	Director Z	3.9
Movie E	Comedy	Director Z	4.1

The genre, director, and average user rating of each film are listed in this table.

With content-based filtering, suggestions are generated by examining the characteristics of films and looking for trends or resemblances. Assume a user has seen "Movie A" and appreciated it. The user now requests recommendations for films that are comparable.

Applying content-based filtering looks like this:

Feature Extraction: Feature extraction is a fundamental concept in machine learning that involves transforming raw input data into representative features that capture important features of the data. This is a critical step in machine learning, as it aims to extract relevant information and discard irrelevant or unnecessary information, thus improving the effectiveness and efficiency of learning algorithms.

The purpose of feature extraction is to identify and create a compact and meaningful representation of the input data that can effectively distinguish between different classes or categories. This process involves applying various mathematical or statistical techniques to transform the original information into a lower dimensional state while retaining the most important information. The extracted features should ideally have discriminative power, robustness to noise, and should be independent or uncorrelated with each other. Feature extraction techniques depend on the data type and the problem to be solved. Common numerical data techniques include principal component analysis (PCA), which finds orthogonal axes that maximize the variance of the data, and linear discriminant analysis (LDA), which aims to maximize between-class variance and minimize within-class variance. These techniques can effectively reduce data dimensions while preserving the most characteristic information.

For text or natural language data, feature extraction involves converting the text to a numerical representation. This can be achieved by techniques such as a bag of words, where the text is represented as a frequency distribution of individual words or n-grams, or more advanced methods such as word input, such as Word2Vec or GloVe, which capture semantic meaning. of words mapping them into a continuous vector space. Image and audio data also require special extraction techniques. For images, approaches such as Convolutional Neural Networks (CNN) are often used to automatically learn hierarchical features at different levels of abstraction. These networks can collect local patterns and textures as well as global shapes and structures. Similarly, for audio data, techniques such as Mel-frequency cepstral coefficients (MFCC) are used to capture spectral information and represent audio signals in a more characteristic way.

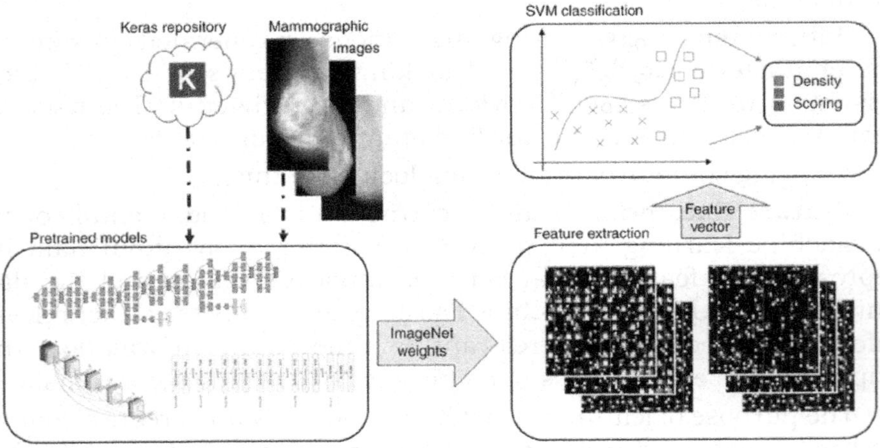

Feature Extraction

In general, feature extraction plays a crucial role in machine learning because it transforms raw data into a more meaningful and compact representation. This allows the learning algorithms to focus on the most important aspects of the data, which improves the accuracy, efficiency and interpretability of the models. Choosing appropriate extraction methods requires industry knowledge, experimentation and an understanding of the specifics and requirements of a given dataset and learning.

Create User Profile: User profiling in machine learning refers to the process of creating a comprehensive description or representation of an individual user based on their characteristics, preferences, behaviors and interactions within a system or platform. This involves collecting and analyzing various data points and patterns to gain insights into user preferences, interests and needs, which can then be used to personalize user experiences and tailor recommendations.

The user profiling process usually begins with data collection, which gathers information such as user demographics, browsing history, purchasing behavior, social media interactions, and clear feedback. This data is then processed and analyzed using machine learning algorithms to identify related patterns and extract relevant features. These characteristics may include attributes such as age, gender, location, interests, hobbies and purchasing power. Machine learning techniques such as clustering, classification and collaborative filtering are often used to group users with similar characteristics or behaviors into different segments. These segments allow organizations to better understand their user base and deliver targeted content, recommendations and advertising.

User profiling has a significant impact in various fields. In online commerce, it helps businesses understand customer preferences and behavior, enabling personalized product recommendations and targeted marketing campaigns. On social media platforms, it helps deliver tailored content and ads based on users' interests and online activity. In healthcare, user profiling can help develop personalized treatment plans, early detection of health risks and intervention strategies.

However, it is important to address privacy issues and ensure open data access and user consent. Organizations must adhere to ethical practices, comply with regulations such as GDPR and empower users to manage their data and privacy settings.

Overall, user profiling in machine learning plays a key role in improving user experience, increasing engagement and improving business results by providing personalized and relevant content and services tailored to users' unique preferences and needs.

Similarity Calculation: Similarity computing is a fundamental concept in machine learning and plays a key role in a variety of tasks such as clustering, classification, recommendation systems, and information retrieval. It involves measuring the similarity or similarity between two objects, whether they are text documents, images, audio signals or other types of data.

In machine learning, similarity is usually measured using distance or similarity metrics. These metrics provide a numerical representation of how similar or different two objects are to each other. The choice of metric depends on the nature of the data and the problem. Commonly used distance measures are Euclidean distance, Manhattan distance, and cosine similarity. Euclidean distance measures the straight-line distance between two points in n-dimensional space, while Manhattan distance calculates the sum of the absolute differences between the corresponding coordinates. Cosine similarity, on the other hand, measures the cosine of the angle between two vectors, representing similarity in their orientations rather than their sizes.

In addition to these basic metrics, domain-specific similarity metrics can be used. For example, in natural language processing, text documents are often represented as vectors using techniques such as TF-IDF (expression frequency-inverse document frequency) or word embedding. Similarity between text documents can be calculated using a metric such as cosine similarity in these vector representations.

It is worth noting that similarity computing is often used in conjunction with dimensionality reduction methods such as Principal Component Analysis (PCA) or Singular Value Decomposition (SVD). These methods help reduce the dimensionality of the data while preserving its internal structure, which improves the efficiency and effectiveness of similarity calculations.

Calculate Cosine Similarity: Cosine similarity is a popular similarity measure used in machine learning and information retrieval tasks to determine the similarity between two vectors. It calculates the cosine of the angle between the vectors, which indicates the similarity of their orientations.

In machine learning, vectors are often used to represent documents, images, or other types of data. Each element of the vector corresponds to a feature or attribute, and the value of the element indicates the size of that feature in the data. By comparing the cosine similarity between two vectors, we can quantify their similarity or difference. To calculate the cosine similarity, we must first represent the vectors as n-dimensional vectors, where n is the number of features or attributes in the data. The cosine similarity is then calculated using the dot product of the two vectors divided by the product of their magnitudes. Mathematically, the cosine similarity of vectors A and B is given by the formula:

cosine_similarity = (A · B) / (||A|| * ||B||)

Here A · B denotes the dot product of vectors A and B and ||A|| and ||B|| denotes the magnitude or length of vectors A and B, respectively. The dot product measures the similarity of the vector alignment, while the magnitudes normalize the values and ensure that the similarity is between -1 and 1.

The resulting cosine similarity value ranges from -1 to 1, where -1 means exactly opposite vectors, 1 means identical vectors, and values near 0 mean little or no similarity. By comparing cosine similarity between multiple vectors, we can identify the most similar or related items in a dataset.

Cosine similarity is widely used in various machine learning tasks, such as text classification, document clustering, recommendation systems and image similarity analysis. It provides a computationally efficient and intuitive way to measure the similarity of vectors, making it a valuable tool in many real-world applications.

Recommendation Generation: Machine learning recommendation generation refers to the process of creating personalized recommendations for users based on their preferences, behavior and history. Due to the increase of available data and the complexity of user preferences, recommendation systems have become important in various applications such as e-commerce, content streaming platforms, social media and online advertising.

The main purpose of generating recommendations is to provide users with relevant and personalized recommendations that improve their overall user experience. This process typically involves analyzing large amounts of data, including user interactions, product attributes, and contextual information. Machine learning techniques play an important role in extracting meaningful patterns and relationships from this data to generate accurate and effective recommendations. One of the main methods for making recommendations is collaborative filtering. This technique uses past behavior of similar users or targets to predict user preferences. Collaborative filtering can be divided into two main types: user-based and product-based. User-based collaborative filtering recommends items to a user based on similar user interests and behaviors, while object-based collaborative filtering recommends items that are similar to those the user has interacted with in the past.

Another popular technique is content-based filtering, which focuses on the characteristics and properties of the objects themselves. By creating user profiles based on their preferences and product profiles, content-based filtering can be used to recommend items that match the user's preferences and interests.

In recent years, advances in machine learning have led to the emergence of more advanced recommendation generation techniques. For example, matrix factorization-based methods such as singular value decomposition (SVD) and matrix factorization by gradient descent (MF-GD) can effectively capture hidden factors and provide accurate recommendations even in sparse data scenarios.

In addition, deep learning approaches, including neural networks and deep collaborative filtering models, have shown promising results in making recommendations. These models can learn complex patterns and representations from raw data, allowing them to capture complex interactions between users and objects and generate highly personalized recommendations. Overall, recommendation generation in machine learning is a dynamic and evolving field that combines various techniques and algorithms to provide personalized recommendations to users. As the amount of data grows and user preferences become more diverse, developing advanced recommendation systems to improve user experience and increase engagement across multiple industries is critical.

1. User provides input (eg liked the movie).
2. Significant features are extracted from the input.
3. Similarity is calculated between the input and other objects.
4. Recommendations are made based on similarity scores.

Using a sample table and a content-based filtering method, recommendations for a user who liked "Movie A" (action, director X) might be:

Recommended movies:

Movie C (Drama, Director X) - Cosine Similarity: 0.97

Movie D (Action, Director Z) - Cosine Similarity: 0.82

Based on genre and director similarities, "Movie C" and "Movie D" are recommended to the user. Content-based filtering can be a powerful method for providing personalized recommendations, especially when target features play an important role in user preferences. This allows systems to make recommendations based on item content, regardless of popularity or user behavior, making it particularly useful in cold-start scenarios where user data is sparse.

7.3. COLLABORATIVE FILTERING: USER-BASED AND ITEM-BASED

In order to give consumers personalised recommendations based on their tastes and behaviours, recommender systems frequently use the collaborative filtering technique. User-based and item-based filtering are two widely used techniques in collaborative filtering

User-Based Collaborative Filtering

User-based collaborative filtering is a technique used in machine learning and recommendation systems that provides personalized recommendations based on the behavior and preferences of similar users. It exploits the idea that users with similar tastes and preferences are likely to have similar preferences for goods or products.

The process begins with the collection of information about user interactions with specific products, such as ratings, reviews or purchases. This information is used to construct a user product matrix, where rows represent users and columns represent items. Each entry in the matrix represents a user's preference or interaction with a particular item. To create recommendations for a specific user, the system identifies other users with similar communication patterns. This is done by comparing the user-item matrix using similarity measures such as cosine similarity or Pearson's correlation coefficient. After that, the system identifies the k most popular users similar to the target user.

Next, the system looks at items that similar users have interacted with, but the target user has not. It recommends these items to the target user, assuming that if similar users liked those items, the target user is likely to enjoy them as well. Recommendations can be based on a simple average of ratings or more complex algorithms that consider the weight of user similarities.

One of the advantages of a user-based collaborative filter is its ability to dynamically capture user preferences. As users interact with multiple targets, the system can continuously update the user's target matrix and change recommendations accordingly. In addition, user-based collaborative filtering can provide excellent recommendations, exposing users to items they might not have discovered on their own.

However, user-based collaborative filtering also has some limitations. One challenge is the sparseness of the user-product matrix, as users typically only interact with a small fraction of the available units. This may result in insufficient data to find reliable similarities between users. The scalability of the approach can also be an issue when you are dealing with a large number of users and targets.

Table 2: User-Item Interaction Matrix

	Item1	**Item2**	**Item3**	**Item4**
User1	5	4	-	2
User2	-	3	5	1
User3	2	-	4	5

Item-Based Collaborative Filtering

Object-based collaborative filtering is a popular approach in machine learning used in personalized recommender systems. It is based on the idea that users who have similar preferences in the past will have the same preferences in the future. The main goal of object-based co-filtering is to predict a user's interest in a certain object by exploiting the preferences of other similar users and objects.

The process begins with the creation of a user product matrix, which records user ratings or feedback on various items. Each row of the matrix represents a user, each column represents a product, and the values of the matrix represent the evaluation or interaction of the user with the object. This matrix is the basis for finding similarities between items.

Various similarity measures, such as cosine similarity or Pearson's correlation coefficient, are commonly used to identify similar objects. These metrics calculate the similarity of target pairs based on user ratings. Items with a high similarity score are considered similar, indicating that users who liked one product are likely to like the other.

Once item similarities are established, a collaborative filtering algorithm predicts the user's preferences for a particular item by combining ratings of similar items. This is achieved by calculating weighted averages or other techniques such as matrix factorization.

Object-based collaborative filtering has several advantages. First, it is computationally efficient because similarity calculations are performed based on objects, not users. Second, it well solves the cold start problem, where there is limited information about new users based on the similarity of goals. In addition, it can provide accurate recommendations even in situations where there is little user data. However, object-based collaborative filtering also has limitations. It can suffer from popularity, where popular products dominate recommendations and long-tail products get less exposure. In addition, it struggles to capture user preferences for new products or products with limited reviews in a narrow category.

Here is an example of a similarity matrix for item-based collaborative filtering:

Table 3: Item Similarity Matrix

	Item1	Item2	Item3	Item4
Item1	1	0.6	0.8	0.3
Item2	0.6	1	0.4	0.2
Item3	0.8	0.4	1	0.5
Item4	0.3	0.2	0.5	1

Each cell in the similarity matrix represents the degree of similarity between any two things. Greater similarity is indicated by higher values.

The mathematics and the ideas behind user-based and item-based collaborative filtering are better understood with the aid of these tables and matrices. Please be aware, nevertheless, that the offered tables are simplified samples for explanation only and might not accurately represent real-world datasets.

7.4. SINGULAR VALUE DECOMPOSITION (SVD) AND MATRIX FACTORIZATION

Singular Value Decomposition (SVD)

Singular Value Decomposition (SVD) is a powerful matrix factorization technique widely used in machine learning and data analysis. It divides the matrix into three different matrices, resulting in a compact and meaningful representation of the raw data.

If the input matrix is usually represented as X, SVD divides it into three matrices: U, Σ, and V. Here, U is an orthogonal matrix containing left-singular vectors, Σ is a diagonal matrix with singular values, and V. is orthogonal matrix containing right-singular vectors. Unit values in Σ are ordered in descending order to indicate their importance in the data representation. SVD offers several valuable applications for machine learning. One of the most common uses is dimension reduction. By choosing the top k unit values and the corresponding unit vectors, the original matrix X can be approximated by reducing its dimension. This enables efficient storage and computing while preserving the most important information in the data.

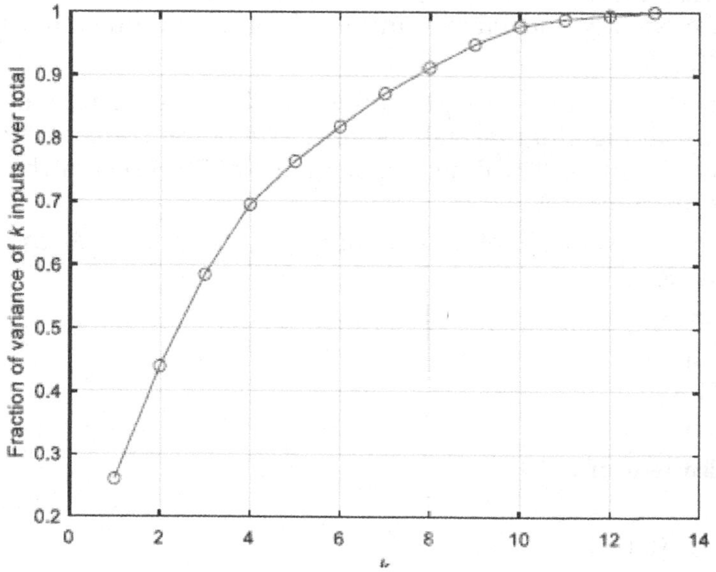

Singular Value Decomposition (SVD)

Another application of SVD is in recommendation systems. In collaborative filtering, where user-entity interactions are analyzed to make recommendations, SVD can help uncover hidden factors that capture underlying patterns in the data. By decomposing a user's destination matrix, it is possible to estimate missing entries, predict ratings and recommend destinations to users based on their preferences.

SVD is also closely related to principal component analysis (PCA), another technique widely used in machine learning. PCA uses SVD of a data matrix to find orthogonal directions, called principal components, that explain the most variance in the data. It helps visualize high-dimensional data and identify important features for classification or regression tasks. In addition, SVD has applications in, for example, image processing, natural language processing, and data compression. It can be used to denoise images, add text documents and even efficiently solve systems of linear equations.

Despite its usefulness, SVD can be computationally expensive for large datasets. To address this limitation, various approximation and optimization techniques such as truncated SVD and random SVD have been developed, which provide efficient and scalable solutions.

In summary, Singular Value Decomposition (SVD) is a versatile matrix factorization technique widely used in machine learning. It enables aspect ratio reduction, filtering, data compression and more. By splitting a matrix into orthogonal components, SVD enables efficient analysis, modeling and interpretation of complex data structures.

A = UΣV^T

where U is an m x m orthogonal matrix, Σ is an m x n diagonal matrix containing singular values, and V^T is the transpose of an n x n orthogonal matrix. The diagonal elements of Σ represent the singular values of the matrix A.

Here is an example of a table showing the matrix A and its SVD decomposition:

Matrix A:

| 2 3 |

| 1 -1 |

| 0 4 |

Breakdown of SVD:

U:

| -0.42 0.41 |

| 0.20 -0.82 |

| -0.89 -0.41 |

Σ:

| 4.62 0 |

| 0 3.14 |

| 0 0 |

V^T:

| -0.76 -0.64 |

| -0.64 0.76 |

The individual values of Σ are arranged in descending order, and the corresponding columns of U and rows of V^T are arranged accordingly.

Matrix Factorization

Matrix factorization is a powerful technique used in machine learning to split a matrix into two or more matrices with certain properties. It has gained considerable popularity in various applications, including recommender systems, collaborative filtering, and data mining.

The basic idea of matrix factoring is to represent a matrix as a product of two lower order matrices. By doing this, we can capture the latent factors or characteristics underlying the original matrix. These latent factors are often hidden or implicit in the original data, but they play a crucial role in understanding the relationships and patterns in the data. In the context of recommender systems, matrix factorization can be used to model user-object interaction. An input matrix typically represents user item ratings or preferences, where each row represents a user and each colu mn represents a product. By multiplying this matrix, we obtain 1 o w-dimensional representations of users and objects, effectively reducing the dimensionality of the original data.

	Item 1	Item 2	Item 3	Item 4	Item 5
User 1	0	3	0	3	0
User 2	4	0	0	2	0
User 3	0	0	3	0	0
User 4	3	0	4	0	3
User 5	4	3	0	4	0

Matrix Factorization

Matrix factorization techniques use optimization algorithms, such as gradient descent, to iteratively estimate the latent factors. The goal is to minimize the reconstruction error between the original matrix and the product of the coefficient matrices. In this process, the optimal values of the latent factors that best describe the relationships in the data are learned.

One of the main advantages of matrix factorization is its ability to handle sparse and incomplete data. Because real datasets often have missing records or sparse information, calculating matrix factors can fill in missing values based on patterns learned from existing data. This feature makes it particularly suitable for recommender systems where not all users have rated all items.

In addit i on, the matrix f actor enables individualized recommendations through user- and product-specific functions. It can identify similarities between users and objects based on their latent representations, enabling accurate prediction of user preferences and product recommendations.

Consider a user-target interaction matrix R of size m x n, where m is the number of users and n is the number of targets. Matrix factorization represents R as the product of two matrices:

R ≈ P * Q^T

where P is an m x k matrix representing user factors, Q is an n x k matrix representing item factors, and k is the desired latent factor dimension.

Here is an example of a table illustrating the interaction matrix of user objects and its factorial representation:

User-object interaction matrix R:

| 5 3 0 1 |
| 4 0 0 1 |
| 1 1 0 5 |
| 1 0 0 4 |
| 0 1 5 4 |

Factored representation:

Q:

| 0.77 0.78 |
| 0.58 -0.27 |
| 0.96 -0.76 |
| 0.98 -0.64 |
| 1.43 1.08 |

Q:

| 1.27 0.85 0.39 1.09 |

| 1.02 0.13 0.95 0.51 |

The magnitude of P and Q are determined by the desired latent factor dimension k. The resulting factored matrices P and Q capture the underlying user and product configurations.

7.5. HYBRID RECOMMENDER SYSTEMS

To produce more precise and varied recommendations, hybrid recommender systems incorporate various recommendation methods or models. They overcome the drawbacks of particular techniques and make use of the advantages of many ways.

Overview of Hybrid Recommender Systems

Hybrid recommender systems are a remarkable approach to machine learning that combines multiple recommendation techniques to improve the accuracy and efficiency of recommender systems. These systems exploit the strengths of different recommendation algorithms to overcome the limitations of individual methods and provide users with more personalized and relevant recommendations.

Hybrid recommender systems typically integrate two or more types of recommendation techniques, such as collaborative filtering, content-based filtering, knowledge-based filtering, and context-aware filtering. Collaborative filtering analyzes user behavior and preferences to identify similar users or items and recommends items based on the preferences of those similar users. Content-based filtering, on the other hand, focuses on the features and characteristics of items to recommend similar items based on user preferences. Data-driven filtering uses domain-specific data or expert rules to make recommendations. Context-aware filtering takes into account contextual information such as time, location, and the user's current situation to provide personalized recommendations.

By combining these techniques, hybrid recommendation systems can address various challenges faced by individual methods. For example, collaborative filtering can suffer from a cold start problem where it is difficult to make recommendations to new users or targets with limited data. Content-based filtering can face challenges in capturing different interests of users. Hybrid methods can mitigate these limitations by using both user behavior data and product features to provide more accurate and versatile recommendations.

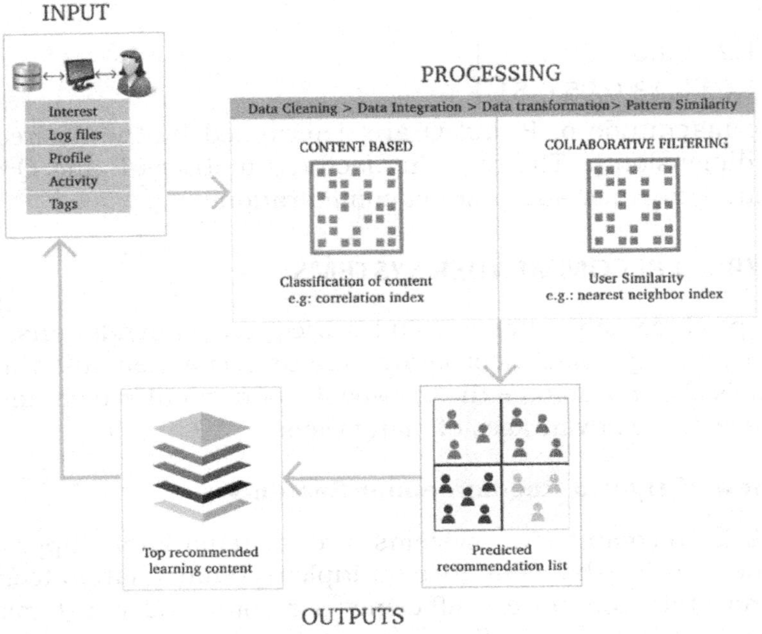

Hybrid Recommender Systems

Hybrid systems have different ways of combining recommendation techniques. One approach is called the exchange hybrid approach, where different recommendation methods are applied separately and the final recommendation list is formed by combining the results. Another approach is a weighted hybrid approach, where each recommendation method is given a weight based on its effectiveness, and the final recommendation is a weighted combination of the individual recommendations. There are also techniques such as feature pooling, cascading, and meta-level hybridization that combine the strengths of different recommendation techniques in a more sophisticated way. Overall, hybrid recommender systems provide an effective solution to improve the accuracy, variety and personalization of recommender systems. By combining multiple recommendation techniques, these systems can overcome the limitations of individual methods and provide more effective recommendations, improving user satisfaction and engagement across industries such as e-commerce, movie streaming, music platforms and more.

Techniques Used in Hybridization

Hybridization in machine learning means combining different technologies or models to create a more sustainable and efficient solution. It involves integrating several algorithms, methods or approaches to exploit their strengths and overcome individual limitations. Hybridization aims to improve the efficiency, accuracy or effectiveness of machine learning systems by exploiting the complementary characteristics of different technologies.

One common approach to hybridization is ensemble learning, where multiple models are trained independently and their predictions are combined to make a final decision. Ensemble methods such as random forests, gradient boosting and stacking use a combination of different models to improve prediction accuracy and generalization. By combining predictions from multiple models, ensemble methods can reduce bias, increase stability, and handle larger data patterns.

Another technique used in hybridization combines multiple data sources or categories. In many real-world applications, data is available from various sources, such as text, images, audio, or sensor measurements. Hybrid models can be designed to process and integrate these different data types to capture richer and more comprehensive information. For example, a self-driving car system can combine visual data from cameras, data from lidar or radar sensors, and text data from GPS or maps to make accurate and reliable decisions. Hybridization can also involve combining different learning paradigms or algorithms. For example, combining rule-based expert systems with machine learning models can leverage human expertise and industry knowledge to improve the performance of data-driven approaches. Reinforcement learning can be combined with deep learning techniques to create hybrid models that learn from both simulation-based interactions and the large-scale real world.

In addition, hybridization techniques may involve integrating machine learning with other computational intelligence methods such as evolutionary algorithms, swarm analysis, or fuzzy logic. These combinations allow the exploration of alternative search strategies, optimization techniques or decision processes to efficiently solve complex problems. In general, machine learning hybridization aims to use the strengths of different techniques, models or algorithms to create more efficient and sustainable systems. By combining complementary approaches, hybrid models can overcome individual limitations, improve efficiency and provide better solutions for various real-world applications.

Benefits of Hybrid Recommender Systems

Hybrid machine learning recommendation systems combine the strengths of multiple recommendation techniques to provide users with more accurate and effective recommendations. These systems use both content-based and collaborative filtering methods, as well as other techniques to overcome the limitations of individual recommendation methods. The benefits of hybrid recommendation systems are many and increase user satisfaction and engagement.

One of the main advantages of hybrid recommender systems is better recommendation accuracy. By combining different approaches, these systems can mitigate the weaknesses of individual techniques. For example, content-based filtering can suffer from the cold start problem, as there is limited user data available to make accurate recommendations. Collaborative filtering, on the other hand, is based on user interaction and can struggle to recommend items that are not part of the user's set preferences. By integrating both approaches, hybrid systems can leverage the strengths of each to provide more accurate recommendations, even in scenarios with little or incomplete data.

Another advantage of hybrid recommendation systems is their ability to handle different recommendation scenarios. Different referencing techniques are great in different contexts. Content-based filtering is particularly useful when the characteristics or attributes of an object are important for a recommendation, such as movie or music recommendations based on genre or artist. On the other hand, collaborative filtering can be effective in capturing user preferences and recommending items based on similar user behavior. Hybrid systems can adapt and select the most appropriate recommendation technique based on the characteristics of the data and the specific recommendation task, resulting in more personalized and relevant recommendations in different domains.

Hybrid recommender systems also offer better clarity and novelty in recommendations. While collaborative filtering tends to reinforce existing preferences, content-based filtering can reveal new and different elements. By combining these approaches, hybrid systems can achieve a balance between exploiting user preferences and exploring new possibilities. It can increase user satisfaction by presenting users with unexpected and exciting suggestions and encouraging exploration and discovery.

In addition, hybrid recommendation systems can deal with the "filter bubble" or "echo chamber" effect, where users receive only a limited selection of recommendations that match their current preferences. By combining different recommendation techniques, hybrid systems can expand the recommendation space and open users to a wider range of objects, helping to reduce the echo chamber and promote surprising discoveries.

7.6. EVALUATION METRICS FOR RECOMMENDER SYSTEMS

Rating Prediction Metrics

Grade prediction metrics in machine learning are evaluation metrics used to evaluate the accuracy and performance of grade or grade prediction models. These metrics give an idea of how well the model can estimate or predict the numerical ratings given to different items such as products, movies or songs.

One metric often used to predict ratings is the mean absolute error (MAE). MAE calculates the mean absolute difference between predicted and actual estimates. This provides a direct measure of the average forecast error, regardless of the direction of the error. Smaller MAE values indicate better prediction accuracy.

Another widely used metric is Root Mean Squared Error (RMSE). RMSE measures the average size of the differences between predicted and actual classification, taking into account both the direction and size of the errors. It penalizes larger errors more heavily than MAE and is popular because it is sensitive to outliers.

Also, MSLE (Mean Squared Logathmic Error) is a measure that is often used when scores span a large range and their distribution is skewed. It calculates the average log error between the predicted and the actual score. MSLE generally reduces the incidence of large errors and can be useful when the rating scale is highly biased.

Addition a lly, R-squared (R^2) is a quantity that estimates the proporti o n of variance in actual ratings that can be explained by predicted ratings. R^2 ranges from 0 to 1, with larger values indicating a better fit of the model to the data. This provides insight into how well the model captures the underlying relationships between predictors and ratings. These predictive evaluation metrics help machine learning researchers and practitioners evaluate the performance of their models and compare different approaches. Based on these metrics, they can refine their models, identify areas for improvement, and make informed decisions about which model performs better for a given classification prediction task.

Method	MAE	RMSE
Method A	0.752	0.974
Method B	0.639	0.823
Method C	0.523	0.687

Ranking Metrics

Machine learning ranking metrics are evaluation metrics used to evaluate the effectiveness of algorithms or models designed to rank items or documents in a certain order of relevance or importance. Unlike traditional classification or regression tasks that focus on predicting a single outcome, classification tasks involve ranking a set of items based on their relative importance to a given question or context.

One widely used ranking metric is the average accuracy (MAP), which is often used in information service systems. MAPA calculates the average accuracy of all relevant items at each item in the sorted list and then takes the average of these average accuracy values. It provides a comprehensive assessment of placement quality, taking into account both accuracy and location of relevant objects. Another important investment metric is NDCG (Normalized Discounted Cumulative Profit). NDCG measures the quality of a ranking by assigning higher scores to the most important items that appear at the top and gradually decreasing scores for items further down the list. It takes into account both the importance of the items and their position in the list and provides a more accurate evaluation of ranking algorithms.

Precision in K (P@K) is a simpler ranking metric that measures the proportion of significant items among the top K rankings. This is usually used when the focus is on getting the most important items within certain limits, rather than evaluating the entire list. Other ranking measures are Precision-Recall curves, which describe precision and recall values at different points in the list, and the Kendall Tau or Spearman rank correlation coefficient, which estimates the relationship between predicted and actual ranking.

The choice of an appropriate ranking metric depends on the specific task and the objectives of the system being evaluated. Different metrics describe different a spects of a ranking, such as precision, recall, location bias, or overall ranking quality. It is important to choose a metric that matches the goals of the application to ensure accurate evaluation and comparison of investment algorithms or models.

Method	**P@5**	**R@5**
Method A	0.6	0.75
Method B	0.8	0.4
Method C	0.7	0.6

Novelty Metrics

Machine learning news metrics refer to evaluation activities and techniques used to assess the novelty or uniqueness of generated results (such as text, images or recommendations) compared to existing data or previously seen examples. As machine learning models become more sophisticated and capable of producing diverse and creative outputs, it is imperative to quantify and understand the level of novelty generated by those outputs.

One common approach to measuring novelty is to use measures based on similarity or difference. For example, in natural language processing tasks such as text generation, researchers often use measures such as BLEU (Bilingual Evaluation Analysis) or ROUGE (Recall-Oriented Understudy for Gisting Evaluation) to compare the generated text with reference data. These metrics examine the overlap of n-grams or linguistic patterns between the generated text and the reference text and provide a quantitative assessment of novelty. Another approach to news metrics involves the use of information theory techniques. One such measure is confusion, which measures how well a language model predicts a given set of test data. More clutter means lower model performance and potentially more novelty in the generated outputs.

Made in the USA
Monee, IL
04 November 2026

67381276R00128